Relationships

Steve Berman
and
Vivien Weiss

A Brooklyn street punk describes his relationship with the first girl he deemed worthy of anything more than sex; the wife of a famous actor discusses the pressures inherent in the overwhelming thrust to stardom; a Jewish couple speaks of the first three years of their marriage, spent in a Rotterdam attic hiding from the Nazis.

Relationships is a mosaic of intimate and revealing impressions. It offers us a privileged glimpse into other people's affairs. It is a sourcebook that can be read straight through or sampled at random. But however it is approached, be assured that the breadth and variety of its perspectives will provide occasionally whimsical, often dramatic, sometimes shocking, but always enjoyable reading.

In nearly fifty interviews culled from hundreds, you may take advantage of a singular opportunity to peer behind the protective façades of men and women, gays and straights, widows and teen-agers, a rock star and a former nun, the promiscuous and the "pure," and listen as, in their own words and from their own personal perspectives, they talk about the people thay have tried to love: how the relationships started, how they were sustained, how they sometimes ended; how things like sex, money, and success affected them; how particular aspects of their relationships shaped—and often destroyed—them.

Relationships: They both obsess and mystify us. They have been the object of speculation, analysis, and theory. Yet the dynamics of sharing space continue to confound us. In *Relationships* Steve Berman and Vivien Weiss offer a unique approach to the enigma. They postulate no theories and draw no conclusions; instead, they let people speak for themselves—and the cumulative effect is more revealing than any neatly conceived theory ever could be.

Peter Simon

Steve Berman is a Boston-based free-lance journalist whose articles have appeared in the *Boston Globe, New Times, New Age, People*, and *Science Digest*. He is the author of *Southern New England for Free* and *The Northeastern Outdoors*. **Vivien Weiss** is a therapist. She is currently counseling cancer patients and their families.

Relationships

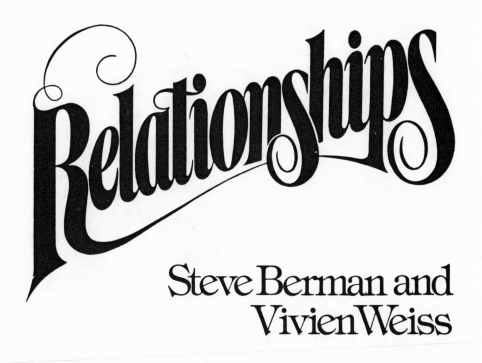

Relationships

Steve Berman and Vivien Weiss

HAWTHORN BOOKS, INC.
Publishers/NEW YORK
A Howard & Wyndham Company

RELATIONSHIPS

Library of Congress Catalog Card Number: 76-53391

ISBN: 0-8015-6269-4

1 2 3 4 5 6 7 8 9 10

To Hannelore—
for finding the romance in it all,
even when there was none.

MARIANNE: Johan.

JOHAN: Yes.

MARIANNE: Sometimes it grieves me that I have never loved anyone. I don't think I've ever been loved either. It really distresses me.

JOHAN: I think you're too tense about this.

MARIANNE: (*Smiling*) Do you?

JOHAN: I can only answer for myself. And I think I love you in my imperfect and rather selfish way. And at times I think you love me in your stormy, emotional way. In fact I think that you and I love one another. In an earthly and imperfect way.

> —from *Scenes from a Marriage*
> by Ingmar Bergman

. . . As there are as many minds as there are heads, so there are as many kinds of love as there are hearts.

> —from *Anna Karenina*
> by Leo Tolstoy

Contents

ENTERING

"It just kind of touched me. She was so completely innocent. She was so beautiful to look at."

"I always wanted something different. I just never knew what it was until I found it."

"I'd just arrived in Paris and there she was—walking in a big rush-hour crowd. Then she passed by my table and was gone."

ENJOYING

SUFFERING

WORKING IT OUT

Acknowledgments

We assembled this book but it was written by the people we interviewed. Hundreds of people welcomed us into their homes and spoke with us. People deposited their lives with us. We're grateful to everyone who allowed us into their private worlds.

We'd also like to thank our editor, Joan Nagy, who was wise in her comments and recommendations, warm in how she sometimes had to handle two frazzled authors, and always a concerned rooter and appreciator for what this book was trying to do.

Stanley and Florence Berman offered an enthusiasm that in ways unbeknownst to them helped make this book more precious. And thanks to Stephen Forman, Ivy Colbert, Jeff McQueen, Amy Kahn, Sandra Choron, Henry Weiss, Pamela Mills, Peter Simon, and Renny Pritikin for reading the manuscript in its various stages.

Again, to everyone who opened their lives for the rest of us, we're deeply indebted. And it's the hope of this book that the rest of us will somehow benefit from your candor.

Relationships

Introduction

For two years we listened to hundreds of people talking about their love relationships: a couple who'd lived in an attic, hiding from the Nazis, an eighteen-year-old paper mill worker from Maine and his eighteen-year-old pregnant wife, a sixty-year-old woman who after three failed heterosexual marriages had finally found love with a forty-year-old woman, a forty-four-year-old paraplegic and his twenty-year-old wife, a couple who'd lost their life savings of more than a half-a-million dollars, a woman whose husband had recently died of a brain tumor.

We interviewed more than three hundred people. We interviewed stockbrokers, press agents, bakers, rock 'n' roll stars, doctors, housewives, psychologists, nurses, editors, novelists, movie stars, bartenders, veterans, teachers, artists, prostitutes, ex-cons, bankers, caterers, travel agents, and junkies.

Many of the people we interviewed wanted our book to somehow tell them where relationships were at in America or, more often, how their own relationship compared to all the other relationships we'd been privy to. But making comparisons or aerial-view statements about love relationships was never our intention. We were simply two people who found their own relationship the most intriguing and most perplexing thing in their lives and who wanted to know a little bit more about how other people's relationships worked or didn't work.

We were interested in what the psychologists and sociologists call *primary* relationships—husband-and-wife type living arrangements; relationships that were either legalized or not by a marriage certificate and ones that were either hetero- or homosexual. In short, any relationship where people were sharing their lives.

People spoke to us for a variety of reasons; some because they found our project interesting and wanted to contribute, others because they needed to talk. We spoke with both individuals and couples, and in many cases, we ended up meeting the former lovers, children, and friends of the people we interviewed.

The interviews lasted anywhere from one to four hours. We had no format, no lengthy questionnaires, no rigid interviewing techniques. We simply tried to listen to the stories people were telling us, interrupting only when an irrelevant tangent threatened to eclipse the essential material.

Recurring patterns naturally presented themselves to us: women complaining that their husbands or lovers weren't communicating with them enough, men feeling that their wives didn't take enough of an interest in their work, everyone expressing the need to be loved and to love. But we weren't looking for these sorts of recurring patterns. We were simply collecting stories.

We weren't looking for answers either. Every relationship, we knew, had to find—and then continually refind—its own extraordinarily peculiar set of answers. People's experiences and their insights into those experiences were all we wanted. In assembling the book, we always looked upon it as eventually being a tool, a resource book: a place not so much for answers as a place where people could come to compare notes. We designed the book so that it could be read at random or straight through, and we assumed that people at different times in their lives, at different stages of their relationships, would be reading different sections of the book.

All of us enter, enjoy, suffer, and leave our love relationships. Our enterings are invariably exciting, our enjoyments and sufferings often commingled, and our leavings almost always painful. We divided the book into these very generalized sections: " Entering," "Enjoying," "Suffering," "Working It Out," and a fifth section, "Leaving." Included in this last section are stories about how people have struggled to minimize the suffering in their relationships. Since some of the interviews fit into all five categories, others into just two, and some only into one, we tried to discern each interview's major emphasis and then placed it into its proper section.

The preponderance of interviews in the "Suffering" section of the book, it's important to note, is not reflective of how many unhappy relationships we encountered in our two years of research. If anything, it's only an indication that people paid more attention to and spoke more volubly about their tragedies than their joys.

The three hundred interviews we accumulated accounted for so many mood changes (both individually and collectively) that we sometimes felt as if we were being granted some preternatural peek into relationships. We'd knock on people's doors and within minutes we were being entrusted with secrets. One woman confided that she'd perforated her diaphragm in order to have the child her husband never wanted. Another woman told us of her husband's insane desire to have her grow two inches, a desire he forcibly (and abortively) tried to carry out by nightly stretching her. Other revelations, less sensationalistic, were painful for people to tell us and painful for us to hear: a woman telling us that her husband of twenty-five years had just left her; a man, fifty-three, telling us that he'd hated his wife for years but was afraid to leave her.

We listened to blatant self-deceptions, lopsided versions of why a relationship hadn't worked. We heard rages: a fifty-two-year-old man still incensed by what his ex-wife had done to him fifteen years ago. And we heard too many people too easily describing the dynamics of their relationships, believing that the teachings and shibboleths of some new or ancient school of thought could neatly explain away ten or twenty years of living together.

We were shown hundreds of photographs. From closets and drawers, albums filled with ten- twenty- fifty-year-old snapshots were taken out for our inspection. We stared at a forty-year-old black-and-white photo of a bosomy nude woman—a woman who only moments before had told us that her old age felt like a prison and she was now waiting to die.

We cried when a sixty-eight-year-old woman told us she'd spent her entire life with a man always too busy for her. Two women told us how in the quiet, restful moments after orgasm, they said things to each other they never thought they could say. We feigned nonchalance, listening to a tale filled with what were for us previously unheard of sexual acts. A fifty-eight-year-old man told us how he still felt like a teen-ager ''every time'' when he got into bed with his wife. A couple excitedly described their morning ritual to us—wrestling for an hour, followed by interminable hugs. And the wife of a recovered alcoholic told us of her husband's first smile in years.

Moments when people told each other how much they loved one another, when they said that by doing the interview they'd reappreciated their loved one, were special. In mid-conversation, a couple might look at one another and tenderly, tearfully embrace.

Four months after we interviewed one couple, both of them were dead. Four weeks after interviewing another couple, a seven-pound baby boy was born to them. A couple we admired, we felt they were honestly trying to deal with their problems, split up six months after we spoke with them. We fixed two people up, both of them having told us they were lonely and wanted to meet someone. And in the middle of writing this book, its authors, after living together two years, married.

We observed the kaleidoscopic diversity of human relationships, glimpsed at the common urges and needs that glue two people together, and ended up respecting the love (however confused, insecure, or arrogant that love may have been when we saw it) that brought two people together and made them want to share their lives. We listened to the "gossip," to the day-to-day transpirings of people's lives, and we saw that the love people feel for each other, however it's expressed, is really something all of us want; it's what we need to give and need to receive.

Very few people in our society are ever given an honest, unpadded glimpse into the daily workings of someone else's relationship. Only professionals—psychiatrists, psychologists, and social workers and sometimes an occasional parent or friend (and then usually when things are desperate)—are ever allowed into another's world. The rest of us have to settle for novels, movies, plays, or at best a little gossip that by the time it finally reaches us is imprecise and lifeless. The closest many of us ever come to an intimate knowledge of someone else's relationship is in hearing the wife-maligning routines of some nightclub stand-up comedian.

The majority of us just don't sit down and talk about our love lives, especially men. It's threatening, too revealing, better discussed behind the veils of fiction; or worse, mangled behind the veils of gossip. As a result, there are no places or very few places to learn about what goes on in a love relationship (excepting, of course, in our own relationships). There are no schools, no forums, no magazines that offer an opportunity to listen to others honestly and uninhibitedly talking about their romantic lives; nowhere to hear thoughtful reconstructions of people's careers in love.

But it's something we so obviously need. Superfluous, we feel, to quote here all our nation's oft-quoted divorce statistics, our figures on wife beatings, child abandonment. This book, we hope, is a modest beginning at making the intimate workings and dysfunctions of people's love relationships more accessible to the general public.

ENTERING

Ah, in those earliest days of love how naturally the kisses spring into life. How closely, in their abundance, are they pressed one against another; until lovers would find it as hard to count the kisses exchanged in an hour, as to count the flowers in a meadow in May.

from *Swann's Way*
by MARCEL PROUST

Becky and Adam

With the help of photo albums and scrapbooks, Becky and Adam give us a pictorial history of their forty-seven years together. About four weeks after we interviewed them, we learned that Becky had died. She died suddenly, unexpectedly, and in the arms of her husband. She was sixty-seven when her heart gave out.

Four months after Becky's death, we learned that Adam, too, was dead. He died of cancer.

Becky: I was dancing at the Roxy on Fifty-third and Broadway in 1927. It was the most beautiful, biggest music hall. I was in the ballet that opened the show. All the big theaters back then—the Strand, the Rivoli, the Capitol, the Colony, and the Roxy—had a ballet company and an orchestra, a big orchestra that played for the movies because there were no talkies yet. When we met I was dancing in the ballet company and Adam was playing in the orchestra. This was when I was seventeen and Adam, twenty-three.

Adam: As I was playing my violin—and after playing the same show over and over I could play it from memory—I began to look around a little. From the orchestra pit, though, I could only see legs, forty dancing legs on the stage. I couldn't see any faces. Now I'm what they call a leg man, so I'd count all the dancers' legs and I'd look at all of them but my eyes would always stop when I got to this one particular pair of legs. I kept doing this, looking at all the legs—and they were all very beautiful—but somehow I always ended up stopping at this one pair. So one day, very quietly, I raised myself from my seat so I could see from the pit who this girl was. And there was Becky, this youngster, so young. And, you know, it just kind of touched me. She was completely innocent. She was so beautiful to look at. Truthfully, I knew that day that I wanted to marry her.

I was a handsome man. This is not bragging. This is factual. I had many offers for the movies. I had to fend off the girls. I even used to pay the doormen at the theaters I worked in to tell the girls that I'd already left. I just didn't want to be bothered with them. Also, I had played mood music for Warner Brothers in Hollywood in 1926, and we had parties out there with starlets. It was wonderful. I had many, many affairs, lots of fun. I never dreamed of wanting to get married. But Becky was so beautiful, so innocent. I'll tell you, and this is true, that over the years, and it's been forty-seven years and that's a very long time . . . well, I won't tell you that I love her more today than when I first met her, but I will tell you that I love her as much now as when I first saw her—legs first, then her face—that day at the Roxy.

Joe and Susan

Five well-groomed black cats were playing on a thick red-colored carpet in their living room. The apartment's walls were completely covered with paintings— all created by prisoners and ex-cons. Joe is thirty-six; Susan, forty-three. They've been married a year.

Susan: If you look out the window of my apartment, you can't see anything except other high-rises. The only thing you *can* see, besides all these other tall buildings, is into the window of an apartment in the building next door. The apartment's on the same floor as mine. Well, that's where Joe lived and I watched him from my bedroom window for a whole year and I thought he was gorgeous.

At first, we'd just look at one another. But then, after a while, there'd be a wave here and a wave there—all through the windows. Eventually, we started talking to each other. We had our first conversation, I remember, while Joe was washing his windows. When I saw him washing *his* windows, I decided to go out on the fire escape and wash mine. And I finally turned around and said, "Hi," and he said, "Hi."

Joe: No. You said, "Hello there." I was actually shocked that she would say hello to me because I had been watching her, too, for that whole year and I was also very interested.

Susan: After I said, "Hello there," I didn't know what to say next, so I stupidly said, "Hey, I didn't know anybody lived in that building." And at that point I guess he must have thought, 'dum-dum'; and he closed the window. I was uptight about even talking to him then so it came out kind of clumsily. What I was really trying to say was, 'Hi, are you married?' But I couldn't think of anything.

I remember thinking at one point that he was a fag because I could see all these guys going in and out of his place all the time. But then I saw some girls and I thought, 'Hey, I'm hip. So what if he's bisexual? I don't care.'

Joe: I was very paranoid about talking to her. I figured that since I obviously could see into her bedroom, if I were to speak to her, she would think I was weird or something. I figured that anything I was going to say might be misinterpreted, and I didn't want her to think that I was looking to rape her. People in New York City are so paranoid that if you look sideways at a strange woman, they'll all yell, ''What are you looking at?'' So I never tried to talk to her after that.

Susan: Often I would sort of semiconsciously not pull my shades down so he could see what I was doing. Or at least I didn't go out of my way to pull them down.

Joe: And *I* didn't have any shades.

Susan: Everybody knew about Joe. I told everyone that I was in love with him but that I just hadn't met him yet. Even the people in my office all knew. I told everyone how he was really terrific and how much I wanted to meet him.

I sat on the phone with a friend one night, looking at him from my window and *he* was looking at me, and I was telling my friend, ''I don't know how to meet him. What should I do?'' Finally, I hung up the phone and I just got up and I opened the window and I signaled with my hand he should open his and he did and I said, ''Hi, do you want to come over for some tea?'' And he said, ''I'll be right there.'' So I called my friend and said, ''Call me every twenty minutes, and as long as I answer the phone, you'll know I'm OK.''

I had a vision of what was coming over. I imagined he was tall and handsome and an architect. And probably rich. I also assumed he was Jewish. So he rings the bell and I ask, ''Who's there?'' and he answers, ''Joe Dougherty,'' and so not only is he not Jewish but he's Irish. My God! Anyway, I opened the door and there was this person who was much shorter than I expected, and I said, ''I thought you were much taller.'' And he said, "That's because my window is higher than yours." And it is; his window is about a foot higher than mine. So then he sat down and he took off his jacket and I saw that he had tatoos all over both his arms. So I responded very cleverly with, "Oh, are you a sailor?" and he said, "No. I'm in prison reform." And then he said, "I'm an exoffender." And I said, "Oh, what did you do?" And I thought to myself, 'If he says rape, I'm going to faint?' I mean, I was really very nervous at that point. But then he said, "Armed robbery," or something like that. And I thought, 'Oh, that's OK.' You know, as long as it wasn't murder or anything like that. Armed robbery just sounded so nice and impersonal.

Joe: It was an interesting evening. I wasn't about to push, but I took an immediate liking to her. She's very vivacious with a really great sense of humor. But I also saw that she was a little overwhelmed in that I was nothing like she expected. I could sense that. But we did feel very nice at the end of the evening and really glad that we'd finally met.

I should probably explain where I was coming from when I met Susan. There's a lot of aftereffects to being in prison, especially in regard to how you relate to women. It's amazing when you haven't spoken to a woman in eight years. You think that you're ready and then you sit down and here's this kind of soft creature. You don't know what to say and you're afraid that anything you say is going to sound very gruff because you're not accustomed to speaking rationally, intelligently. So I went through a series of changes when I got out of prison. I decided that it was too easy to get hurt in a love relationship. Partly I felt that way because of my own experiences before prison and partly because of a lot of stories I'd heard about people who get out and in six months they get married and two years later they're in the divorce courts. So what happened was I never went out with just one woman. I always went out with two or three women at the same time so that anytime I started feeling too much for one of them, the next day I'd be sure to be with someone else. And in those first six years after I got out of jail I never really got hooked up to a degree where I latched onto someone or where someone latched onto me. When I met Susan, as far as I was concerned, she would just be another one of them. But that didn't happen. I just kind of met her and liked her and all those other women fell by the wayside without me really consciously doing anything. Suddenly there she was and it was OK. I didn't get shook up by it. And I'd never lived with a woman before, never been in love with a woman before. But it turned out to be an amazingly smooth and comfortable transition.

Susan: It was funny the way it all happened. The day after we met was my birthday. I had gone out to dinner with my old boyfriend and his family, and what happened was that after I came home, Joe came over and we just kind of screwed around all night. And I don't know if it was so romantic, but it sure was terrific. We talked, got a little high, and absolutely enjoyed the hell out of each other.

Joe: I don't believe in the lightning-bolt love affair but somehow we just hit it off in a really big way—so I guess it *was* a lightning bolt.

Susan: But we did have two hurdles we needed to deal with. The first was that I was seven years older than Joe and I hadn't told him. I didn't lie—it was just one of those things that I hadn't mentioned. It was my birthday when he came over, and what's the first question someone asks you on your birthday but, ''How old are you.'' So I said, ''How does the year thirty-four sound?'' which was the year I was born, 1934. And he said, ''That's exactly how old I thought you were.'' So I wasn't really lying.

Then we had a money problem. I made a lot more money than Joe, and Joe's background is such that he's very macho: The man is the provider; the woman is dependent on the man.

Joe: I didn't have any problem with a woman working. I just didn't want a woman to earn more money than I did. I mean, I felt like a man's got to earn more money than his wife.

Susan: So I lied about my salary. I finally told him both things—about my age and about my salary. He didn't mind the age thing at all. We went through that part fairly easily because we were pretty close by then. And I was relieved about that. I was very fond of him at that point, and I really didn't want to be rejected for some silly reason like age, an artificial thing that I had no control over and couldn't change. But then I told him that I earned more money, and forget it. It was days before he would talk to me after that. There was a strain. He was inhibited; he was pulling back.

Joe: Suddenly, I felt like this whole thing was wrong because she wasn't supposed to earn more money than I was. It was a put-down. I was earning $15,000 and she was earning $25,000. And there was no way I knew of at that time where I could possibly catch up. And I knew that I wasn't into earning a lot of money because I was enjoying what I was doing. The sense of gratification I got from my work was worth it. Intellectually, I could say like, 'Hey, it doesn't really make any difference.' And it was even flattering because it meant the woman I was with was worth a lot, that she was very bright and intelligent. But that was on the intellectual side. On the emotional side, it was very threatening. I really went through a whole emotional trauma. But finally I said, 'Hey, this is all bullshit. What's the difference if she makes more money than I do? I oughta be glad.' And once that settled in, then of course the intellectual side won out and I thought it was terrific. And I also saw that Susan wasn't rejecting me for not earning more, that she wasn't even thinking about it, and that she was saying, 'Hey, what's the difference? Who the hell cares who earns more money? I'm interested in you.' I realized that she could have reversed that whole situation on me and then I'd really be in trouble because then I'd really go through a trip of how I'd been rejected because I wasn't earning enough money. So finally I realized how really fine it was that I was with such a bright lady who really cared about me.

Susan: The thing I really know about this relationship is that I can be absolutely me in it. I can be mad, I can be funny, I can be loud, I can be goofy, I can cry. Sometimes, when Joe gets mad at me, sure I'll need the reassurance that he still loves me because I'm insecure, and that part of me will never change. But I know I'm absolutely totally me with Joe. For the first time in my life, I feel at home. And I'd been married twice before and both my husbands were very nice men but I never should have married them. I was always struggling in those marriages. I was always trying to be perfect for them and as a result, I was never me. I always wanted something different. But I never knew what it was until I found it. And now that I have it, it's really fantastic.

Joe: You know, this may sound funny, but the littlest things make us happy. Maybe because I was in prison and because Susan was never really happy with a man before, we're like that. Like when we look up at the stars at night or when one of our cats does something cute or just taking a walk together. And Susan, she likes to cry a lot when she's happy. It took awhile for us to find each other but we've got a good life now.

Felix

Felix is sixty-five. Before retiring, he was a globe-trotting silk salesman.

I arrived in Paris on a Friday afternoon in 1948. I was staying at a hotel right on the Champs Elysées. I unpacked my baggage, went downstairs, and in front of my hotel there was a sidewalk café, so I sat down. I was waiting for a friend who said he'd pick me up at seven o'clock for dinner. So I'm sitting, it's five, five-thirty in Paris, and a woman walks by. I had never picked up a girl on the street. All of the women I met, I'd met socially, through friends. I had never in my life picked a girl up. But this girl walks by, and for the first time in my life I want to talk to her. I want to stop her and talk to her. I can't explain it to you. I'd just arrived in Paris and there she was—walking in a big rush-hour crowd. Then she passed by my table and was gone. I sat down and tried to forget about it.

Later, my friend came and we had dinner together and then went to a very good musical. We got out of the show at about eleven, and we'd planned on meeting some of his friends at a bar afterward. We walked to the bar. It was a beautiful night, a warm night, and all of a sudden, I don't know, I cannot explain it to you, but something came over me. I don't know what it was, and I said to my friend, "Listen, I don't feel well. Do me a favor. You know these people. Go there without me. I'm going home." This was about eleven, eleven-fifteen. So I took a cab. I don't really know why I left. Then I got out of the cab, paid the driver, and I turned around and there she was. We started talking. She told me her name, a beautiful French name, and she was lovely. I told her about what had happened to me and she said she believed in things like that. It was so fabulous. I could have gone with my friend and never have seen her again. It was too much of a coincidence. She came back to my hotel that night without any ado, without talking about it, and she didn't leave. We were together for four weeks in my hotel. She never even wanted to go out, not even to see Piaf or Dietrich. She just wanted to stay in that hotel room.

Terry O'Connor

Terry's sixteen. Cars, beer, pot, "chicks," music, and fights are his social life. And hangin' out on the streets of Brooklyn, just goofin' off near subway stations, candy stores, and school yards comprise his day.

I've been going out with this girl named Diane for about a year and a half. She comes from a very exclusive family. They live in Bayside. It was a constant thing with each girl I'd meet—that I'd try to get down with them, sleep with them. But like with Diane it was different, she was more on my level whereas with everybody else I was bringing myself down to their level. For once somebody was pulling me up, and that turned me on. Diane knew what I really was, what I was good for, rather than just what I had to give her sexually in bed.

I'd buy her coffee, we'd go places together, we'd go to Carnegie Hall. I never did that with a girl before. We wouldn't go to hear rock music, we'd go hear classical music at Carnegie Hall with her parents. This is at fifteen, sixteen years old.

I met her at a keg party on this golf course. I was sitting around with my friends and these girls came up in a group, about five or six of them. So I had my headband on my head and this girl walked up to me and she takes my headband off and she sits down next to me and she hands it to me. She just hands it to me. So I'm hangin' out smokin' joints with her and I get up to get a beer but I forget my mug. So I came back and I sit down and I say, "I forgot my mug." And I look down and I see my mug is broken. She broke it. I was too gone to think about it, so I end up sitting in a field with her and we're just holding each other and I had on my mind that I had a lot of money on me and a lot of dope. And I'm thinkin', 'Hey, maybe this girl just brought me out here so somebody can hit me on the head and rip me off.'

It was dark and it was this beautiful night, four in the morning, and everything's wide open, the trees and birds, and like I thought I was flying. I didn't make it with her that night but I went home to this friend's house and I thought about her a lot. But I couldn't think of her name. So I realized that the reason she broke my mug was because she didn't want me drinkin' no more. Obviously she cared about me, that's why she did it. And I say I gotta get this number.

So after about two weeks this girl walks up to me in school and she says, "You're Terry O'Connor, right?" A lot of people at school know me. So I say, "Yeah, I'm Terry O'Connor. Don't bother me. I'm gettin' my lunch, man. Don't bother me." So she said to me, "Do you remember a girl named Diane?" And I said, "No, I don't." You always say no, you know. Then I started thinking, 'Hey, maybe that's her.' So I said, "Hey, I know her." So she says, "622–4807" I went home, made a phone call, and we went out.

Soon as we talked to each other, we dug each other. Dug each other. She was a virgin and I wasn't; so it was awhile before I could explain to her what I wanted and that my idea of a relationship is a lot of love and I dig a lot of affection. Whatever term you want to use, she was a virgin and then she wasn't after a while. She got really upset afterwards just because she thought she had done a wrong thing. I was trying to explain to her that no, it's not wrong. Society says it's wrong; society says you can't go to bed with somebody if you're not married. And I really loved her. She was like the first girl I said, "Hey, I love you, too."

I loved her for what she was and not what she was in bed. I slept with her only two or three times. I'd take a bus and a train to see her and then I'd only be able to spend fifteen minutes with her. Like I knew her parents wouldn't leave us alone for more than fifteen minutes. So I used to go all the way to her house for those few minutes.

And all during this time I'd be gettin' laid by other girls. She knew there were other girls but she never knew how far I went with them. I mean, I've slept with many girls and like I couldn't wait to get out of the room afterward because there was no love behind it. Whereas they say macho men would walk out like big men, you know, with big smiles on their faces—like 'Wow, I just got laid.' Some of the girls would want me to stay there overnight. I couldn't wait to get out of the room. I'd be pissed off at myself because I'd be doing exactly what I didn't want to do.

I feel that I can share myself with many people. And with Diane, I could do that more than I can with most people. I love her tremendously, especially when I don't see her—that's when I dig her. I spent over $250 on this girl. I went down to the Bowery and I bought her a diamond and a sterling silver heart. I bought her all these things. In the beginning it was a material relationship, and then it built up to a love, and then I didn't have to prove anything to her anymore.

When we were alone it was like an intense scene. It was beautiful love. It was like we'd talk; we'd just sit down and I didn't have to do anything with her to love her. She'd come up to my house and we wouldn't say anything for half an hour. We'd just look at each other. And when we'd leave each other, I'd just say, "Thank you." But see, she was different people—different with whoever she hung out with. Different faces; she wore masks. And I saw through them and she knew I saw through them. But like when we were alone she wore no masks. The same with myself. Whenever we were with other people, zap, we'd put our masks on and we'd fight.

So other people started coming into our lives and ruining it for us. Things started snapping for me at school. I started to meet people. I started to go places. She didn't dig it. I started going to concerts, playing football. It was always like "Terry's always doing things, going places. Terry's always having a good time." It became a hassle to do all those things with her. I mean, she lived so far away and I didn't have a car. She's got to come to terms with herself, and I have to get a car before things can work out between us. If I had a car we'd be gone by now. We'd be off. If we had a 1969 Monte Carlo, we'd just get into it and go, man.

Amy and Carol

Amy and Carol are both junior high school physical education teachers. They're in their late thirties. They live with their six children (each of them had three children before they met) in a roomy, one-family house just outside of San Francisco.

Amy: Carol and I met five years ago. We met at a summer bungalow colony. We were both married then. As couples, we really had a lot of fun. We'd all socialize together. We'd even sometimes get together during the winter months. About a year and a half after we met, we were all together for New Year's Eve, and my husband started playing footsies with Carol by the fireplace. A few weeks later, after Carol and I played some tennis, I spoke to her about the incident and that's when she confessed to me that she was actually more attracted to me than she was to my husband.

Carol: When I first thought about Amy and the whole idea of homosexuality, it was very hard for me to think beyond kissing. My thoughts never really went further than that. But during the summers, when we'd been together, we sort of mentioned to each other that the idea of women being lovers didn't seem so terrible. And whenever we spoke, I sensed that Amy left open enough of a crack to make it seem possible. And we had always shared a great deal, told each other all of our secrets.

Amy: I had never looked at that side of myself. I had either stayed away from it consciously or unconsciously. But my response to all of Carol's provocative suggestions was to have an open mind. Carol and I became very close friends, and one day I remember telling her the greatest secret of my life—that I had

had an affair with somebody during the second year of my marriage. It was a big thing for me to tell her that. And when I told her, she was really wonderful about it. She didn't judge me. Well just as she was about to go home, that same day I'd told her, I suddenly put my arms around her and started kissing her. And a minute later, my husband came out and saw us. He had heard a few noises, pleasure sounds coming from us, and he was very angry. He said all kinds of nasty things about what I might want to do with another woman. So I told him we were just hugging and it was just nice.

Carol: I think our first kiss really had to do with a buildup of feelings and sharing. It was something we'd been thinking about for years even though it wasn't a primary thing. And I just loved Amy so much as a person. I really respected her.

Amy: It was a very turned-on and panicky feeling. All of a sudden I had the courage and the need to kiss. It was something I couldn't have pictured myself initiating but I did. I surprised the hell out of myself.

After that first kiss, we spent a lot of time negotiating on the phone whether or not we wanted to get together again. We finally agreed to spend an afternoon together and that's when we got to know each other's bodies. We started by kind of sitting next to each other and hugging and kissing a little bit. And then we sort of wondered what happens next. I just remember those feelings of saying, 'What the hell am I doing here. What am I getting myself into.' But it felt good, so I figured I'd just see what happened. I let myself experience feelings that I hadn't experienced for a long time. I felt like a turned-on teen-ager. It was very powerful. I remember us saying after the first experience that it was nice that we had both been married and were experienced and had experimented to some extent in our marriages so that we didn't have a lot of hang-ups about how much we could experiment.

Amy: At the time, we definitely didn't think that this would jeopardize our marriages. We felt like this had been very nice and we would try to get together and do it again. But there was no question about how much richer we felt when we were together than when we were with our husbands.

My relationship with my husband had always been very non-communicative, quiet, hostile, and superficial. I was definitely in love with him but very unhappy sexually which I blamed him for. I couldn't get any sexual satisfaction in our relationship and I had suggested he go for help. But I didn't push hard enough, so we just kind of rolled along. It was just the kind of thing where we should have done a lot more talking to each other. It was strange. He was easygoing. We never got angry. We never yelled at each other. We just simmered. And I'd never told anybody that I wasn't terribly happy.

Carol: I think I always felt that my marriage was a rather good one. But when Amy and I were together our relationship was just incredible. There was just so much more there than there had ever been with my husband. It's remarkable the things you start to feel when you finally love someone so much. It was also very exciting because it was obviously taboo and on the sneak and hard to arrange.

Amy: We ended up getting together so often that our husbands eventually knew that we were having a sexual relationship. But they were willing to let that be and it was OK. Then we made arrangements with them about how many hours a week it was OK to be with each other. But after a while it just became obvious to everyone that we were in love with each other.

Carol: Both of our husbands were highly civilized most of the time. I don't think they ever really expected us to end up together. What happened was we both split up with our husbands, but not because we were gay and not, at least as far as they knew, because we wanted to be together. I knew that I wanted to be with Amy but she wasn't sure she wanted to be with me.

Amy: I knew that I wanted to end the relationship with my husband. I wanted to get out of that bad relationship before I even thought about entering another one. And it took about another year and a half for Carol and her kids and me and my kids to all move in together. That's when Carol and I and our six kids all finally merged into one household.

The reason that both of us left our husbands was because we knew that there was something better between two people than what we had had with them. But we didn't know if we'd be able to pull off all the kids living together as one household. We hadn't dared think about it because we were so scared of losing custody of the children.

Carol: We told our kids that we wanted to live together, and we told them that some people in the world wouldn't like that idea. We told them that not everyone knows about our relationship but that most of the people that they know do. We told them that it was OK to tell anybody they wanted about it—*anybody* meaning the other kids on the block and their teachers at school.

Last year two of our kids were in the same class and had to write a composition about their family. They found that a little difficult partly because their family's not like most kids' families.

Amy: And sometimes that's really difficult. Our hardest problem is that each of Carol's kids are not officially mine and my kids are not officially Carol's, and unfortunately that's something their fathers are constantly reminding them of. So it's very confusing for them. They live in a family setting but are told by their fathers that they're not a family. And their fathers are very much into doing that. Our husbands have laid certain things on the kids that they never would have done if each of us had remarried another man. It's a problem we have to live with but we've become pretty good at dealing with problems. We've had to.

Pauline

She's forty-three and has been married and divorced three times.

I must have met Bobby when I was twelve. In fact, we were going steady by the time I was thirteen. My parents forbade me to see him and this made him very, very attractive. They didn't want me seeing him because his mother was the neighborhood prostitute. They never told me this back then because I was supposed to be sheltered. All they'd ever say was that she wasn't a nice lady. But as far as I could see, she was a very nice lady.

Then Bobby moved to Florida; his father lived out there. And I was young and, you know, you don't remain faithful to a guy who's living 1,400 miles away. So I started seeing other guys. But every time he came back we'd go steady again and my parents would flip out. I'd have to lie to them so I could see him. He went into the army, to Korea, and when he came back he looked like a young Robert Wagner; he was gorgeous. He was in uniform, but he didn't wear an army-made uniform. He had all his army clothes tailor-made. And he had the silver star and the bronze star and he was absolutely gorgeous. And he said, "Let's run away and get married," and I said, "No. I can't do that." So I said to my father, "Look. I wanna marry Bobby, but I will not marry him until you give me permission for him to come to the house and pick me up." I was getting tired of sneaking out. It was like four and a half years of sneaking out. My parents said, "No way will we give you permission to bring him to the house." So we eloped.

I was eighteen, he was eighteen and a half when we got married, and everybody was banking on us splitting up. But I was very much in love with Bobby then. It was like a forever thing. I got pregnant right away and then he was sent to Germany; he still had time left in the army. Anyway, when he got out of the army, he got a job and he worked for about five months. But after that job ended he didn't bother looking for another one, and that's when all the trouble started. I had an apartment, I had a baby, and Bobby was out of a job. So my father started giving me money every week for myself and the baby with the stipulation that not one cent was to go to Bobby. He said Bobby was a bum, and by that time I was beginning to think that Bobby was a bum too. Everything was deteriorating by then. I would have gone home a long time before I did except that everybody was saying to me that one day they'd be telling me "I told you so," and this I didn't want to hear. So I figured, no matter what, I'm gonna stick it out.

So one day Bobby came home and I'll show you how dumb I was. He had been gone all night long. He comes in and he says, "Don't you want to know where I've been?" So I say, "Not particularly." I mean, what was he doing all day anyway? Like nothing. He'd drive around in his car with the boys. So anyway when he asked me if I wanted to know what he'd been up to I really didn't care. So he says, "Well, for your information, I just pulled a robbery in Maryland and I've got a gun." So I'm very smart, right? I have a little baby. I go to the phone, and I say, "Operator, give me the police." I'm reporting him. So he runs out of the apartment. So I tell the police that I don't know whether it's true or not but my husband told me he pulled a robbery in Maryland and he's got a gun on him. I didn't even ask what kind of robbery. I figured he had a gun on him, he'd been in a robbery, and I didn't want him around.

I was really very upset. I left the apartment and I didn't want to go back because I thought he might have a gun, even though I didn't know for sure. I was too dumb to be scared for myself but I was worried because of the baby. I mean if he took a wild shot it could go off and there'd be no more baby. So I called my father from a pay phone and I told him what happened, and he said to me, "Pauline, pack everything you want because I'm going to take you home." And I was crying because I just didn't want to face people. You know, everybody saying that they were right and I was wrong.

I've only seen Bobby once since then. About ten years ago, I was standing at a subway station and all of a sudden I got lifted up in the air and who was it, it was Bobby. I think you always have a soft spot for your first love. I think your first love always remains your first love. Something's special about it. It's like the first time you ever felt a certain special way about someone. When I think of Bobby now, I think of the good times, the crazy times, the fun we used to have. Crazy things like running under the boardwalk in Coney Island and kissing. Or like our song, "Too Young." It's really strange how or why you remember certain things. Bobby I remember with kindness, with nostalgia, and I hope he's happy. The others that came after I don't give a damn about one way or the other. You know, just bug off and don't bother me. But him, I really want him to be happy. Maybe it's because he's the first person I loved.

Ron and K~~athe~~

The bookshelves—preassembled ~~...~~
look like wood—are crammed u~~...~~
living room is small with one w~~...~~
canary cages. (Raising and selling ~~...~~
told, is one of several of Ron's ~~...~~ ...ney-in-
your-spare-time projects.) Ron is thirty-five; his wife,
Katherine, thirty. They're members of a Seventh-Day
Adventist Institute located in the foothills of Massachu-
setts's Berkshire Mountains. Along with thirty other
adults—some married and with families, others single
—they live semicommunally on forty acres of land. Ron
runs the community's vegetarian restaurant. They've
been married for six years.

Ron: We met at an Adventist school down in Georgia. The founder of our religion, Ellen White, has given lots of counsel on courtship and marriage and all that type of thing. It's counsel she has given to make a happy and perfect marriage. Katherine and I actually entered a courtship, one that lasted several months.

Katherine was getting missionary training, nurse's training, and I had just finished being a student at the school in Georgia. Now, when I first considered beginning a courtship, I asked myself certain questions like: Am I ready? Is it time for me to have a companion? Have I proven myself in my parental home to have a home of my own? Then the next question we're all told to ask ourselves when we consider courting is, Do I *need* a companion? If the answer is yes, the next question is, To whom? That's when we go to seek advice from our elders, our Christian counselors—those with age and experience.

After I had seriously started counseling about marriage and before Katherine knew anything about it, I prayed that the Lord would help me. I'd spend time in the woods. I believe that God can direct in many different ways. Then, after I thought that Katherine might be the one, I wrote to her mother and father and asked permission to court their daughter. If they had said no, I couldn't have done it. I think Katherine still has the letter I wrote to her parents asking for permission. A letter or a phone call or some means of communication has to take place between the parents and the young man. The principle is that Katherine actually belonged to her parents, and had I won her affections unbeknownst to her parents, I would have stolen her, and that goes against the Decalogue—"Thou Shalt Not Steal."

They told me in their letter that they thought that Katherine was old enough to make up her own mind and they were willing to trust her decision in the matter.

Katherine and I were both at a committee meeting right after I got the reply from her parents. After the meeting, she was walking home and I ran beside her and I asked, "Did you get a letter today?" I thought she was going to get a letter from her parents first and that they were going to tell her all about my wanting to court her, and I was scared to death. So I said to her, "Did you get a letter from your folks?" and she said no, and I breathed a sigh of relief. I said, "Well, I have a letter for you to read." So anyway I handed her the letter her parents had written me and she said, "That looks so much like mama's writing." By this time we were walking down the road and were getting close to her house. She read the letter and her face was just as red as a beet. Well, then she got to the driveway and she handed the letter back to me and said she had a lot of thinking and praying to do. So she ran into the house and left me standing at the side of the road.

Anyhow, she went in to pray and later that day she called me on the phone and said that I could come and see her that night. So I went down there that night and we discussed it all a little bit more, and she decided that she would consider courting me. That's how we started out.

For us, courtship's really a period of time to get acquainted but the intention is definitely marriage. We studied the books together, books telling what a real Adventist home should be about. And we had a chaperone, too, an old lady.

I wanted to use the courtship time to talk things over. We spoke about children, diet, everything. I wanted to know some of the things Katherine felt about her own Christian relationship and her relationship to the church. And I knew that it was very easy for me to get attached. So right from the very beginning, I made it plain that there was going to be nothing that was going to form a relationship or an attachment before we actually knew for certain that God wanted us to be husband and wife. We didn't hold hands. We didn't kiss. We didn't—I don't know—whatever you want to call it, we didn't. We didn't exchange gifts, nothing.

I was working at the community's bakery and had white shirts that needed to be washed and ironed. My niece usually did that for me. One day my niece didn't have time to get 'em done, but that evening when I visited Katherine my shirts were all ironed. And I said to Katherine that as far as I was concerned ironing my shirts was a no-no. I knew that because we're human it was possible for her, even by just ironing my clothes, to form an attachment to me. I wanted nothing like that in case the Lord didn't see fit for us to be husband and wife. I didn't want that to be a problem for us—that she would have to undo or to untie some connections we made if we didn't end up marrying. And that's why we didn't even exchange pictures or anything like that.

Katherine: Eventually, through a lot more time on our knees, we knew we should marry. It's so hard to keep your head straight when you're coming that close to so strong a magnet. And we also kept real close to our counselors. They all knew us real well.

Ron: I wanted my counselors to tell me if she had any faults, and I wanted them to be frank with her, to tell her what she was up against. Our counselors spoke with one another. And in some cases, we even had the same counselor.

Katherine: Our instructions in courtship were that courtship is the time to watch every development, weigh every sentiment, watch, ask questions, find out. So we studied a lot, prayed a lot, and discussed a lot. We'd go out and pray in the woods together, on our knees, with our eyes shut. And we'd take turns praying aloud.

Ron: You want to know how I popped the question? We were going into town one day and I asked her if she'd mind doing a little ironing, and she said, "Well, no. I wouldn't mind."

Katherine: And then he asked me if I could mend some of his pants and would I do his laundry. Then he asked what about cooking, and I said, "I thought you didn't want me doin' anything like that before we were, you know, married." And he said, "Well, I mean can you do my cooking, my mending, and my ironing forever?"

Ron: We feel very, very strongly that God has one man for one woman. In the Ten Commandments, one of the commandments, the seventh—"Thou Shall Not Commit Adultery"—says that when you're married everything else is taboo with another woman. We believe this: that God places a sacred circle around the husband and wife and there are certain activities that only belong to these two.

Before I was a Christian, before I was a Seventh-Day Adventist, I had relationships with other women. This was when I was in the navy and so forth, and these were activities that I should have never done, that only belonged to my wife. Now, because of those past relationships, I can't share certain things with Katherine. I'll be frank with you. There's a type of close relationship that a husband and wife have in the area of kissing. And this is hard to say, but when I was young and inexperienced and foolish, I entered into some of those kissing types of things with other women. Now, even though I would like to share this type of kissing with my wife, I can't. I can't because I immediately think of it in these old, bad contexts, and it's put a scar on my mind. Eventually I hope the Lord will take that away so I can share it with my wife. I've cheated my wife out of that; it's something that rightfully belongs to her.

I've shared this with some of the young men in our community, trying to help them see that they need to be very careful in their relationships and that God wants them to have just one woman and that they should save all of that for her. This special love we represent as a daisy, and if you pull off a petal and give it to Jane, and another to Sandy, then when you finally find *the one,* you hand her this daisy but it only has a couple of petals left.

Katherine: A lot of people say they develop the ability to love as they go from one person to the other but that isn't true. They might learn some things, but when they finally try to settle down with *the one,* it's pretty hard to forget all those other things. You'll find yourself comparing when you could and should be completely satisfied with the experiences you're having with that one person. Sometimes somebody else might have satisfied you just a little bit better on this point or that point, more than the one you settled down with. But you wouldn't know that if you hadn't tried so many others.

Ron: It's really so beautiful when you do it the right way. You know, the proper way, when you know that God is leading you.

Ivy

Ivy's fifty-one. Janice, her lover, is thirty-seven. They've been together for three years, and both of them are convinced that they'll "remain together for this life and any future lives to come."

I have a thorough belief, a complete faith that this relationship was the relationship I'd been working my entire life to be worthy of. I'll tell you a story—an incredible story—and then you can judge for yourself.

About five years before I met Janice, I was thumbing through the *Los Angeles Times*. For whatever reason, I stopped turning the pages when I came across a huge three-quarter-page picture of a nun. The picture was part of an advertisement for a parochial college, and the nun in the ad was someone who taught at the school. There was a blurb accompanying the picture and it described everything this particular nun was doing at the college —teaching a dance course, organizing an art gallery, bringing guest lecturers to the campus. The photo was powerful. She was wearing a habit and it was the eyes that got me. I looked into them and I fell into them. And then I said to myself I have to meet this woman. I just fell into the picture. So I cut it out and filed it away. And I'd never done anything like that before in my life.

Years later I was going through all my old papers, cleaning up my apartment, when I got to the pile of papers with the photo in it. I'd totally forgotten about ever cutting anything out of the newspaper. Well, I looked at the picture and . . . I can't even begin to tell you the impact that picture had on me when I realized it was Janice. I just looked at it and said, "Oh, my God." I'd known Janice had once been a nun but I'd never seen a picture of her in her habit. I took the picture—and this was only about six months after we had started living together—and I hung it up on the back of the kitchen door. When Janice came back to the apartment that night, she saw the picture and it was incredible. She looked at it, turned crimson, paced the floor, and after a minute or two said, "That's the sign," and I knew what she was talking about.

John Meyers

*After a lifetime of celibacy, he decided to marry. He's
forty-seven and works as a hospital administrator.*

While I was in the priesthood I'd think of children—that it'd
be nice to have a family, to have offspring, to carry on the family
name. I was the only son in my father's family, and I knew that
the name would not be carried on. That didn't prompt my move,
but I was aware of it. I always felt close to the idea of a family and
as a priest I did a great deal of counseling with families, children,
and youth activities.

My wife was one of my parishioners and she helped out with
many of the church's activities. She was four years younger than
me. Right from the start she was attracted to me as I was to her,
but there were no sexual exchanges during our courting period.
It was simply a strong feeling of love and regard for each other. It
seemed so natural, the two of us, such a good thing. We were
unable to put a gate on it. We even tried separating several times
at first but that didn't work.

I never discussed any of this with my pastor because my relationship with him was never that open. But with my brother
priests, who I was friendly with, I could open up and get their
response to how everything was developing. I wanted to know
from them if I was blind, if I was making a fool of myself with this
young lady.

During the mid-sixties, when all of this was happening to me,
there was a push with Vatican Council II for a married clergy, but
the pope never allowed the idea to get to the floor. During this
time I was also completing work toward a masters degree in psychology and I think that was a real turning point. I was learning

how to come to grips with things that were going on within myself. There were mostly lay people where I was studying for my masters—psychiatrists and psychologists—and just being able to check out my own feelings with them was a reinforcement of the direction I was going in.

It was a difficult time for me. I had to make a decision. My wife and I knew we couldn't continue with the way things were going. We had to do one of two things: We either had to separate totally or I had to leave the church. I was aware that there had been some precedents where the pope had released certain priests in France from their vows in order to be married. When I sensed that that was possible—that I might be able to get papal dispensation and not have to be excommunicated—I decided to request Rome to relieve me of my vows. Prior to the sixties, if you had left the priesthood it was as a black sheep, a *persona non grata,* or in effect, as a scandalous, sinful renunciation of your vows. Automatic excommunication. There had been men who had left, but they had left under great clouds. Everyone prayed for them very seriously, prayed that they'd come to their senses.

I told my wife that it would be nice if I could get papal dispensation but I didn't know if that would be possible. You have to understand, too, that my ties to the church were very strong and I didn't know if I could handle leaving the church without the dispensation. And my wife didn't even know if she wanted me to leave. But all along there was never any pressure from her. You see, we both came out of a rather traditional, strict life-style within the Catholic tradition, a really traditional Irish background. Priests from the church were very important people, which made things with our families a little sensitive.

My dad died before permission was granted from Rome, and I know he was puzzled and anguished over the whole thing. He was very upset that this was happening to me because I'm sure I was a proud part of his life. Mom, I think, was also very upset and concerned. But she gave her consent, approval, and acceptance of my life even though it did hurt her a bit. She even felt that it was good that I was entering into a family setting. My wife's mother ... well, she accepted it. She accepted whatever her daughter felt was proper. But if she had had her own way, I'm sure she would have preferred her daughter to marry a lawyer, a school teacher, a social worker, or even a sanitation man. Anyone but a former priest.

I'd say that it was all a very easy transition, a very natural transition. There was no real pressure or anxiety or hiding behind corners. The only difficulty we had was when we were so-called courting before the permission from Rome came. We'd go out to dinner and at that point we didn't want to needlessly advertise our relationship because there might be some eyebrows raised by certain parties. So I wouldn't, for instance, wear my collar when we were out. When we'd socialize I'd go incognito as they say. I'd wear just a sweater and a shirt.

I felt for a long time that it was an unreal setting for modern times—to be a celibate priest in the rectory. I felt a person should be more involved with the workaday world, with people, with their problems. I was absolutely celibate until the age of forty-one. I was ordained when I was twenty-six and I was in the active ministry from 1955 to September of 1970 when I left rectory life. I received my dispensation from Rome the following year and I was married in 1971.

They say that around ten thousand priests have left the church in America in order to get married or to live a more involved lifestyle. That figure—maybe even as high as fifteen thousand—includes some priests who've obtained papal dispensation and others who haven't.

In certain cases, some priests who've married have not remained married—priests have no better rate of divorce than the general populace—so naturally infatuations come into play here. But in my situation it didn't happen. We were about the same age, late thirties, and our seven years of marriage with a family shows, I suppose, that it wasn't just an infatuation.

The release from Rome finally came and we were married at

the bishop's chapel. At that time, even though the papal dispensation had been granted, we still weren't allowed to be married in our local parish church. We had to be married rather secretively in the bishop's house where there wouldn't be too much notoriety. Today that's all a lot more relaxed. After the marriage we just set up house and everyone seemed accepting and open to us. What was said behind closed doors . . . well, that's other people's problems.

I feel that reaching out is what life is all about. Reaching out to somebody, having a tie with somebody. I really think that relationships are the root of everything. And now, with my wife and children and my work, I'm able to enjoy a fuller relationship with both man and God.

Bart and Kathy

They live in a small town in southern Maine. Bart works the night shift in a nearby paper mill. They're each eighteen and they're married. At the time of this interview Kathy was eight-and-a-half months pregnant.

Bart: I had a bad experience with one girl right before I met Kathy. I got the cold treatment from her and it blew my mind for awhile. I was feelin' lonely and I needed somethin' to get me out of the feelin' so I went to the Portland Rollerdome, the roller-skating rink.

Kathy: That same night, I was goin' out with this guy, Billy, and we went roller skatin'. When we got there, Billy was treatin' me bad—like he was tellin' me to sit on the bench and have a good time while he'd go off roller skatin' and pickin' up girls. So I said, 'Okay, I'm gonna make him jealous.' I saw this guy sittin' nearby and I figured I'd start talkin' to him. The guy sittin' there was Bart. So here I am tryin' to make this guy jealous and I'm talkin' to Bart and Bart starts tellin' me to break up with Billy. I'd only been goin' out with Billy for a couple of weeks so I was confused. Well, I ended up tellin' Bart that this guy's treatin' me like shit and what should I do. And that night ended with me breakin' off with Billy and me drivin' Bart home.

Bart: I really liked Kathy but what I liked most about her was that she had a car. That was the deciding factor of our relationship. I swear to God! I said to myself, 'Wow, this chick has a car.'

Kathy: I liked Bart. I thought he was a nice guy. But what really got me was that he kept callin' me after that first night and every time he'd call me I wouldn't be home and he kept callin' and I wasn't there. And that really impressed me—that this guy's been tryin' to call me and I'm never there but he never gives up. So finally I called him back and we got talkin' and we made a date to see each other the next day. I was a senior in high school then.

I picked him up the next day and brought him over to my house and two days later he asked me to marry him. He was a fast worker. I was shocked. I said yes but I almost didn't know what I was sayin'.

Bart: I asked her to marry me partly because that's usually a sure fire way to get some action. It really is. It really works.

Kathy: I didn't know how serious he was—and I didn't know how serious I was. It was a real shock because I'd just met him. We did hit it off pretty good. We got along together; we could talk to each other without hurtin' each other. We could be open with each other. I don't really know what made me say yes to marryin' him—but I did.

Bart: I think what Kathy just said about both of us not hurtin' one another explains a lot of stuff. We're both eighteen and to understand all this you have to go back a couple of years. When I was twelve, my mother married a guy who'd been married five times and we didn't get along. It was just conflict all the time. I wasn't gettin' along with my mother then either. So when I was twelve I moved out. I broke my stepfather's nose before I left—I was defendin' myself. He used to haul off on me all the time. So I was takin' care of myself ever since I've been twelve. I lived with relatives, friends, on the street, whatever.

I never had anybody say somethin' nice to me. And I'd always gotten into a lot of trouble with girls. They seemed like they cared for me so I always felt that what they were sayin' was comin' from a deep place—but they really didn't care. Maybe I thought all that because I needed it so much. But I believed it. These girls showed me affection but I'd be interpretin' it on a much deeper level. But Kathy really gave it to me. I felt I had security with her. And before her, I'd been bounced out of every house I'd been in. You know, when I was six months old my old man was beltin' the shit out of me.

Kathy: And I'd really been hurt by men too. One guy I was with was really screwed up in the mind. He treated me real bad. He used to hit me all the time. We'd be sittin' in study hall and he'd hit me—you should of seen the bruises on my legs. He'd hit me for no reason, just to get his anger out. But Bart's not like that.

Bart: We decided to get married when Kathy was in her fourth month of pregnancy—but we didn't get married because we had to.

Kathy: After I got pregnant, I decided to keep the baby because I loved Bart and I knew he wanted to marry me. I'd been pregnant with another guy's baby and I'd had an abortion. But when I found out that Bart had gotten me pregnant, I really was excited.

Bart: What happened was that we were over some friends' house and they had a baby, a year-old baby. And when Kathy looked at that baby, her face glowed. I never saw her face glow quite like that. So then she expressed to me that she'd like one—and I said I'd give her a baby as a birthday present.

Kathy: I knew Bart loved me and I knew I loved him. And even though he didn't have a job then, I knew that somehow it would all work itself out. I was so happy about it.

As much as I was happy about it, though, it was also a little scary. I was seventeen, still in school, and I was scared to death to tell my parents. I think my mother knew that I was pregnant all along but she didn't want to come right out and say it. She was droppin' little hints, though. Like I was sittin' in a chair one day and my stomach was hangin' out—this was in my fourth month —and she said, "What is that? It better not be what I think it is." My parents weren't—and aren't—too happy about everything. They're both alcoholics and so they get upset real easily about everything.

Bart: When I found out about the baby, I said to myself, 'I've tried a lot of different things but this is something I've never tried.' But I'm also scared. Our finances are out of balance. I make a hundred dollars a week at the mill and that's not much. And sometimes it just seems like everything's happenin' to me at once. First there was one new person, my wife, now this other one on the way. It depresses me sometimes. I even left Kathy for a few days a couple of weeks ago. I didn't know if I could go through with it.

Kathy: When he left me, I was scared but I knew he needed to get away for awhile. I guess I understood him because I'm the same age and this is scaring me too. You know, all the responsibilities. So I know how he feels about it, the good and the bad feelings. When I'm down and depressed about something, I also think, 'What am I doing here? I'm young, I could be out enjoyin' life.' I feel like that sometimes but it doesn't ever last. Then, when I look at the other side—that we're going to have a baby in another three weeks—well, then, deep down I know that this is what I want to be doin'.

Bart: What really convinced me to stay and have the baby was seeing a friend's baby. This kid was about two years old and his father had left when he was born. I watched this friend with her baby and I saw that if I left Kathy, then this is who'd she'd be. And that's how it is a lot of the time: The man leaves and then the woman has to take care of both herself and the baby. And it's always bad for the kid because of all the hassles when another man gets close to the mother. The kid suffers and I didn't want that to happen to my kid. You know, I wouldn't want to leave my kid the way I was left. I had so many bad experiences with my father and my stepfather that I think by now I know what not to do to a kid. I don't know what *to* do and that scares me. But I do know what *not* to do. I could write an encyclopedia about it.

Kathy: Bart doesn't trust himself but I do. He knows what he's been through and he doesn't want to put his little son or daughter through the same thing. You know, he's not gonna pick the kid up and throw it against the wall when it's six months old like his father did to him. He's gonna think twice.

Jack and Helena

We met Jack and Helena on a ferry ride from Woods Hole, Massachusetts, to Martha's Vineyard. When we told them about our project, they immediately asked if they could do an interview. Within five minutes our tape machine was recording. For the next half hour we sat on a sunny, windy deck—just enough time for them to tell us the story of how they met.

At the time of this interview, they'd been together eight months.

Helena: I was meeting lots of men but there was nobody who was falling in love with me and nobody who I was falling in love with. I spent a year and a half just running around like a maniac, screwing around a lot. Finally, I was getting really lonely and I was admitting it to myself. So I figured what have I got to lose, and I put a personal ad in the local underground newspaper. The ad read:

WOMAN 28

Attractive, gentle, making satisfying living through art, seeking individual who's also fulfilled by their work and who enjoys music, movies, theater. Companion-lover wanted. Someone who enjoys poetry, outdoors, and believes in growth and open communication. Write Box #47 ^c/o this newspaper.

I thought that most people would think it was odd that I was putting an ad in the paper because I was a fairly attractive woman and why couldn't I find a man? I'd met a lot of attractive men, but no one I felt I could have a relationship with. So I tried the ad.

I had twenty replies and Jack's was one of them. His letter was fantastic. It really communicated his wit, his charm, his intelligence, his honesty. And he told me all about his shortcomings.

Jack: I was surprised that I was responding to one of those ads. But that particular ad came right out at me. Something about it seemed very sincere. I guess I'd gotten disillusioned with the superficial ways I was meeting people. Being a musician, you're always in bars and having a sort of meaningless discussion with somebody who you know nothing about. You look at them and they look at you, and well that whole pickup scene is just ridiculous. So I wrote my response to Helena's letter, then I looked at it, threw out a couple of sections, and made a second copy. Actually, I didn't expect anything to happen. I sort of hoped, but I didn't expect. On one level I thought she'd probably dismiss my letter, and on another level I figured . . . well, most of the other letters she'd get won't be as detailed as this one. It was the type of letter that gave her a chance to find out what I was like.

Helena: Before Jack and I finally met, I think I'd met maybe three of the other men who'd sent me replies. And surprisingly, all of them were really nice men. There were no sleazy replies at all. I had just assumed that there'd be a lot of that because a lot of the ads are pretty sleazy to begin with. Well, eventually I called Jack after reading his letter and we spoke on the phone. But the call was really awkward. He didn't sound very friendly.

Anyway, we made a date to meet at a restaurant, and as soon as we saw each other, sparks flew. When I saw Jack, I couldn't understand how all the women in the world didn't just fall at his feet. I thought he was the most adorable man in the world.

Jack: I was charmed, too—very much so. We had a two-and-a-half-hour lunch and drank an entire bottle of wine which loosened both of us up a lot.

Helena: We spoke for hours that first day and I think both of us knew that something was going to happen.

Jack: Yeah. After that luncheon, I knew I was interested in pursuing her.

Josh

He's thirty-five.

I decided to go to a park and it so happened that this park was having a rock concert. This was in '68. There was a love-in there and it was chaotic. Just people all over the place and no one making any kind of contact with one another. It was like everyone was so isolated yet they were ideally there to establish some kind of link with one another. So I was walking and I saw this woman wearing this purple shawl, this shawl that looked like velvet. She was coming up to all the people and talking with them. And then she came closer and closer and then I heard her say to someone, "Come on. Aren't we supposed to be dancing and getting together. Why's everyone just standing around?" And I was amazed. And then she started coming up to me and she came up to me and I looked at her right in the eyes and she had these butterflies painted on her face. And when she came up to me I just grabbed her and looked at her and she didn't say a word and I didn't say a word. It was only for a moment but it seemed like an eternity had flashed in front of my eyes. I mean, it was like a moment, yet so many things were happening in that moment. And I said to her—and it was like I was observing myself saying this— "We're going to be together for the rest of our lives."

Three days after their initial meeting, they were married. And two kids and eight years later, they're still together.

ENJOYING

As they lay close together, complete and beyond the
touch of time or change, it was as if they were at the
very centre of all the slow wheeling of space and the
rapid agitation of life, deep, deep inside them all, at
the centre where there is utter radiance, and eternal
being, and the silence absorbed in praise.

from *The Rainbow*
by D. H. LAWRENCE

If I don't love you baby,
Grits ain't grocery,
Eggs ain't poultry,
And Mona Lisa was a man.

LITTLE MILTON

Joan and Barry

They're married. Joan is twenty, Barry, forty-four. At the age of eighteen Barry contracted encephalomyelitis and was left paralyzed from the waist down. Joan met him while doing volunteer work at the hospital in New York City where Barry was a resident. At the time of this interview they'd been married for six months, but they'd been emotionally involved with one another for almost two years before their marriage. They're both native Brooklynites.

Barry: I hadn't been disabled before my nineteenth birthday. It was a disease, encephalomyelitis. It just came overnight. So I've spent more than half my life in hospitals.

Well, Joan was a student and was doing volunteer work at the hospital where I was a patient. I had seen her around but we didn't really know each other. We were on a hello basis but that was it. I'd been living at the hospital for twenty-four years at that point.

Joan: Besides doing volunteer work, I was doing fieldwork for college. So I started working with the adults more, mostly with the bowling and camera clubs at the hospital and Barry was working in medical photography. He had gerbils which he kept up in the photo lab and I love animals, and that's how we got to know each other. Every night, after I came back from school, I'd go visit him and the gerbils.

Barry: It became a hangout for her. It started out that it was my birthday and she brought my gerbils a present. That was really the icebreaker. She always used to come up on the pretense of being interested in my gerbils, and from there it progressed— more so on her part. She was determined. I was more reluctant.

I was reluctant because . . . well . . . through my stay at the hospital I encountered a number of volunteers or just friends and some were platonic, some weren't; but I never allowed it to become too serious, at least on my part anyway. I just felt there were too many physical complications and I really didn't want to burden or share my problems with anybody else. So usually it got to a point where I just let it cool off and that was it. And I still am friends with a few of them now.

Joan: All his friends were female. He had no male friends. I had to get used to that. It used to drive me crazy. I'm insanely jealous. Whenever I would see him, he was getting another letter from some girl or other woman he knew, and a lot of them were already married with children. But they'd still keep in touch with him for years and years.

Barry: This was part of my existing at the hospital. I mean, there weren't that many patients at the hospital that I could talk to, not that we didn't have that much in common, but you get together and talk about all the little things. We had *too* much in common. So I looked elsewhere. The hospital always had a volunteer program and volunteers were always coming and going. Because they were new, they weren't always talking about the same stuff. And when one phased out another one always came on. A couple of them were really serious about me and a couple of them contained their feelings for me. I found out females mostly get carried away more than males—I mean as far as emotions go. I told a friend of mine who worked at the hospital that this thing with Joan was not gonna last, that we'd just enjoy each other's company for as long as it lasted and that'd be it.

Joan: Boy, was *he* surprised!

Barry: I really was. She was very determined.

Joan: He really couldn't put an end to it. He couldn't just say tomorrow you can't come anymore. He kept thinking that eventually I'd wear out, that I wouldn't want to come anymore, and it just didn't work that way. I enjoyed being with him. I don't think I missed a day. I felt myself falling in love with Barry immediately. I just never liked too many of the guys I knew from school and stuff. Most of them were very immature. In Barry I found someone I could really talk to. Barry wasn't used to opening up and talking either. He never wanted to tell me anything at first.

Barry: It wasn't easy. At first I was very hesitant.

Joan: I waited till he was ready to tell me the things he wanted to tell me. I knew I'd have to give him time.

Barry: She was ready to explode, trying to find things out about me. And I don't know whether I was afraid because I knew it would scare her or because she might not accept some of the things I had to tell her. But anyway, she took things like a pro.

Joan: There were a lot of physical things that he didn't want to tell me about his illness—like why he spent so much time in a hospital.

Barry: She used to tell me that I had institutionitis and that I was a classic example. And in a way it was true.

Joan: I would point this out to him—that maybe he was afraid to leave the hospital.

Barry: When you've been in an institution for so many years, you accept it as your home and that's the way it is. I never ex-pected to marry or to be able to really love someone—you know, openly—and I was resigned that this was going to be it for me. I had everything I wanted in the hospital's photography room. I had a hot plate there, I had my stereo, and I had a lot of privacy.

Joan and I started seeing each other in January, but we really didn't get that close for another month or two, and I remember telling this friend of mine that I'd call it off after her exams because if I called it off before, I might be responsible for her fail-ing. And then I figured, 'OK, the summer's here, why break it off?' At least we'd have something for the summer. After the summer I'd do it. Then she started her last year of college and I figured I didn't want to louse up her last year.

Joan: And he kept on going like that.

Barry: I've never been able to easily express my feelings, and Joan expresses herself very easily, and she opened up to me right off the bat. She'd write me letters that she'd hand me or mail me and she'd get embarrassed when I'd read them and she'd go into another room until I'd finished. So sometimes she was a little afraid to speak her feelings but she'd always write them down. When I got the letters I felt good. I just didn't feel I'd be able to handle this whole situation. I felt that Joan was really competing with the hospital. It sounds funny, but all my ties were there.

Then I started seeking professional help at the hospital about Joan. I was trying to find out about the different ways of getting support if I moved out of the hospital—medicaid, SSI, welfare. I'd meet with a fellow I'd known as a patient at the hospital who'd left a few years before. He'd tell me some of the things I wanted to know. He was also a paraplegic and was married. And I talked to a psychologist about my fears of leaving the hospital. It wasn't so much my fear of being with Joan as it was of leaving the hospital. I had my ties there. I started thinking that maybe I'd try it out for a year, living outside of the hospital, and then if Joan didn't like it, I could always go back.

Joan: But deep inside me I knew he loved me—someplace—but he was just afraid to say it. He was afraid to say it to himself.

Barry: Then we had a weekend out of the hospital. We wanted to see if we could possibly manage. So when her parents went away one weekend, she sneaked me home.

Joan: That was really his first time away from the hospital. The only other time he'd ever gone away was when he'd go out for the day with an orderly.

Barry: I was scared to go away even for the weekend.

Joan: Yeah, and as I was taking him across the street—my parents only lived across the street—I kept expecting him to say 'Turn around.'

Barry: Anyway, I figured that maybe after a weekend we'd be able to decide. The weekend was very nice. It worked out and Joan was able to do the things and handle the things that I needed to have done for me.

Joan: It's my cooking that did it.

Barry: Then we did it one more time. We had another weekend that worked out too. And then we really started talking seriously. I'd been a clam all my life, very difficult to pry open. But now I'm probably at the point where she was when we first met.

I told my family about Joan and it was very hard for them to accept. They figured I was safe in the hospital, secure, and that Joan was just a kid and how was she gonna take care of me. Our age difference is a big one. I'm about twice Joan's age. She's twenty and I'm forty-four. I would have thought it would have been more difficult for Joan's parents because I could understand how they felt about their youngest daughter accepting so much responsibility.

Joan: Yeah, it was one long night of screaming. I think my mother's still waiting around for something to go wrong so she'll be able to say ''I told you so.'' But she knew that if she didn't accept it, then she'd lose me in the end. I have a will of my own, a mind of my own, and she ended up giving us a very nice wedding.

Barry: Joan had never mentioned anything about me to her parents. All they knew was that she was a volunteer at the hospital.

Joan: But my mother got word back from other people at the hospital, people who she knew that worked there, that had seen us together. When she found out, she said, ''Remember, don't get serious with him. You'll only get hurt in the end.'' So I never told her that I was still seeing Barry.

Barry: Joan felt that if she made it definite, they would really give her a hassle. So until it was final, she just didn't say anything. The same thing happened with me with my family. It hit my mother very hard. She wondered, 'can Joan do this and can Joan do that?' I don't really know whether my mother was concerned about my sex life or not, but she said to me, ''You know, I never really talked to you about it.'' Then I told her, ''Ma, Joan knows.''

Joan: We can have regular, normal sex, but it's easier for us other ways. Really, we could write our own books about it.

That's what all the counselors in the hospital worried about—how our sex lives were going to be. We had other things on our minds, but that's what they were worried about.

Barry: They didn't seem that interested in our being compatible, liking each other, being able to talk to one another. It was just sex plus my other physical things. And Joan . . . I guess it has to be just because of her love for me that she was able to do the things she had to do for me. I know it wasn't pleasant for her then and it isn't pleasant for her now, but she does it. And if she didn't do it, then to tell you the truth I don't think I'd be here now.

Joan: Changing bedpans and all that really didn't bother me from the beginning. I didn't mind it at all. It was just so great to have Barry here. I mean, it's a small price to pay.

Barry: I had read in these articles that people's wives turned up their noses at having to do certain things. So in this one article they said that if your wife had to be your nurse, chances of it working out were not that good. It's one thing to be a wife, but if you have to be a nurse as well, the responsibilities are just too much. If you need certain things done, the article suggested that you have somebody else come and do them. And I have a problem with urine and bowels and so they said get somebody else to take care of these things, so I did. I used to have an orderly come over once or twice a week.

Joan: I disliked that even more. I mean, I had to wait for someone else to do these things and I figured, 'If I'm here, I can do it.'

Barry: And I still can't believe it. People I bump into from the hospital, they ask me, "So how's married life?" and I tell them that it's really a dream for me. I can't believe it's happening.

For example, we went on a trip. Before she met me, she never drove out of Brooklyn. She still can't even believe that she drove to Florida and back, and that's how I feel just about our being together. I mean, not now, but when we first were married, I figured sometime I'd wake up and I'd find myself back in the hospital—as though nothing had really happened at all. It would have been just a dream. But Joan's really been the deciding factor as far as our relationship goes. She wears the pants around here. She did the planning of the trip. I was excited inside, but for years I'd found out that every time I'd get excited about something and it backfired, I'd be very disappointed. So Joan would be sitting in bed with the AAA Triptik, planning the mileage and the hotels, making all the reservations, plus handling me, loading and unloading the van.

Joan: I don't think he really knew our trip to Florida was gonna happen. I don't know if I knew it was really gonna happen. We'd be in a hotel saying to each other that we couldn't believe that it was really happening—but we got the slides back, so now I believe it really happened.

Barry: We just like to pick up and go. I mean like yesterday was a nice day, so we said, "Come on, let's go to the aquarium in Coney Island." So we went. We went out on the boardwalk. We went out to eat in a restaurant. And we just do things, go places. It doesn't matter what we do, we just like going.

Marcia and Rita

At the age of fifty-eight Marcia, a psychiatrist and grandmother, fell in love with Rita, a thirty-eight-year-old museum curator. At the time of this interview, they'd been together for two years.

Marcia: I had always been heterosexual. I never would have dreamed of anything not heterosexual, particularly at my age. I have grandchildren. I'm sixty and have been married three times with many men in between. All my relationships ended in divorce. I was married for about a year and a half when I was in college. Then my major marriage was for twenty-three years. That relationship was very rich and very full, intellectually and culturally. In fact, people were just amazed when we broke up. Everything was shared in terms of values but it was really very detached on a human level, emotionally. I was very distant and I was hungry for closeness. But Don was basically content and if it hadn't been for me, we'd probably still be together. There was a lot of hostility between us that came out as competitiveness and muteness. Once we didn't talk for *six* months. After a while, it just became a really ugly relationship, and it didn't matter how much we shared intellectually. I also found Don to be asexual. Well, I shouldn't say asexual, we did have sex. But I certainly found that his passivity and detachment carried over sexually.

My third marriage was for four years. It was, in a way, the converse of my other marriage. Allen was very unintellectual but very sexual and very attractive and very exciting. He was married, by the way, when we met and he left his wife for me. It was very exciting with Allen at first because of his charisma and charm and the kind of romantic, sexual aspect we shared. It was also fun. I think if we would have continued it as an affair it would have been a great one. But the romance vanished after not too long. After four years, the marriage ended with Allen leaving me. I've described his leaving as being precipitous but not sudden. Like my second husband, Allen was also someone who feared intimacy. But I remember at the time feeling very threatened at the prospect of breaking up yet another marriage, and unlike any of my previous marriages, I was the one who was clinging and begging him to stay. The last time I saw Allen was in court, and I was delighted that he looked so terrible.

I never had any intimations on the conscious level of wanting to be with a woman, not until Rita came along. The only experience I ever had, which was most abortive, was in high school with this lesbian student who really had a thing for me and she had me sleep over and so forth. I was very threatened by the whole thing, and on one occasion she and a friend sort of cornered me and I resisted. Other than that I had the usual adolescent crushes but there was absolutely nothing on the conscious level.

I met Rita at a party, a fund-raising party, two years ago.

Rita: We started talking because I was on my way to the jungles of Guatemala for a vacation. I was going to places nobody ever heard of and Marcia had been there ten years ago. That freaked me out. When we met I was in the process of breaking up with Judy who I'd lived with for seven years. It was a bad relationship but I guess I needed it. I never really wanted it. I just sort of backed into it. By the time I met Marcia the relationship had already been over for at least two years but it just kept dragging on. We owned a house together and there was a lot of untangling. But she probably would have stayed on forever.

I had spent a year being totally and absolutely isolated before I met Judy. I mean, I must have read four hundred books, that's all I did. I didn't see anybody. I met Judy through some mutual friends at a party. I'm bisexual but I found that it was easier to meet people in the gay world. So I met Judy at a gay party. Anyway, she moved into my apartment and I just didn't protest and we got more and more involved. I made it work somehow but I always knew that it was sort of a second-rate thing.

Marcia: Anyway, when we first met, I found Rita very interesting. I was excited. I remember telling a friend that there was a woman pursuing me.

Rita: Which I definitely was doing.

Marcia: I was very uneasy about it, yet I didn't discourage her. At first it was so disconcerting. It was a totally new experience. I was very excited, very uneasy, and didn't quite know what was going on. But at the same time I was getting more and more interested in Rita.

I would come home and my doorman would give me a beautifully wrapped package, so aesthetic. They'd be little gifts from Rita, like homemade hot mustard.

Rita: Meanwhile, we were meeting every other week for lunch. We would just talk about different things, not about our relationship. I remember Marcia was talking one day about some problem she was having with her daughter. We had a lot to say to each other.

Marcia: And it was always very rich. And then Rita said, "Why don't we meet every week instead of every other week?"

Rita: I was in a quandary. I sort of knew that Marcia was straight and that she'd be shocked if she knew about me. I just assumed the whole thing was out of her realm.

Marcia: And then Rita wrote me some marvelous notes because she was just bursting. It got uncontrollable.

Rita: I was falling in love and I didn't know what to do with it. I didn't want to scare Marcia off and I'd rather have her as a friend than nothing. The notes probably sound very sophomoric now.

Marcia: Not at all. I still have every one.

Rita: One night I told Marcia I'd be over to her house at about ten o'clock. I was terrified.

Marcia: That was April 11. I sensed that something was going to happen that evening.

Rita: You certainly did. You changed into something very sexy. I couldn't believe it.

Marcia: I was just very excited and bewildered.

Rita: I never had done anything like this before. I never, as the gay world calls it, brought anybody out. It was very new for both of us.

Marcia: And I just couldn't believe it. You know, here I am, fifty-eight years old, and it was so foreign to me, so different from anything I'd ever experienced. I don't know how else to say it but I had to get used to it sexually. It just had to be an experiential thing. It took a while before I felt really comfortable. You know, I was enjoying it very much and I had such strong feelings for Rita, such affection and tenderness, but it was awhile before I really felt wonderful about the sexual aspect. Some of Rita's gay friends, I remember, were sort of suspicious. I was looked upon by them as a straight woman who thought it was chic to have this sort of adventure.

Another thing, I was very self-conscious about in the beginning was our age difference.

Rita: Oh yes, you were very nervous about that. But I've been with people of all different ages and I don't understand age. It doesn't matter to me.

Our relationship really evolved very openly. There were never any strings. And neither of us are hiding the fact that we're together. Maybe me a little because I've had trouble in the past. My first relationship with a woman was when I was twenty-nine, and the man that I had almost married suddenly became impotent because he found out that I was gay. In the beginning of our relationship, Marcia was blindly telling everyone about being gay and I thought we were really going to get into trouble. But we didn't.

Marcia: My colleagues certainly don't know. They don't have to know that I'm gay. Some of my patients do know, though. In fact, one of my patients, a homosexual woman who was in the midst of deliberating about whether or not to tell her parents that she was gay, once looked at me and asked, ''Have you told *your* parents?'' And I said, ''No, but I've told my children.''

Rita: I really think that most of my experiences in the past would have led me to be cynical about love. People have just eaten me up alive. I'm sure there's a reason why I sought relationships like that, but I always found myself in these relationships where I was just giving everything I had and there was nothing coming back. I felt that you couldn't have a good relationship like Marcia's and mine. I felt it really didn't exist in real life. Marcia thought that it existed but that she just hadn't found it yet. I've really never been in any kind of relationship that's so wonderful. We have problems but we can deal with them.

Marcia: We talk to each other every night when we're not together.

Rita: There's so much to speak about, always.

Marcia: Both of us feel that we've found the right person, and it doesn't matter if that person happens to be a man or a woman. We've just found the right person and we don't feel that we're in any category.

Anne Byrne Hoffman

She's a dancer, an actress, a writer, a mother, and in no way does she fit any stereotype one might have of a movie star's wife. Still, her story is very much the story of how she became just that—one of Hollywood's leading men's first ladies.

We've known each other for nearly fifteen years and we've been married for eight of those years. We met in 1963 and we fell in love immediately. It was one of those across-the-room—well, across-the-table—infatuations. I was so much in love with Dusty when I met him that I didn't know he was short. It took me about a month to realize it. One day we were walking across the street and I saw our reflection in a store window and it was quite a surprise.

We were in this bar and he was sitting there and I thought he was the end. I just looked at his face and said, 'Wow, this is it.' At one point we were stuck at the table alone and I couldn't talk to him. He'd say, "You're a dancer?" I'd say, "Yes." I was sure that he probably thought I was stupid so I made sure to be even less talkative. But it turned out that he'd been attracted to me the same way I'd been attracted to him. So it worked out. We saw each other constantly for about a month. Then I went to Philadelphia to dance and while I was there I guess I had second thoughts about him. He was really in love with me and he wanted to get married right away, so I dropped him. I was in love with him but he scared me. He was very aggressive and—I thought at the time—very sure of himself. It was a very painful break for him. Years later he told me how hurt he was.

And that was it for three years. I came to New York twice during that time and I thought of looking him up because I was feeling kind of guilty. I wanted to explain to him why I'd done what I'd done, but I never did.

So three years elapsed and I met someone else while I was in Philadelphia. I had become terribly lonely. I met this guy who was a lawyer and I decided I'd marry him. And I knew—I mean I think people have the right impulses—I knew the minute that I said yes that it was no. It's never a surprise when those things don't work out. I mean there's a feeling in your stomach that tells you. But you mask it; you rationalize it. This was before the days when people had the nerve to not show up at the church. I mean, I think now maybe I'd have the guts to call it off the day before, send back all the gifts. But I was caught.

Dusty didn't know anything about it; we'd had no contact. Then after I became pregnant with my daughter I went into therapy and I saw that it wasn't going to work out and that I didn't want it to. So I moved back to New York and moved into my parents' home with my newborn baby. My husband had taken all the money out of our joint account and he'd left me with only forty-two cents, so I was completely broke. But I started dancing again and my parents were helping me. Well, one day I was looking at the *New York Times* and I saw a picture of this old guy and I recognized the face immediately. I looked at the caption and it was Dusty. He had done this thing on TV and off-Broadway where he had played this old man. I immediately wrote him a note. In the note I mentioned that I had this new little thing in my life. As soon as he got the note he tracked me down to a theater where I was rehearsing for a concert. So we started seeing each other again and that went on for another three years.

We'd both been through sort of parallel crises while we were apart. We'd both given up smoking and we'd gone into therapy. And he was very nice to my daughter right away and they developed an attachment to each other quickly. The relationship between Dusty and me was still very much the same as it had been.

He didn't play it any cooler than he had the first time around. Maybe the only difference was that he was making more demands on me.

I finally got into the New York City Ballet and Dusty got the lead in an off-Broadway play. The play got great reviews and it began looking like something might really happen. Then somehow somebody heard about Dusty and thought he should test for *The Graduate*. The producers and casting people had seen everybody and they were really scraping bottom when they got to Dusty. So he went out to California and it was awful. He was so nervous he made everybody else very nervous; but when the director saw the rushes it was exactly what he wanted.

The whole experience was a disaster. You see, I didn't know anything about Hollywood. I wasn't brought up on Hollywood. My parents didn't take me out to the movies. All I knew was that it was this special place where all the people were beautiful and interesting and so I thought this was it for our relationship. I figured, 'I'm this ugly kid. *They've* got him now. He's probably having an affair with Katharine Ross.' He was so excited but scared and he couldn't really be reassuring to me. I was afraid to go out there and be with him.

It was really terrible. First of all, we were shaky in the relationship. I mean, at first we had this basic love and this passion. It was not an intellectual passion at all. But, as in all relationships, the passion changes. It stays but it changes, and we were in that passionate stage where we'd be hurtful to each other and then feel guilty about having been so hurtful. It was a hard time. So I went out to California, this little ballet girl. I was so afraid they'd find me out. They'd find out that my clothes were cheap, that I didn't know how to dress, that my hair was dirty. I really felt like that ugly girl from down the street. But I did it all that to myself. People were actually very nice to me. They even thought I was pretty.

It was a different world. Hollywood had what seemed like an endless expense account—zillions of dollars—and here I was coming from this dance company where we had to do everything on $97.50 a week. I couldn't believe it. It just seemed so out of proportion. And Dusty was feeling as ugly and unhappy as I was. So basically we were nervous and tense during the whole time he was filming out there. The idea that he would become a big star didn't even occur to us until a few weeks later when it actually happened. When I first saw *The Graduate,* in fact, I couldn't relate to it as a film because there was so much personal stuff in it and so much tension involved. I mean, I liked it, but it kept reminding me how painful a time it had been.

I remember the night the film opened. We had to get all dressed up and Dusty didn't like my hair. There were a million photographers there. I mean, it's not fun. It's like going to a party where you can't laugh. I can see why people get stoned before they go to them, but in those days we weren't into that—we missed the whole drug scene. It was like we were doing something in our sleep, like zombies. Dusty was tense. I was tense. We weren't having a good time. People were pulling on him. I wasn't used to that. I was threatened by it.

Dusty didn't quite know what to do with me, so sometimes I would just be left out—I'd just be standing there. And people are very rude. They really do push you aside and they eliminate you and when you're very insecure you think it's because you're not interesting. You don't realize that they're insensitive. So when people ask us isn't it exciting and isn't it wonderful and aren't you thrilled, I really do feel *no,* it isn't. If your personal life is the way ours was at that point, which was very precarious, all that success only wreaks havoc on you.

That's when we started having the problem of Dusty thinking I didn't care about his career, that I didn't focus in enough on his work. I used to say it wasn't true but now I see he was right. I can understand him to a point, but I'm not him. I mean, I care about his work, but what he really feels is that I don't feel it the way he does. And, of course, he's right. It's taken years for me to understand that in myself, that there's no way I can see it as though his eyes were my eyes. In the beginning he'd be angry with me and tell me I couldn't understand and I'd say, "Yes I can, yes I can." But then I realized I couldn't understand what he was telling me about his acting any better than he could know what it felt like physically for a dancer to be able to stand on pointe every day. He wanted me to be emotionally affected the same way he was.

We actually split up for a while then, although we spoke a lot. Dusty was beginning to like all the fame and I felt horribly threatened by all the women who were available to him. I had no way of knowing that these other people weren't any better than I was. He was a lot smarter than me about all that; he knew the bullshit of it all while I didn't. But then again, he had to have his freedom at that time. He just had to have some time where he was going to sort out what he was going to do next. The thing that really saved him was that he was a serious actor and that was his number-one focus.

For quite a while he didn't work because he was waiting for the right part, so he had a lot of free time on his hands. Also, suddenly this guy who had always felt he was this ugly person was like Robert Redford or Paul Newman. He was Mr. Gorgeous and everybody wanted to be with him—where each woman would become more clinging than I had ever been. So we maintained our friendship during all of that time. We communicated a lot and I still remained the only one he could really talk to.

I was pained by the whole split-up, but at the same time I was beginning to realize that I wasn't such a schlemiel and that I did have some value as a human being. I was also beginning to enjoy being with my daughter more. In a way the whole thing was good for me as well. It gave me a certain freedom because I had let go of the thing I was clinging to, a fantasy of security. I'd gone from one very insecure situation—my first marriage—and jumped right into another, still fantasizing that this one was secure.

I wasn't making a conscious effort to get back together with him during this time, but I liked him—so it was easy always to be his friend. Sometimes I would think of the absurdity of it. Like he called me the night before the Academy Awards because he was depressed. I wanted to go with him and I was hurt. First of all, I thought it would be wonderfully glamorous and exciting and fun, plus I felt I deserved to go. He didn't take me because I guess he felt I would have made him feel uncomfortable. It would be another tense situation. Anyway, the night before he left he called me up because he was very depressed and I was genuinely sympathetic. The next night some of my friends came over to my apartment to watch the awards with me, and I said to one of them, "You know, Dusty's very depressed." She said, "Are you kidding me?" And I said, "He really is." She said, "He's gone to Hollywood, maybe to win an Academy Award, and you're sitting in this shitty one-room apartment with no money and you're feeling sorry for *him?*" And I guess she was right. But still, he *was* depressed and I guess I didn't mind patting him on the head. The one thing that Dusty's admitted many times is that when he thought about marrying me, he was sure he'd be marrying someone who really knew him. He'd never have to worry about why I'd married him. He knew it wasn't because he was famous. And that problem has never come up.

So we were off and on for about a year. He made *Midnight Cowboy* and he got me a little part as an extra and we had our problems. I couldn't stand it when I saw him hanging out with other women. But I started to get more confident, and some of the men on the film actually asked me out. And when Dusty finally realized I was going out with other men, he didn't like it at all. "What do you mean, you're dating? You go *out* with them?" "Yeah," I said. "Just like you. You go out with people; I go out with people." And then he began to look at me again.

He called me a little more often because he didn't like the idea of me seeing other people, and he started asking me questions like "Who did you go out with? Is he handsome? What did you do?" And I'd say it was none of his business. I didn't want to know about his people; he didn't need to know about mine. I really wasn't looking for anyone. I was just beginning to feel less tense about the new situation with Dusty: that whatever was going to happen to that relationship was just going to happen, that I wasn't going to go under, that I could make my own way. I had recovered from the humiliation of being a divorced mother, and that had taken a long time.

Then we started getting along very well. He was leaving for Florida to do some filming for a couple of weeks and we had a very nice dinner together. But then the next day Dusty was feeling really tense and depressed, and he told me that he thought it could never work between the two of us, that I just didn't understand his work, that I would never really understand what he goes through. I guess what he wanted at this point in his life was somebody who would really absorb herself in his life. And there was always that little part of me that was her own person. So I think that made him a little bit fearful. And at that point, he really left. And I remember calling up a friend who had just split up with her boyfriend and telling her how depressed I was about it, how I still loved him so much, and how I wasn't ready to accept that I might never see him again. Anyway, I had a date the night he was coming back from Florida and I had hoped he'd call while I was out, but the baby-sitter said he hadn't and I felt bad. And then, at about two o'clock in the morning, the phone rang and it was Dusty. And he was so cute because he was nervous and he said, "Where are you?" And I said, "Well, I'm home. You just called me. Where do you think I am at two o'clock in the morning?" And he said, "Well, I wanna come over." So he came over and he said, "Did you go out tonight?" And I was so pleased to be able to say yes. And he said, "Well, I've been thinking and I don't want you to go out anymore and I don't want to go out anymore either. Let's try it again." So I said, "OK." Then he said, "All right, I want you to move in," and I said, "No. I can't do that. I think I should stay where I am and we'll date and we'll see each other every day and I won't go out with anyone else, but I'm not ready to move in." So we started seeing each other again.

That was the beginning of a very nice time. He started doing a play on Broadway so he was in New York all the time and I was dancing. He used to come over and I'd help him with his lines and it was just a lot of fun. I really enjoyed seeing him on stage. It was a much more real experience for me than the movies. And by this time his manager really adored me and he kept saying to Dusty, ''Why don't you marry her already?'' Then New Year's Eve came around and I knew it—I just knew he was going to propose. So he did propose and we were married in May.

Because Dusty's always making films in different places, we spend a lot of time apart. We try not to go more than four weeks at a time without seeing each other. We speak to each other a lot on the phone, just about every day. I think the separation is not really as difficult for Dusty and me as it is for the kids because we have a level of communication that doesn't change, but with the kids that level changes almost by the week. I suppose on that level our communication is difficult because I carry the burden of the children and I have to remind him to talk to them when he's away. It's easier for him to talk about his day with me, about his problems, his frustrations, his tensions on the set, rather than talk to the kids because naturally they don't care about any of that. They're only interested in how he relates to them on their level. That's the hardest part about his trips away.

I kind of prefer having him away when he's working because if he's working and we're together, we're still apart because he's the kind of man who works in such an obsessive way that it's almost like having just a body there. It's easier when we're away from each other because I'm not frustrated. I know he isn't there and I know that when I speak with him it'll be for maybe ten or fifteen minutes but during those minutes he'll really be there. It's so much better than when I see him wake up in the morning and he's somewhere else.

As for Dusty's sudden success, we were initially very fearful of doing things; not so much of spending money—I was at least familiar with the more affluent way of life and I knew it was pleasant—but Dusty really didn't know. And, of course, the scary part, too, was that it was *us* doing it and spending *our* money at it, being able to afford to do it, which was an adjustment. Buying our house, I remember, was a traumatic experience. We bought it and we were very happy but then we had to do things with it, and so when we moved into it we all lived in one room. We were all stuck in the dining room because we were terrified to move around the house. The house seemed so large. But after seven years we really have grown into it and we've learned how to use it. And Dusty knows what he wants to do and now he's more focused on it. Being a serious actor is his security blanket. If he was an entertainer it would be harder.

The only thing I sometimes have a bit of a hard time with is my need to be a baby with him, to have the child in me taken care of. Sometimes I just want to come to him with that part of myself. In the beginning, the relationship was very much like that. When I first met him I was unsure of myself and he was very supportive and very much a friend and I believed everything he said. After a while, though, I started to realize that what we both really needed was for me to be able to stand on my own two feet and assert myself because I couldn't keep depending on him—and he was getting tired of it anyway. So I started withdrawing some of that stuff. I didn't keep saying, 'Take care of me, take care of me, I'm helpless.' And it was interesting because this change in me really paralleled this tremendous jump in his career. So he needed me to be able to take care of my own needs that much more. Anyway, now when I come to him with that stuff every once in a .while, he's not used to that child in me and it's not always so easy for him to give in to her.

I think our relationship has changed a lot through the years and it probably keeps changing. I know that after our second daughter was born I was very much stuck in the role of being the wife and mother. That was when I had postpartum depression. I was unhappy because I had nothing to do. I barely had to take care of the apartment we had and he was busy working on a film. He was uptight, too, that I wasn't doing anything. I had all the security I needed and I had no excuses.

Then one summer, six years ago, we went to Europe because

Dusty was filming in Rome and that was when I realized I wanted to go home. I wanted to live in our house and I wanted to sort myself out. So the kids and I went home and that was the first time we'd been separated since our marriage. It was bliss, absolute bliss. I realized there was no reason why I had to be a housewife. I mean, money frees you of that. Then the tables turned for Dusty. He was in Rome and he was on his own, without his family. It was a different situation for him. I fact he called me one day and said, "I feel like I've died and you've adjusted very well." It became really hard for him. He didn't realize that people can be apart and still include each other in their lives. Everything I did somehow included him. I mean, it wasn't just for me that I left, it was for both of us. And I wasn't going away from him, I was just growing.

I really do want to be here now—in this relationship. I can't see being with another kind of person. I suppose if I did lose Dusty, I'd probably find somebody very similar. And I think he feels the same way.

Rose

She's eighty-six and was widowed thirteen years ago. She lives in the Canarsie section of Brooklyn.

I was nineteen when I got married and I was married for fifty-four years. He was my cousin, my first cousin, and he came over to our house and he fell in love with me instantly. It just happened and we got married in a few months. I went with other fellas and my father didn't like any of them. But Harry, my father liked. Everybody liked him. My father saw that Harry was a nice fella and he saw that he made a living. Back then, that was the first thing you asked about the boy. Was he a good provider? Could he make a living? It was a different world then. Today, you don't ask your parents about who you marry and who you don't. But we asked our mothers and fathers and we listened to what they said.

Harry was good to me, he supported me, and we always had it nice. I knew he was a hardworking man and I knew that when he came home, he was mine. I didn't have to worry about him going out with others.

He worked hard. We all worked hard. He used to get up at five in the morning and he used to have to travel on three or four trains before he got to work—and he always worked seven days a week. He never had a day off. He worked Saturdays and Sundays.

I knew he had to work and that's all, so I never missed him. I never called him at work and he never called me. I'm telling you, it isn't like today. What do the women have to do today? Or the men? They just think of having good times and going out.

He worked until half-past seven and so when he got home he was tired. We had dinner and if we were able, we'd take a walk.

We'd just walk, not even saying anything because we'd both be so tired from the day. Then we'd go home and go to sleep. Remember, he had to get up at five in the morning, sometimes even half-past four. And he never complained and neither did I.

When he was at work, I was washing the clothes. We had no machines, we had no Frigidaires so we waited for the ice man. And we had to feed the children, and we knew that we had husbands who came home, and we knew we had to treat them nicely. It wasn't like today's generation. I always say I like my old times better. It was nicer then. We knew we had to take care of a home. We knew that our husbands came home and that they were the bosses. We didn't send them out to shop. We didn't tell them we wanted money. Whatever they brought home, that was enough. We didn't say, "Let's eat out. I can't cook today." It was a different life then entirely.

Today's life—I don't see what's good about it. We lived nicely, that was the main thing. Harry didn't call me "darling," "deary," "honey," or "sweetheart." And I didn't have to run over to him and hug him and kiss him. That was for a certain time and place. If you loved the person, you just loved them. So what if today they call each other "honey," or "deary." I see how they do it—they argue and fight and then they call each other "honey." I'm telling you, it's a different life today than then.

He was just a hardworking man and that's all. He was very quiet. He never insulted me, never. We never had a fight, only talks. He never even raised his voice to me or me to him. It was a true life and that's all, and all of us worked hard.

Jackie and Linda

Jackie and Linda are in their early thirties. Jackie's a secretary, Linda, a travel agent.

Jackie: It will be two years this January that we've been together but we met prior to that. It was a kind of romantic meeting on the subway about six years ago. The train was empty and Linda got on. She was a very attractive lady. I didn't know if she was gay and I was a very shy person, but I couldn't stop looking at her, which made her a little uncomfortable.

Linda: I felt very vulnerable. Women don't usually look at each other in a cruising way. Usually they look at you more in a critical way, like 'Where did she buy that dress?' When a woman really lingers on you it's kind of uncomfortable because you know it's definitely more than just a critical look.

Jackie: I was actually making *myself* uncomfortable staring at her, so then I'd look away. But there was definite eye contact and some smiling. I was thinking, 'If I don't speak to this woman now, I'll never see her again.' But what could I do on the subway, just walk over and introduce myself to her? So finally I got off the train and she continued on. That same night I went to a gay bar downtown and lo and behold, Linda walks in. I couldn't believe it. I was in shock.

Linda: I really hadn't known what to think of her on the train. She looked so young. I thought perhaps she was just a kid playing a game with me. I never even dreamt that circumstances would bring us together that night. So someone introduced us and I asked her if she wanted to dance. I didn't realize that she was in a relationship with someone else at the time. She was very nervous and very aloof and I liked her but I didn't like her. There was

75

some kind of tension there. And that was it really. Sometimes we'd hear about each other from a mutual friend but we didn't see each other again for four years.

. Then two years ago, January fifth, I was in the process of breaking up with my lover. She decided to go out to a gay bar and I thought maybe I'd join her later, maybe not. I felt very indecisive about it. Then suddenly I had this feeling like I had to go somewhere, and I decided to go to the bar. And there was Jackie. I'd forgotten all about her, and she said, "Linda," and she hugged me and I looked at her and I said, "I'm sorry but I really don't know who you are." So she said, "Don't you remember— the subway?" And I said, "Oh my God. Yes." We went home together that night and that was it.

Jackie: I remember waking up the next morning and feeling fulfilled in a way I had never felt before. I just had a feeling.

Linda: There's such great empathy and communication between us. Jackie is my best friend. Other lovers have never been my best friend before. I can tell her things about my childhood, painful things, dreams, fears, hopes, everything. So there's total communication and it was like that for both of us from the very beginning. We've said many times that it had to be planned, that it was something that was meant to be. I feel that the love she's brought into my life has turned my entire life around. When I was involved with other people, I would tend on one level to be saying the things that were supposedly expected of me. But I always felt that on another level this little voice inside me would say, 'How can I be doing this? I don't really mean what I'm saying.' You know, when you're quietly brushing your teeth, little things pop into your mind. But it's not like that with Jackie.

Jackie: We kind of take it one day at a time. We have a little anniversary every month and we renew our contract, so to speak. On the fifth of every month one of us will bring the other flowers or mail a card or we go out to dinner, something special.

Linda: I feel more of a commitment than I've ever felt before. Jackie and I still have fantasies about other attractive people, but we know now that it's only that. Like when I say *I'd* like to buy a house, it's not *I* anymore, it's *we.* It's no longer like the grass is greener on the other side. There is no more other side.

Jackie: We can't really say that in five years we'll feel the same way. I feel that I will, but I don't think it's fair to promise, to make vows. I like some time to myself and Linda does also. That's one reason why we took a two-bedroom apartment, two bedrooms and two bathrooms.

Linda: We each use different toothpastes, deodorants. You can maintain your own individuality that way. It's very important to us because our previous relationships had not been like that. Instead of our lovers being happy for us about our outside interests, they were resentful of the time we spent away from them. And then you feel torn inside, like should I stay or should I go. The break of my last relationship came when I realized, Hey, I'm only going to go through this life once so I really better do it my way.

We feel that each person should be completely in and of themselves. We share the rent and utilities but we don't have a joint savings or checking account. In previous relationships we had joint accounts and found tremendous difficulties with them, so we just avoid these little hassles by keeping them separate.

I suppose our relationship sounds almost utopian, but I really think that people can have this type of relationship if they just leave room for growth. I say to Jackie "I love you," but I love myself first. Anybody who tells you different is just bullshitting. If I don't love myself, I can't love her. I've spent too many years of my life not being true to myself or trying to be somebody I wasn't. Another thing I wanted in this relationship was to be me. I have a saying: "Love me when I'm bad because it's easy to love me when I'm good. But if you can love me both times, then you really love me." I feel that you have to just let go and be yourself in your own home; you have to have that person at home who will help you renew yourself. Then you can go back out and face the world. No matter how many hurts I have from the day, I can come back home and say, "Hold me. I need you," which I've never been able to do before.

SUFFERING

"Oh Ashley," said Scarlett, "Nothing's turned out
the way I expected."

from *Gone with the Wind*
by MARGARET MITCHELL

There is nothing on earth as cruel as a rotten
marriage.

JOHN CHEEVER

Gretchen and Phillip

Both of us being postwar children, we have only cinematic ideas of what Phillip and Gretchen Schindler endured during World War II. For two years the Schindlers hid from the Nazis in a darkened, cramped attic.

This interview, conducted in Brooklyn in the Schindler's small three-room apartment, understandably touched upon painful memories, and what may appear in print as uninterrupted dialogue was, in actuality, a halting, pause-laden interview replete with moments too painful to retrieve.

Gretchen: We had known each other since '32 and we got married in '42. From '39 to '42 we even worked together. We were both editors of a magazine. I was also a photographer and Phillip wrote short stories. This was in Amsterdam. But we were married only four weeks before we went underground. We married in August '42 and in September '42 we went underground.

Phillip: We were married in the zoo.

Gretchen: In the Amsterdam zoo. Jews were not allowed to marry at the place where decent people married.

Phillip: We were not allowed to use any means of transportation, either. We had to walk an hour and a half in order to get to the zoo.

Gretchen: That was like walking from here to the Bronx. We walked with our families on our wedding day and that was the last time either of us ever saw our families again.

Phillip: We had to wear the Star of David then, so we had to walk to the zoo in very small numbers. Too many of us couldn't walk together.

Gretchen: It was no celebration. We just wanted to get it over with.

Phillip: The Germans had said—at least there was a rumor—that if you were married you could stay together if you were deported. Nobody then knew that they were being deported to be gassed. We just thought Jews were being deported to work in German factories.

Gretchen: And not even that was true. You didn't even get into the same train with your husband or wife on the way to the camps.

We knew of the concentration camps but we didn't know of the gassings. We really believed that the Germans needed workmen. They did need workers—but they didn't use the Jews. But we didn't know of the gassings. That we heard much later. So we wanted to get married so we could be together during the deportation.

Phillip: We loved each other and knew we were going to get married anyway. This just made it happen sooner.

Right after we were married we went underground and eight months later we had to move again. At first we were being hidden in Amsterdam by a German SS man. He was a homosexual grocer who had left Germany in fear of being caught for being homosexual. He had been my parents-in-law's grocer back in Germany. In August of '42 we went to this grocer's house. He was a German citizen who had left Germany and who was living in Amsterdam. As a wedding present he agreed to hide us in his house, and he did that for a period of eight months. He was an anti-Nazi and he wanted to go underground himself. But some of his Jewish friends had said, ''Don't be foolish. You can help the people much more with your *goyisha* face and with your SS uniform. It's fantastic what you can do.'' And that's what he did.

Gretchen: When we got married there was a curfew. You had to be home at 7:30. And you needed special permits to live with one another, even if you were married. At that time, we didn't want to ask for anything from anybody, so until we moved into the grocer's house, Phillip and I didn't sleep together. We didn't sleep together the night of our wedding. Five nights after the wedding, that's when we moved into the grocer's house. This grocer, of course, had a big picture of Hitler hanging up which he hated. And he'd turn it to the wall and I was always the one who would turn it the right way.

Phillip: After eight months he was called up for duty in the German army. After the grocer left his boyfriend started to black-mail us. He wanted money from us. He was a Dutch homosexual and all he wanted was our money. That's when we had to move to the attic in a small village near Rotterdam.

The circumstances there were the circumstances of Anne Frank. It was basically the same setup. The only difference was that we were alone. It started out basically as an underground contact which didn't cost us anything. We were just supposed to stay there for the two or three months . . . until the war was supposed to be over. But the war continued and we had to live on only a thousand calories a week. The woman who was feeding us had rations, so she had to buy our food on the black market—which cost a fortune. This woman who brought us our food lived on the first floor of the house. Other people lived on the second floor, so the woman could only come to us when the people on the second floor were out.

Gretchen: We were together in the attic for twenty-four hours a day.

Phillip: We were so starved that after awhile all physical relations between us stopped. The body didn't menstruate anymore, nothing. We slept in one bed, on straw. Each one of us had a little part of the straw but we were too weak to ever embrace.

Gretchen: I was a little stronger because I had more fat reserve. But I slept or dozed practically all the time. Phillip couldn't sleep at all. We just stayed in this rotten bed all the time and we ate a thousand calories a week. Today, if I ate a thousand calories a *day* I'd lose weight.

I'll tell you what we ate. We had onions, so our breakfast con-sisted of a teaspoonful of chopped onions. We had bread, but by the time we got it it was black. There was no yeast in it. It was dripping wet, tiny, and after a day it was full of mold, which in the beginning we would try to scratch off but then, when we were so hungry, it didn't matter. And one of these tiny loaves had to last us a week. Can you imagine how thin those slices of bread were? Nothing. But we measured it all very mathematically so that it would last.

Also, to take against diarrhea we had taken dehydrated apples. With a little bit of water you could make this into applesauce. It has horrible tasting. And somehow we had some artificial vanilla. And for my birthday I got a *whole* slice of the bread. Phillip had sacrificed his portion for me and he cut it up into eight smaller pieces. Each piece had some of this horrible tasting applesauce on it. And that was really the most wonderful birthday present I've ever received. He kept saying he was full, that I should eat it all. And I knew he was starved. Other times we ate potato peels, dirty salad. And we had hardly any water. We had to go to the bathroom on the roof, at night.

Phillip: During our time in the attic, I dictated to Gretchen some children's books and two detective stories and these were published after the war.

Gretchen: He couldn't sleep so that's what he did with his mind.

Phillip: Actually we didn't talk that much during this time. There was no necessity for long talks because we knew each other, we understood each other. The only talks we had were when we consoled each other, when the other couldn't take it much longer. We'd tell each other that we needed each other to survive. And after the three years we spent there, I think nothing can ever upset our marriage.

One thing was harder than anything else. People who were in the concentration camps and who survived . . . well, of course, objectively, it was much harder there. There's no doubt. But they had one advantage, they had camaraderie. They had the feeling of mutual destiny. But we were cut off from everything. Also, we were being kept by a very unwilling person. These people just wanted our money, our jewelry.

Somehow you forget very fast that you once ate 1,000 calories a week to keep you alive. You never forget the experience, though. But now, when I'm on a diet and when I have 1,250 calories a day, I scream bloody murder. Because I've forgotten I lived on 1,000 calories *a week.* But as for our relationship . . . well . . . it was a very unnecessary but positive experience.

Gretchen: There, in the attic, even a toothache was a catastrophe. Phillip had grown a beard—not because it was fashionable as it is now but because he had gotten an infection, a skin irritation. There was no soap there. So he had this red beard. And he got a toothache, one that he was practically going through the wall with and he had to go to a dentist. He was ready to give himself up. The pain was unbearable. So the woman who lived downstairs told him he could go to the dentist if he shaved his beard off. And that was really ghastly because when I started to cut off his beard, I saw that his head had shrunk to absolutely nothing—just bone and skin. He had a skinny face to start out with but there was absolutely no flesh whatsoever. He said he couldn't stand how he looked but I told him he looked so nice and that he was just used to seeing himself with a beard and that's why he looked so different. But I was so afraid. I didn't think he was going to make it much longer.

Phillip: We were told one day that everything was over. Everyone was on their roofs, applauding. Americans were flying over Holland and dropping food parcels. Everyone thought that was the end of the war. But it was only an agreement between the English and the Germans. The Germans were allowing American planes to deliver food to the Dutch people. The Dutch were starving in the streets then. It was the fifth of May and everyone was singing in the streets. And the woman from downstairs came up to us and said now it's time to come down. I was carried down because I couldn't walk and Gretchen put on a skirt.

Gretchen: It was funny. I put on a skirt and it fell down. I had lost so much weight.

Phillip: So they put me down on the street. These people had never seen a Jew before. Everybody came and brought us cookies and what can I say—it was very touching, it was very, very emotional. But after two hours the SS came with guns and started to shoot everyone. Lots of people were killed. It was the German SS in Rotterdam who were shooting. The commander of the SS had declared that even if there was to be an armistice he would never come under British or American rule. So we ran back to the attic but it was useless. Now everyone knew we were in there. Our first reaction was . . . well, we had only one can left of something—spam, I think—and we said we'll eat this can and then just not eat.

Gretchen: We had no feeling of joy or anything. Nothing. Just hunger. We figured that we lasted through the entire war and now everybody knows there are Jews in the village. The commander wouldn't surrender. But Rotterdam was finally freed three days later on the eighth of May. And for those three days we were in fear, we were miserable. There was lots of killing during those three days—tanks, machine guns.

I'll tell you something: While you are there you have the feeling that the world owes you something; that you went through what nobody else went through. But that's what everyone said. Everyone said that what they went through was the most terrible experience. So we made up our minds pretty fast not to talk too much about it. I wouldn't believe that people who are still alive could have gone through what we have gone through.

When you think of that time in your life, do you marvel at each other's strength?

Phillip: This sounds beautiful. The question sounds beautiful. And I could give you just as flowery an answer which would bring tears to your eyes and, no doubt, to your readers' eyes. And most people would give you this type of answer. But it didn't do a thing. It only gave me insight into myself and it showed me that this is the woman I would marry if I had to marry again today.

Gretchen: I mean, we were not so preoccupied then with finding ourselves and, how do you say, communicating and all that. We were just very preoccupied with surviving.

Phillip: And we were together. The pressure from outside and the pressure from inside . . . we didn't have any release. It would have killed most marriages in similar circumstances. But basically our marriage stayed together there because Gretchen is a strong person.

Gretchen: Phillip didn't think it was worth it. He didn't want to go on.

Phillip: Without her, I wouldn't have survived. It wasn't worth my while to survive. I needed paper and pencils to survive, to write. But I couldn't even get those. I think I would have killed myself or I would have given myself up but I had the feeling that Gretchen needed me. She wanted us to survive.

Gretchen: I, alone, don't know what I would have done. I might be strong and might give the impression of knowing my way—but I'm the most insecure, dependent person under the sun. And I was the happiest person even with all the misery in that attic because I was constantly with Phillip. With all the disadvantages and the hunger and everything—to me he was the strong one.

Phillip: After the war we started to work together. This was 1945. And we had arranged in the attic that we would always work together. So we chose to be together twenty-four hours a day even after the war. We work on a project together, we keep house together. I cook, do the dishes, and do the shopping. And there's no competition, just respect for each other.

Gretchen: I love it that we're together but I must get out of the apartment sometimes. It's like when I was in the underground, I had to get out sometimes. So we travel. We're amateur archeologists. We travel to the jungles of Mexico, the jungles of Guatemala. We go to concerts, theater.

Phillip: It's interesting but I have no friends. I have a very active social life but no confidants other than Gretchen. And Gretchen, too, is the same.

Gretchen: Because of the war both of us have different values than most other people. One woman once asked me, Who am I friendly with? Who do I complain to about my husband? And I told her that if I have any complaints, I just tell him. And she marveled at that. She told me she needed a woman friend to complain to about her husband. And that was so strange to me.

Phillip: Our relationship was good when it started out. I think if there would have been any real doubts about each other, our relationship wouldn't have survived what it did. Also, you asked before, did the experience enhance our knowledge of each other. Naturally, it did. I mean, we had other *tsuris* then. We weren't in the attic just to get to know each other. But, of course, by being together twenty-four hours a day, we more or less know each other's thoughts. I know what she's thinking now before she's even thinking it.

Gretchen: And Phillip knows what I want long before I even realize what I want. He's very intuitive about me.

Phillip: It gave us a very deep insight into each other. We know things about each other that few people ever have the chance to find out.

This was a forced twenty-four hours and we hoped everyday it would be over tomorrow. I know I took a tremendous beating during this time because I accepted every whim of Gretchen's, thinking that once the war was over I wouldn't have to be so overindulging. If the war is over tomorrow or if the war is over next week, you can correct it—this habit of giving in to your wife's every need. But if it takes three years, it's hard to alter those patterns. How could I tell my wife that I wanted to be in the bathroom alone, for instance, after the war.

So a lot of things that in a normal marriage would lead to friction, like having no private time to be alone with yourself, don't affect us. When I came out of the attic I was just so used to this lack of privacy that I figured why shouldn't I just accept it. So now, whatever we do, we do together. I used to play chess but Gretchen doesn't. So I gave it up. And she's done those sort of things for me.

Gretchen: We had agreed with our families that after the war we would meet at a specific place. But we were the only ones to come.

Phillip: A lot of friends, good friends, important people—I mean, important for the world, not only for me—were dead. And to this day I cannot see why I survived. So after we came out of hiding I couldn't take the empty Holland anymore; all these people were gone. I was being reminded constantly of the fact that I survived. Somebody who doesn't feel this, like Gretchen, cannot understand it. I mean, in the first few weeks after I got out, I went after people in the street thinking it was . . .

Gretchen: OK, enough. Enough of this.

Phillip: It's OK. I thought if I changed where I lived—but I should have been more intelligent—I might get rid of this feeling. So this was the reason why we went to America. It was a new start.

Gretchen: You have to appreciate the fact that we never talk about these things so much. I usually cut it off sooner. Usually, it's quite upsetting for Phillip, much more than it is for me. So why don't we ask new questions. No more about this.

Phillip: You know, we cannot make someone else feel what has happened to us during these years. If you hear that a volcano in Indonesia has erupted and that it has killed twenty or thirty thousand people, and you sit and you read it in the newspaper, you say, "Horrible!" But you cannot imagine what the people feel who are seeing the lava coming.

Rose Hellman

Rose Hellman is fifty-two years old. She has three children and a husband she doesn't live with. She's a nursery school teacher in New York City.

The real problem and the real reason why my relationship with my husband had to change was that there was no relationship. There were no arguments. There needed to be arguments. Arthur, like his mother, is very proud of the fact that people cannot argue with him. He boasts about that. You can't pick an argument with him. He wanted to hear no criticism, no violence, no anger. He'd say, "What's so bad? Why are you so unhappy? What's the matter?" A perfectly good husband. He'd support you, a lovely home, two-car garage, PTA, healthy children. What's wrong?

Arthur grew up in a family that just didn't talk to each other about things like that. You just didn't. Nobody ever screamed at anyone. If you needed something, you got it. Why not? It was a family.

I grew up in a very independent family. First of all, I lost my mother when I was eight years old. She was bedridden until I was eighteen years old—then she died. And I remember my mother being very physical. She would pinch us with the same passion as she would hug us. Very different from Arthur's household. And also we came from a socialist background where politics were discussed in the house. Everything outside the family was as important as everything inside the family. But Arthur came from a very low-key kind of family.

They were so different from me. I could have married a Mongolian and it wouldn't have been so different. I was constantly modifying my behavior to fit theirs. And we were never alone. When we were first married we moved in with his parents. Then we had our first baby and moved into an apartment. But we were never alone. And I never remember really getting to know him. But I do remember him thinking that some of the questions I asked him were stupid. So I started thinking I was crazy and I started going to a therapist.

I knew it was wrong, the marriage, since the first year. I always knew it. But I didn't think I could do anything. I had no conception of what to do. I was terrified. I would crunch my thoughts and I'd get black and cry. I used to have nightmares. I knew I didn't love him but I was afraid. I never loved him.

I don't know whether or not he ever loved me. I don't know because it doesn't mean anything to him. It's a different way of looking at things. It's like, ''What do you mean, do I love you? You're my wife!''

I had been going out with a number of boys, very unsuccessfully. And I began to get pressure from my family, especially from my grandmother, to get a husband. There I was, twenty-one, twenty-two, twenty-three. All my friends were married, the war was on, there were no men, and each time I'd meet someone I'd go with them for a week or two, maybe a month, and all of a sudden something would happen. I would just say, 'That's not for me. That's not for me. That's not for me.' This went on until I met Arthur. I was very taken with him when I first met him. I thought I loved him the first one or two weeks. I was a WAC on the ward and he had been wounded. This was 1945, right near the end of the war. And there he was, wan and pale, thin, with his leg up in traction. Everyone else playing blackjack and gambling, cards, dice. And, you know, these guys would yell ''Hey, WAC'' all day. But there he was, this quiet guy, Arthur, reading poetry. At that time he was reading Henry Miller; you couldn't even get Henry Miller at that time in the States. You know, he was just interesting. He was writing things, reading poetry. Very pale, blond, and blue eyed.

Then I started going to visit his family and I started to get too deep into something I wasn't ready for. He should have been another one that I discarded like all the others. And I remember how it happened, when I lost it for him. Just like that. We were coming back from a writer's meeting that the Red Cross had organized and we were in a corner and he was going to kiss me goodnight and he was on crutches at the time. And suddenly a nurse passed by and he pushed me away. He was afraid that someone was going to see us. And in that instant I knew that this was not the person for me, because of his uptightness around authority, which is exactly what he's like today.

I was afraid. My grandmother said, ''You'll break up with him like you did with everyone else. You'll never get married.'' So I thought, 'Maybe it's me. Maybe I *am* crazy. Six, seven men I've been going with and I can't find anyone. Something must be wrong with me. Maybe the magic with Arthur will come back. Let me keep it going.' But the magic never returned.

I remember saying, 'It's too late. I'll marry him, then—afterwards—I'll divorce him.' That's what I had been telling myself. So strange.

My crying was always an affront to him. He was always against it. He couldn't understand it. I used to run out the door, symbolically, but then I'd come back hours and hours later. And he'd be disturbed, the children would be upset. We'd never talk about what was bothering me. He'd just get mad that I was running away. It's like you hit a kid, he cries, then you hit him because he's crying. You forget what the original hurt was.

In 1967 I ran out in a bigger way. I went to a conference out in California and I stayed the whole summer. I met a young man. He was much younger than I and he took to me. I couldn't believe it. I suddenly realized that I was a woman. I had had attractions to people but I was terrified of them. I was a married woman. What would the neighbors say? So Arthur came that summer to rescue me. And I remember when he came to the hotel where I was staying, I was crying. I said, ''Arthur, I'm not sure if I want to go back.''

And he said, "You're crazy. My mother's staying home with the kids. What am I going to tell mama?"

I said, "I don't care what you tell anyone. I don't think I want to go back."

He said, "What are you going to do here?"

And it was true. I didn't have any job. I didn't have any savings. I was in a hotel room by myself. And so he came back the next day and I said I wanted to sell our house. The house was like an albatross around my neck. All these things, these possessions that we owned together. But I never told him I wanted to leave him. I wanted to sell the house. I wanted to go away. I said a lot of things but never: "I don't love you. I want to leave you."

Then that summer something happened that changed me entirely. I didn't know how or when but I knew that I was going to leave Arthur. I had a neighbor, a neighbor who lived three houses away who also had three children. She was an exquisite redhead. Irish. You know, one of those real Irish redheads. She had married one of these wife beaters. She used to have marks and she never wanted to talk about it. Weekends she'd always run to her mother. She seemed to find some peace there. Well, that summer her mother was killed. She was coming out of a garage and a truck hit her. And it was a terrible blow to my friend, much more because she had no place to go, to escape. This was about July, I remember. And in August this woman disappeared for two days. They couldn't find her. And then we noticed the police were around the house and they found her . . . hanging in the attic. Her husband never even thought of going up to the attic to look for his wife. She hanged herself there. And to me that was like—God, is that the only alternative unhappy women have—to commit suicide? I used to speak to her. Not too much. She'd tell me she was unhappy. And I knew that her husband was beating her. And I'd tell her a little about me. But we were afraid to expose ourselves. It was like everyone was in their own little isolated worlds, suffering. And we lived so close to one another. Now I know that everyone on the block probably had a similar story. These lovely, beautiful homes. These English Tudor homes.

That was like a rock forming inside me. I remember thinking, how was I going to do it, how was I going to get out. I knew I wanted to sell the house so I started pushing to sell it. I was saying to myself that if I don't leave, then this is how I'll end up. Either I'll go crazy or I'll commit suicide. I mean, I couldn't see any hope of Arthur changing.

I knew that in order to really be free I had to have a profession, so I finished college. And Arthur was always very supportive of all these things. He wanted me to be happy. He was content. He wanted things to work nice. It was important for things to work for him.

I started teaching in the public schools and I began making forays. I'd go into New York and stay at a hotel for a couple of days—just by myself, as a kind of experiment. I was looking for love all the time but always I was frightened when I found someone.

Change is so painful and there's so much fear. Actually, it's not change that's painful; I think what it is is the resistance to it that's painful. It's like being on a boat and holding onto the dock, not letting the goddamn boat go. I'll split myself in two.

I had been in and out of therapy. I couldn't find anybody I really cared for. I couldn't stand the ones that sat there and made little notes about you, and the Freudian thing turned me off, and the screamers made me uptight. In the end, I thought I had to do it myself anyhow. It's just me. I have to do it. And one day I met a guy, a therapist—someone had given me his address. And I went to see him and as soon as I started talking, maybe because he was very busy, he said, "You don't need me. You need a lawyer." He said I was analyzing perfectly what was wrong. I thought that was marvelous. Usually it takes years for you to discover that what you really want to do is leave your husband. I got it right off. That was the last therapist I went to. From then on the only time I really had to talk to a therapist was after this other relationship about which I'm going to tell you.

One of the main reasons that I did not leave Arthur earlier was because I could tolerate it. Arthur was away so much of the time. What it was was that I used to wait for him to leave and then things were better. When we were together it was bad. There was very little yelling. Only when I cried was there yelling. And I never knew what I was crying about. I couldn't express it. I would just cry. And it affected sex, of course. Sex is not anything you can just have. I mean, it's part of the passion of the whole relationship. And after our first few weeks together there was really nothing good about the sex. And I tolerated it and I thought I had to.

So now I'll tell you the one, great, beautiful story of my life. I'm sorry it had to end but it was wonderful.

I was looking for a place to live and I met a friend who told me she knew a lovely man who had been separated from his wife for two years and he had a huge apartment and he wanted to rent out one room. So Judy introduced me to Ben. She gave me his address and his telephone number at work. He worked at some office, a printing office as a matter of fact. And I went up there to his office and I liked him right away. First of all, he was distinguished, fatherly looking. I don't know, maybe I was looking for a father. He was nine, ten years older than I. He was in his early sixties. So I thought I didn't have to worry about that business of him being younger. And he had a lovely voice and there was something about him I really liked. I wanted to see him again. And he said he had a room to rent and would I come up and take a look at it. So he gave me the address and I met him at his place.

And when I arrived, I said, "Oh, my God." It was a real slum on the lower East Side. East Broadway. The old synagogues, the garbage, the old wharves. And *schmutzik* and broken windows. I walked up this hallway—the filth of the halls, the blacked-out windows. I never really knew anyone who lived in a place like that. And he'd been living there for twenty-five years. He raised his family there. He loved it and he wouldn't dream of living anywhere else. But inside, it was like another world. Quiet, far away from everything. And a great big portrait of Lenin on the wall and on the other side, Karl Marx. And this was my childhood, you know. My family were socialists. And the place was real funky. You can't imagine a funkier place. And he showed me this little room.

He was a worker. You know, he worked all his life in a printing office. He never wanted to be a boss and he never wanted to buy a house. He never wanted to own property. He reminded me of my father so much. I mean, really, the whole thing. He was living now as a revolutionary. He was very active during the Vietnam War.

Anyway, about a week later he called me and asked me to dinner. So I went out to dinner with him. It was very pleasant. And he invited me again. We had several dinner dates and once I went to hear him lecture about China. And I just went wild. He gave me books to read about China and he kept calling me and I kept calling him. And when I finally got a good teaching job, a huge, huge bouquet of flowers arrived. Gigantic. The size of this table. Yellow mums, with a card from him. And that was so nice. So I called to thank him. By that time I'd known him a few weeks. That's all, just a few weeks.

He invited me to have dinner at his house one evening and afterward he asked if I wanted to spend the night. And I suddenly went wild. I tell you—I never thought—suddenly—and I don't know what made me do it—I whipped off all my clothes and said, "Would you like to take a shower with me?" Can you imagine that?

I gathered, though, that he was still a little bit hooked on his wife. She had left him. He was still in pain and I could feel the pain. I could feel that anyone who came in the way was not going to get in real touch with him. I knew that right from the beginning and I shouldn't have pushed the relationship as much as I did. But I was in so much need. It was so beautiful. It was just everything I had ever read about. He was a fantastic lover and I was like a child—everything I dreamed about, everything I thought love could be. I used to do wild things. I mean, I used to get up at five in the morning, get a cab, run, and jump into bed with him, you know, before he went to work. It was just absolutely wonderful.

We shared everything. First of all, Yiddish. We spoke Yiddish. He read Sholom Aleichem to me in the original. We'd sit up in bed reading. I introduced him to *The Little Prince*. And we went away together. We went to hotels. Finally, that spring, I had two weeks off and we went to Puerto Rico. And we had a little house, way up, way out there in the hills, in the mountains, overlooking the river. And we both got sick together and threw up on a sailboat. All kinds of things were happening to us. It was beautiful, beautiful. But it was the peak. It was too much. We were really at it, constantly. It was as if we were eating each other up. I should have seen the handwriting on the wall because when we came back from Puerto Rico he was depressed and I stayed away from him for a while. I had enough good sense to do that. But it was just not right for me to pressure him at that time. I detected that it was loosening and I wanted it to stay at the peak that it was. But nothing can. Nothing ever can, and I didn't know that. I didn't want to give up this one chance I had in my life. But it wouldn't stay up there.

And one day, it was October, I had come back from the theater and I was tired. I was in bed already, in my little short gown. And the phone rang and it was him. And he said, ''My daughter is in town from Los Angeles and I want you to come over right away. You gotta meet her.'' This was October 2 and we had been together since January.

And I said, ''I can't, Ben. Maybe I can meet her tomorrow. I'm really so tired.'' I was really dead. But he said, ''I'm coming to get you. You gotta come.'' So he came and he picked me up.

I didn't know that all that day he had been out in the country with his daughter. There had been some big dinner and he had eaten all day long and had drunk lots of coffee and lots of liquor. And, you know, he was entertaining his daughter and he had stayed up all the previous night. He was thoroughly, thoroughly exhausted. Well, we said goodbye to his daughter, it must have been about midnight. She went to sleep at her sister's house.

And we immediately jumped into bed and we started carrying on. . . .

He got a heart attack in the middle of the sex, in the middle of our lovemaking. . . . He didn't die. He got a very severe heart attack. You read about those kinds of things. So I got him to the hospital and I got him there on time. They said that it was very lucky that I was there. But I knew it wouldn't have happened if I wasn't there. I just knew it. He would have gone to bed and maybe that was the extra . . .

And things were never the same between us after that. We were afraid of having sex. So we had occasional sex but very little. And I became frightened. I think I told you that I had a bedridden mother and we grew up with bedpans in my house. And just the sight of a bedpan does something to me. And I suddenly saw myself as being locked up with an invalid for the rest of my life. It really scared me. And I could not communicate this to him because I really loved him. I had this awful conflict going on. And then he got another attack—his second heart attack. And with the second one I knew I somehow had to ease out of the picture. And I think he must have known it, too, because we started playing games then. Basically, I don't have a background of being honest with people so I don't know how to be honest. I didn't know how to say it. You know, I'd say I was busy, that school was keeping me busy. It was very painful for me yet I couldn't stay on.

He had started something in me. I needed to be with him. He had started something that was more than sex. It was such a passion. I found myself demanding things that he couldn't give, physically and everything. It affected everything.

Then he recovered enough to be able to go out. But by that time I wasn't seeing much of him. And I started hearing that he was seeing someone else. That killed me. Someone else was going to take care of him. But I couldn't get back into the picture. And I discovered that this someone else was a very, very young girl.

Last June I called him. We had dinner together. We kept everything very cool, very surfacy. Then he told me that this new woman was moving in with him. So that was finis. I just stopped calling. And the last time I saw him was at a lecture on China. And I didn't recognize him. I was so upset. He had aged. He walked funny. He could hardly walk. And right now, I just heard, he's in the hospital with his fourth heart attack.

I haven't been able to match that feeling I had with him with anyone else. It's still very heavy for me. I'll never stop loving him.

It must happen.to me again—that sort of love connection. And if it doesn't, I have a lot to fill up my life. But I'm not going to tie up with anyone again if it's just going to make me unhappy. I'd rather have nothing. The only trouble is age. As you get older you look in the mirror and you see the lines and you start saying, 'Well, gee, maybe it's better having someone for companionship than being alone. What value is there in being alone?' Know what I mean?

Jerry

Jerry is forty years old and has been a theatrical agent ever since he was twenty-two. Barbara, his wife, age thirty-six, works as a television screenwriter. They live in Los Angeles and as Jerry explained, "We're heavily into the rat race, at least my wife is."

They've been married for fourteen years and have two children.

Right now both my wife and I have reached a sort of plateau and we've seen that we've established patterns. You know, at some time in your life everything is in flux and all your dreams are in the future. But at a certain age you begin to realize that patterns are being formed and that where I'm at now is roughly where I'm going to be in say fifteen years. And at that point people begin pouting. That's where we're at now. So there are great tensions in our marriage now because we're both reexamining what we want. You start asking yourselves how far is all this from where your fantasies were when it first started.

From my point of view, our life isn't too far from where I wanted it to be. But for Barbara it's very far. See, when we were married back in 1962, what was fashionable then for intelligent, hip, aggressive, young people was a sort of Robert Hall beatnikism that you could slip on very cheaply. It meant some disdain for material objects. It meant you were a leftist or a liberal, which was relatively simple then because not much was happening in the world in those days. And that was the context within which we met. I really believed all that. I really didn't want a house, didn't want possessions. I never buy clothes. Well, as it turns out, Barbara is much more middle class than I—or even she—

thought. And now she's prepared to admit that she would have liked—and still would like—the house and the Cadillac and the country club and all that sort of stuff. And I've never said no to any of those things. But I can't see how they'll ever be the motivating force for how I function.

She's a very successful TV writer in Los Angeles, an Emmy winner, so she has a very good income. But we have two kids in private school and all the accoutrements that go along with that. We spend an enormous amount of money on household help. The kids' school bills come to $6,000 a year. The help is like $7,000 a year. So right there is $13,000 right from our net which eats up over twenty grand of our gross. So essentially she wants me to earn more money. That's really the crux of most of our disputes.

I think this desire for the good life was something Barbara didn't know about herself when we first got married. Very legitimately as people get older they begin to examine more honestly what it is they want. So I don't put her down for all this. I don't think there's anything wrong with wanting all these things. But I just don't want to do what I have to do to get them.

By my standards I think I'm a great success—but that's cutting the cloth to fit the body. I enjoy my work. I really enjoy the independence I have. I could certainly make more money from my business but that would make me responsible to too many people which would ruin my independence. God knows, I'd love to be a millionaire. I have nothing at all against money. But if you have to lose too much to get what you want, forget it.

This money thing makes us very nasty to each other. There's lots of resentment. She resents that I don't want to work harder to make more money. I resent her for wanting me to change my life-style so she can have what she wants. And all this resentment leads to punishing-type actions. You know, screw him if he doesn't want to cooperate and so on and so on. Admittedly, I've fallen into a very comfortable niche. I have a business that essentially runs itself. I do no soliciting for business at all. I mean, I haven't done anything really aggressive in years. I love my wife and I'd like to make her happy—but within the limits of my own curious set of principles. It's not as if I think she shouldn't have these things, that these things are immoral or anything. I think it's just that there are some things I can't and won't do.

My wife also thinks that being an agent is not a very challenging business. She'd rather I be something more creative. And, in that regard, I really can't argue with her. A theatrical agent isn't really a very challenging job, intellectually, creatively. On the other hand, I don't know where it's written that I have to choose a challenging, creative career. You know, I like living in the fairly relaxed and comfortable way that I'm living now. What's it all about anyway? Working is just a way to get the things you want. That's all. The problem is that my wife takes her work so seriously. She finds it challenging. It's like life and death for her.

I really think a continuing financial strain could eventually do in the marriage. You know, I really don't object to her desires. I just object to being punished for not satisfying them. And the problem isn't really money so much as it is personalities. On a subliminal level you're always fighting to be the power source in your relationship. And if money was plentiful then we'd both find something else to hassle about.

All these things, from an outsider's point of view, don't seem so heavy—money, status, power. But if they break up a marriage that's lasted for fourteen years, then they are that heavy.

I hate the word adultery. I don't know a better word for it but at a certain level adultery implies cheating, as if there are rules. So I think one can only speak of cheating if someone is being cheated of something. And in my relationship with my wife, my outside relationships don't interfere.

Whatever problems we've had in our marriage, and God knows there's been plenty, they've had nothing to do with outside relationships. There are simply various pressures on our relationship that are caused by the fact that two intelligent people came together at the age of twenty-five or twenty-six and now it's fourteen years later. And they've both grown and developed and changed and had children and have gone through a lot of history on the way. That's what causes the pressures.

Repetition is really the curse of marriage. Like my playing with my mustache bothers my wife. Imagine how tired she must be by now of me playing with my mustache for the past fourteen years. And imagine how tired she is of dirty ashtrays. Things on that level. That's what causes the strains on marriage.

My wife's a very attractive lady and her job is such that there's a lot of men around for her to be with. But I don't get jealous. If I was going to worry about that, I'd go crazy. I have to assume that for a healthy woman or a healthy man the prospect of having a single sex partner for your entire life just isn't reasonable. What she does outside our marriage, I don't know and I don't want to know.

I'm not very sexually active outside my marriage. I would guess that if you took a survey of all the males who are married, I would end up in the bottom 10 percent in terms of the number of times I've had extramarital relationships. I mean, I know married guys who go out casually every night with other women. I tend to get involved in relationships that are close ended before they even start. I tell people right away where things are at, so that no one will be confused. These aren't things that you can control and you're asking for trouble if you don't tell whoever you're with what's going on. The fact is I'm married to a woman I love and I have two children whom I'm tremendously fond of and I've no interest whatsoever in breaking up that family for the sake of my crotch. That doesn't seem to me to be a fair trade. As my father used to say, "The fucking you get in the end isn't worth the fucking you get in bed." And it's true. So generally speaking, I'm very careful about the people with whom I get involved. To be very specific, there are two young women at the moment with whom I have sort of strange relationships, both of whom are very seriously involved in other, very serious relationships. And that's just fine. But one of the two did want to intensify what we had and I told her we better stop now.

Extramarital affairs open you up. You know, love is like anything else. The more love relationships you have the more loving and tender you become. I mean there's an accumulated psychological effect you get from having affairs. Like you feel enormously virile. Which is not to say that I'd recommend extramarital affairs in a textbook as a way to conduct one's marriage.

Obviously, after so many years, passion cools which is one reason why extramarital affairs are almost necessary. It's necessary for sustenance. You know, you're alive. You need it.

As you get older you settle for what you can get. A couple of months ago I was working on a German-made movie and the director and the star came over and he brought his secretary, who was a very pretty young kid who was born in France. It was very obvious that there were sparks between us and we ended up getting it on. But both of us knew it was only for a weekend. I mean, she knew I was married which immediately put certain restrictions on it. And it was very funny because after our second night together she ran off with someone else. She said, ''You know, I just have to keep my balance.'' And there was very little I could say to that. Those sorts of things are terrific. It's great for the ego. It's wonderful just in terms of a transference of energy.

I would suspect that after ten years very few married couples spend an entire day in bed. Certainly when the first kid comes along you just can't anymore. The time just isn't available. Now if the occasion arises and if it's possible, I'll certainly spend the day in bed with whomever. It makes you feel like a kid again. And the danger that something might grow out of that and become threatening is part of the charge. It's sort of a challenge to keep your head. What I try to do when something like this happens, particularly if the woman is single, is to let her know right off that I'm not available for anything long-term. It's a fine line you run, but it's terrible and it's wonderful and it's very difficult.

My relationship with my wife has nothing to do with my extramarital affairs. See, if you're with a woman because the home scene is fucked, then you're doing something else. I'm not looking for other women as a way of getting back at my wife. I don't see that it affects her at all. And this is all relatively new to me. I was absolutely faithful for seven or eight years. I never even kissed another woman. I didn't use to think that you could have both a marriage and outside affairs. I just thought that that was the way marriage was. But, you know, things happen. And what really happened was that women in general got to be a lot more aggressive sexually. It wasn't only the men who were the wild beasts who were starting these affairs.

I feel marriage is wonderful and necessary and it's certainly an institution that will last. But I do feel pressured by being married. First, in the type of emotional commitment I can make to other people. When I was single, if I saw a cute kid somewhere, I'd have no hesitation about trying to get her into bed. So that's a loss; it was available before but it's not available now. It's not something I bemoan but it is a loss. Second, I'm responsible now for three other people so that in a variety of ways my freedom is limited. And my wife feels that loss of freedom much more strongly than I. And she's been feeling that way for the past five years. But that's her story.

Martin and Sylvia

Originally, Martin and Sylvia agreed to do an interview together. We arrived at their house, chatted awhile, then started the interview. But within ten minutes it was clear that the situation was impossible. Martin and Sylvia were bickering, challenging each other's every statement. Things got so uncomfortable that after awhile we had to propose an alternative plan: to interview each one of them separately. Both of them readily consented.

Since their interviews were so similar in content we decided to juxtapose only portions of Sylvia's interview with Martin's more complete narrative. The two interviews can now be read as one continuous story.

Martin's fifty-eight; Sylvia, fifty-six. They have two children—a daughter who's twenty-seven and a twenty-five-year-old son.

Martin: We've been married thirty-two years. I was a GI coming home on a pass and I saw her on a railroad platform. I tried to pick her up but she'd have none of it. Then I followed her onto the beach at Coney Island and ended up making a date with her. I knew right away that I wanted to marry her. I was twenty-five when I met her and I was engaged to another woman at the time, but when I saw Sylvia, that was it. There was no question and she was just as receptive.

We never had real quarrels in the beginning. Our quarreling started later on when our kids were older. I think that in a lot of marriages you don't have time to really get to know one another. You're too consumed, when you have little kids, in just survival. What happens is that when you're both left naked without the kids, it becomes a hassle.

Sylvia: I think we were both so involved in child raising, community involvement, house ownership, and doing the things we both enjoyed, that our problems just didn't crop up for a very long time.

Martin: I think what exacerbated everything, more than anything else in our marriage, was my loss of a huge amount of money. Sylvia is very fearful for security, financial security. She's dreadfully concerned about what's going to happen ten years from now.

Sylvia: We never really planned for the future. We don't have any retirement money except for a tiny bit that I have from a small pension. I don't have a family to turn to, financially or any other way. And where does an older person turn without any resources?

Martin: I had tied in with a partner and had gone into a very interesting business. I traveled a lot and up until two years ago things were going great. Our company really began to move and we went public. But I found out later on that my partner was a thief, stealing public funds and to make a long story short within three years we were broke. We were living very nicely, traveling like there was no tomorrow but then I lost about a half a million dollars.

We had a magnificent home that we were building on the ocean. I went in for a big bundle. It was on a private beach on a bluff overlooking the ocean. It was paradise and I lost it. We couldn't pay to have the house finished. So last year when this thing broke she blamed me. Every time the builder would call and ask if he should put something special into the house I'd say sure because I was sitting on stock that was worth about half a million dollars. Now it's worth peanuts. I was planning on selling all my stock and feeding it into this house. But meanwhile I didn't have any resources of my own. We never even had a bank account. So I was playing with paper.

Sylvia: I knew we lost everything when we had to sell our house, when Martin didn't have the money to pay for all the commitments he made to the builder. It wasn't that he lost a job. Anyone can lose a job. I can lose my job. But he lost the business because he didn't manage it well. It was mismanaged.

We spent a lot of money frivolously. I used to say it was both of our faults, you know, that I never really inquired. Every time I'd inquire he'd just get really angry. Martin just never planned for the future. He never, never wanted to think about it, and when I said something, when I questioned him, when I asked him how he was committing money which I felt we didn't have, he would lie. I sensed it; I sensed what was happening. I kept saying, "Are you sure we can do it, are you sure?" And he'd say, "It's in the bank. We have it." I never checked but I knew something wasn't right. Martin just can't handle directness; he can't handle directness about anything but most especially about money. And, of course, it all went down the drain.

Martin: When things got bad last year, we were just going our own separate ways. I hid from home. That period was impossible. I would just go out to the movies and get lost. We didn't even look at each other for that year and a half. It was terrible. It was easier not to talk. I'd come home, ignore her, sit down and read, or else go out to dinner with some friends.

We exacerbate one another. We're not like friends, which is what a marriage should be. We talk differently, we think differently. We skirt dealing with the real things because I'm always on the defensive. She's an exceedingly honest person, to the point where she really alienates a lot of people.

Sylvia: I can talk easily about this but it's so threatening to him. He feels like it's an attack on him. I can't break through

Martin: We go out to eat frequently; we'll go to the theater very frequently. But the nights when we're home alone together, we have very little to say.

Martin: It's hard to say why we stay together. I've grown dependent on her. She makes all of our social arrangements. Thursday will come and I'll very hesitatingly say, "What are we doing tomorrow night?" And she'll go right up the wall about that. She hates my being so passive. It kills her.

that. We start to talk and it ends up with him saying, "I've had enough of that," and cursing me and things like that. It's very, very hard for Martin to break through that defensive barrier. He's such a needy person, so dependent.

Sylvia: I feel more alone with him than I feel without him. I think he feels the same way. I think he feels alone too. He's voiced it on occasion. I don't ever think there's going to be a resolution.

Sylvia: He just depends on me for every goddamn thing. It drives me up the wall, absolutely drives me up the wall.

He doesn't have any interests of his own, any friendships of his own. He sits and sleeps in that chair or in that TV room whenever we don't have a plan for a particular night. He's always asking me what do I have planned, what are we doing tonight. You know, I do the social number but it would be nice if he took an interest sometimes. I just can't hack being sucked at all the time.

Martin: Maybe I stay with her because there are times when I think she's absolutely fantastic, but when she becomes a shrew I could kill her. For instance, last night. We had had a perfectly nice weekend. Yesterday afternoon we went to see a play and then over dinner, she started getting shrewy. We didn't quarrel; we just went home and each of us withdrew. I went into the den and watched the basketball game and then went to sleep, and she was in bed by nine o'clock.

It was getting so bad for awhile last year that she was even getting to look like her mother. Her mother was a terrible shrew. She had a very unfortunate marriage. And

Sylvia's gotten like this, just this constant picking. You know, I've yet to walk into this house and have her say to me, "Gee, I'm sorry you had a hard day," to be even a little concerned for me. When I was taking this financial beating there was never any compassion from her because she was too concerned with her own hide. I would keep saying to her, "I made it before and I'll make it again. You know it's going to be rough but why don't you try to encourage me rather than discourage me." To this day, if I come home and tell her I've found a new product to manufacture, that I found the greatest product in the world, she'll say, "You can't sell it. You'll just go broke again." There are times I can take her by the neck and strangle her.

I think I still love her. I like to be seen with her and I like to be with her, but she was very rough when things were bad for me. Constant bitching, constant quarreling. I stay because I know what I have and I wouldn't want to get into something that was possibly worse. There are enough pluses to keep me here. We like doing a lot of things together. But as I said before, the drawback is when we go home and we're alone with each other. Why *she* stays I don't know. That has to be her answer.

Sylvia: I think part of it is money because we really don't have any money or any plans. And with the job situation the way it is, I can lose my job any day. With my pension, I suppose I could survive but I'd have to really live a poverty kind of life and I'm not willing to do that. Jobs are very scarce and if I got laid off or something, I don't know where I could get another job. So money is part of it and I think the other part is, you know, we've built up a mutuality of concerns. Mainly, though, I'm not willing to give up the comfort of sharing our incomes at this point.

Martin: We rarely have talks anymore. Anytime we have an extended talk it degenerates into a quarrel. Part of the thing is that I don't think we listen to each other. I know I'm guilty of it and she is too. I find that she's impossible when you start to criticize her. But I can be a son of a bitch too. I can't really put my finger on why we stay together. Maybe at this point it's a challenge.

Sylvia: I think that Martin is never going to change. He went to therapy for so many years but he's never going to change. He's just unable to really deal on a meaningful level, on a gut, honesty level. I'm depressed about it. I know that if I had the financial resources I'd leave. But because I don't, I stay.

Margaret Sanderson

Her life has been a life of extremes: from a brutally poor childhood to being the wife of one of America's most powerful and well-known businessmen. She both looks and moves like Katharine Hepburn—dignified, brisk, utterly elegant. Her home reflects that same graceful old-world strength: marble fireplaces, gardens, and an exclusive library.

She's sixty-eight and has been widowed for many years.

(Her surname has been changed to protect her privacy.)

A friend found me a job at a radio station as a receptionist and switchboard operator. My first morning there, Robert came in and saw me sitting at the switchboard, and he said, "Good morning, little woman." Well, when he left I remember running into one of the newscasters and telling him, "I don't know what this is going to be, but it's going to be something." I just knew it. The newscaster responded by saying, "You'd better leave this place. Give up the job. That man is death on women."

The minute Robert got off the elevator, before I knew who this man was, I remember I had trouble catching my breath. I remember I got red, I blushed. I did more than just get red, I mean I was vivid. I perspired all over. Then, when he came in and stood behind me, I was sort of limp. I swiveled the chair around and sort of looked up at him and that's when he said, "Good morning, little woman." And that was it. He still didn't tell me who he was but when he walked right into the main office, I figured it out.

So after that, whenever women called him, girl friends, I would never put them through to Robert. I would always say he was in conference. He'd come out to the switchboard and say, "Didn't what's-her-name call today?" and I would say, "I guess I wasn't at the switchboard at that time."

There was a very well-known and extremely rich man, Mr. M, who was sponsoring a show on Robert's station, and he began to spend a lot of time in the reception room. Sometimes he would send his car around for me at lunchtime—quite impressive, a Dusenberg. Well, Robert didn't like my seeing him in the least and I knew that. So I'd rub it in even more. I really didn't care for this Mr. M beyond a certain fascination, and it never went a bit further than the lunches and the dancing. And, of course, I was consumed with thoughts of Robert from the start. But anyway, Robert used to tell me what a terrible reputation Mr M had and how I shouldn't be seeing him. And when he'd say things like that, I'd tell Robert how fascinating I found this man. From then on, Robert spent considerable time at the switchboard, and when Mr. M would come in, Robert did whatever business had to be done with him immediately and then he escorted him to the door.

So then Robert said, "We must discuss this. I want to talk all this over with you." And I said, "Lunchtime seems like a perfect time to discuss it." And that's how it all got started. Eight months later we were engaged.

I always had a thing about wanting to rescue the man I was with. And Robert, as far as I was concerned, was on the edge of a cliff when I met him and I was going to save him. He had already had two nervous breakdowns and he had one when we were married, the night our first daughter was born. That breakdown manifested itself in his inability to function. His time was spent mostly in bed. He demanded considerable attention, especially at nursing time. So I had to give up nursing our baby. Robert would call, "I need you *now*," while I was nursing the baby in the next room.

He was a very sick man but he was also an extraordinary man, just absolutely incredible. He was, in the first place, the most beautiful creature that ever walked on two feet. He was very tall. Sometimes I used to look at him and think this is not possible that this is my husband. Very distinguished. When he would walk into a room, the size and the beauty would just take over right away. He would sit at a piano—he played piano—and it would be magical, just magical. There was a relationship he had with the piano; this was his mistress, there wasn't any question about it. In his early days, he wanted to be a concert pianist but was discouraged by his father. In those days, the status of musicians was the same as that of domestic help.

Robert wanted very much to be a whole person but the more successful he became, the more miserable he became. He was in analysis for thirty-some-odd years and he never got anywhere at all with it. He had a specialness, he was charming, unbelievably charming. I never knew anyone who wasn't vulnerable to his charm. And terribly funny, the most continuously witty person. Still there was this terribly tortured man underneath. And I don't think Robert was ever in love with me. I don't think Robert was ever in love with anybody. Sometimes I used to think he was incapable of loving.

I was desperately in love with him and many times that was totally frustrating. I think all the external evidences of his loving me were there. He was most loyal and most attentive, a sweet person. But his intense involvement with himself, his poor health, and his dedication to his work were the dominant forces. Much of his energies went into the creative aspects of the business. Once he told me he wanted to prove to his father that he could be a better businessman than his father had been.

Robert was primarily a soloist. He did not know how to be either a partner in his business or in his marriage. He was a marvelous person if you weren't emotionally involved with him. He was very much the nineteenth-century Victorian male. Things had to center around him. *His* opinion was the important one. *His* decision was the only one that mattered. At a business meeting, if he didn't have his way, he would have palpitations.

With his hand on his chest, he would say, "I don't feel very well." That usually brought on the desired effect. Someone would say, "Oh, go ahead, Bob. We'll do it your way."

I could express my frustration to him but I knew what his reaction to it would be—either totally turned off or he would just not hear. Not being a career person, my nest was terribly important to me: my husband, my children, and my home. The latter two became more and more important to me as things with Robert became more unstable.

Robert was always a guest in his own home, rarely a member of the family. When he came home at the end of the day, I had his cocktail ready, his slippers ready, and I kept the children away. That was the time when I'd meet him in the library and he'd let off steam. He'd talk about the day's happenings in a tone of complaint. I would usually be just a sounding board or I would give him support. He felt soothed by this but there was really no soothing him deeply. He was the original guy with the hair shirt and the corkscrew up his ass that no matter what you'd do, the self-imposed punishment and guilt were what got him every time. He was a sad, suffering person.

When I felt a need to be soothed—I was very close to my children, to animals, and to nature—I'd go out and put my arms as far as I could reach around one very special tree in the garden and think, 'My God, my God.' I could just feel its strength, and I'd think of all the hurricanes and the violent weather over the years and this tree was still standing. This great, strong tree would hold me up and would always fill me with strength.

Once Robert spoke to me about his analysis and he said he had never really opened up, that sometimes he wouldn't utter a word for an entire session. The fact that the cost of each session was fifty dollars did not seem to matter. His reason for it was that if he really gave of himself in analysis, then instead of being up there, he'd be down here with the rest of us. He would be deprived of his uniqueness; he would have to join the proletariat. I was part of the proletariat. He felt he was special, a separate thing. He was in love with that concept, in love with it so deeply that no matter how much suffering he had to go through he would prefer to stay different.

At least five times I told him I had to leave him. But when it came close to my leaving, he'd get very sick. It was finally after about twenty years that I started to feel the buildup of resentment. It took such an awful lot to kill the kind of love I had. I tried to make it work in every way. But there was such lack of love I felt from him. I was really a glorified housekeeper-nurse. That's what he needed as he grew older.

I was so used to demonstrative relationships and he wasn't demonstrative. In the act of lovemaking, I think sometimes we did make contact. And I think—and this may be wishful thinking—that there were certain nights that we'd be making love and I would think this had to make a baby. Those times would be so much more unusually right and connected.

He wasn't aware of his limitations as a partner. He didn't really know. For example, he was an insomniac and needed to sleep alone. He just could not sleep with anyone in the same bed. We'd start in the same bed, but sooner or later there came that goodnight pat that I anticipated with feelings of deep aching.

This boy came to stay with us. I needed help so I put an ad in the paper. He was twenty-one and he helped out with the kids. I didn't fall in love with him then, but I did later. He was a marvelous consolation and I could talk about everything with him. He got me over what, I guess, was the major hurdle. I felt very strongly about him. It wasn't that he was a very emotionally rich twenty-one-year-old. It was the need and the timing. He was undistinguished and uninteresting. Of course, I didn't see him that way then because I loved him. He was big, strong, able, agile. He also was a sad, lonely person in need of support and lots of tender care. And I needed very much the same thing, besides needing help with my family.

Let me tell you that I had decided at the age of eight that if I could find a man that I loved and have a home and children, then nothing else was important. And basically this is what I had. As a child, I had been so used to being hurt or deprived of something or other—food or love or family or a home. You see, I wasn't spoiled. I didn't have to have everything. If even a part of the dream came true, it would be great.

But with Robert I very often felt like a small child in a crowd of adults where there were too many legs in the way and never being able to get through and not enough air to breathe. There was no way at all of getting through to him.

Loretta

She's fifty-one and was widowed five years ago. She lives in Tulsa, Oklahoma.

I'm in the middle of an affair with a man that I can't bring home, can't introduce to my kids or to the rest of my family or even to most of my friends because he's not anyone who's available. This was something I thought would never happen to me. I'm a nice, middle-class woman who never even screwed around before she got married. I was twenty-two and still a virgin—which in this day and age is quite unusual. My husband and I were each other's only lovers until he died. What happened was that I got involved with the husband of one of my very close friends.

I always thought that nice girls don't do things like that. I found out that nice girls do. His wife doesn't know about it and it's been going on for two years now. He and I see each other at least once a week. There's usually one night a week when we're able to see each other.

After my husband died, I didn't go out at all until I started to see Frank. We saw each other at a party and then a few days later he came over to my house on some excuse, and while my son was watching television in the next room, he sat down on the couch and suddenly told me that he'd loved me for the past twenty-five years and he just couldn't not say anything anymore. I'd never thought about it because it had never occurred to me to think about someone else's husband that way. I had known him and his wife since high school. I had always felt that he had a very strong physical presence but that was it. I was stunned and very upset, frightened, hysterical. I told him to get out and never come back

122

again and I didn't want to hear anything like that, that it was crazy. But he ran a very good campaign. He'd call me at seven in the morning, at three in the morning, show up at the door at ten in the morning when he was supposed to be at work and really pursued me in a way that I had never been pursued before. It was very romantic and very flattering.

I kept wondering what he wanted with a middle-aged old bag like me. I kept thinking middle-aged men were supposed to chase young girls. What the hell did he want with me? He said that this had been something on his mind for twenty-five years, that as long as he'd known me he'd felt there'd been something between us. And I finally gave in, not because I thought he loved me, but because I figured if he screwed me once he'd go home and he wouldn't bother me again. But it didn't work out that way. We're very much in love with each other.

It's very hard to be objective about his relationship with his wife because I want it to be nothing more than an empty shell. He talks about leaving his wife on occasion but I don't really expect him to. He has four children whom he loves very much. I plan to continue the affair and the only thing I think that would get me out of it would be if I really fell in love with somebody else. But I don't really see anybody else, even if there are men around. Frank says when you're in love you don't look for anybody else.

There's never enough time for us to be together and things are always disjointed because of this. When I'm away from him, I gather up so many things I want to tell him—but by the time I see him, I forget what they were. I resent that I can't share all these things with him. We both say that the time we spend together is unreal, it's out of time, it's in another sphere because we're divorced from the rest of the world. We can't be anywhere where we're involved with other people who might know us. So whatever we do and wherever we go is sort of not connected with the rest of our lives.

For each of us this is really the most important relationship in our lives. And we'll find the time to be together even if it means conniving and lying to our families. One advantage of a love affair is that it doesn't ever get to be prosaic because you don't really have enough time for it. We've speculated about whether or not the sex would be as good if we lived together. Between this man and me there's a very strong physical attraction—there was from the beginning, almost like electricity as soon as I touched him. We can spend the whole day in bed together having sex seven or eight or nine times—and we say, people just don't do this when they're married. There just isn't time for it. Either this kid is sick or that kid wants you to help her with her homework. When my husband was alive, I never knew to value the time with him. There are a lot of things that I've discovered in the last two years that I didn't know existed and there are a lot of avenues that I've explored with this man that I don't think I would have ever known about were my husband still alive.

My husband and I were happy and satisfied with what we had. But there's a kind of intensity that comes with just spending a whole day or a whole evening not concerned with anything but each other. You know, what you do in bed together is not only fuck. It's the talking to each other, the learning about the things that each of you thinks and feels. My husband was shy and even found it difficult to say 'I love you.' But this man is different. Frank has helped me rid myself of some of the inhibitions that I had. I would never initiate anything sexual on my own because I was afraid of doing something displeasing or distasteful, as far as sex was concerned. But Frank goes by the anything-that-pleases-you-pleases-me philosophy, which makes for a much freer, much more open relationship.

When I'm with his wife or when I'm with the two of them together, it's sort of like the two lives are divorced and I'm the friend of the family. In fact, I was instrumental in arranging a surprise party for their twenty-fifth anniversary. All of this is so crazy. All the things we've done are crazy and they're all things I never thought I'd be doing. The standards are gone. I'm discovering a whole new way of living and I'm not too happy with it because it's upset all my feelings about what I thought were my beliefs. In my marriage, I never fooled around or thought about it. Frank said he knew as long as my husband was alive that if he had tried to pursue me, I would have been horrified.

I believe that Frank really loves me because there have been too many things that have happened to me and too many situations that we've been involved in where the easiest thing would have been to get out. If he just wanted to screw around, he's got a lot of other women available to him who would be much less of a problem.

I've gone out with other men on occasion because I get these feelings of rebellion and damn it, I say I shouldn't be involved in this and I should be doing something about not being involved in this. If an opportunity presents itself in such a way that I can't ignore it, then I might go out on a date with a guy. But I haven't gone to bed with anyone else.

I really don't think that Frank would leave his wife, and so I pray that she doesn't find out about this because if she did that would end it. He has too much at stake as far as his children are concerned and as far as his profession is concerned. It's not realistic for him to give all that up. Sometimes I feel resentment because I think if I'm the greatest love of his life, how come he's not able to walk out on his wife for me no matter what the sacrifice. But when I think about it, I can see his point of view. And sometimes I think for myself that I hope to God nothing happens because it would alienate me from so many people. There would be so many friends who we'd both lose. And on top of all that, I'd lose him.

Stella

She's twenty-seven and lives in a low-income housing project in the Bronx.

I was twenty-one when I got married. We were married on the tenth of January and on the eighteenth of January my husband got busted for doing a robbery. He was sentenced to do two and a half to five years.

I was brought up around people who thought that girls grew up to have babies. There was no love talk or none of that. All my friends were having babies at twelve and thirteen. So when I was pregnant at eighteen, they were saying to me, "Shit. It's about time." This was the conditioning, man. Girls had babies. So I had babies and I didn't know what I was getting into. It was the same thing with my getting married.

I think I wanted to get married because I had nothing else to do. When we met, I was spending all my time at home. I was on welfare. I was being cool, not using drugs. I was just like in a state of limbo. So I think getting married was like something to do.

Marvin had a drug history and he drank a lot. That's where his head was at when I met him. He was just into standing on the corner and drinking. He wasn't about working, nothin' like that. And because welfare was paying for my room, I wasn't getting into his case about not working. He was just available. He was OK with my two kids—he was a kid himself—so I figured I'd marry him.

The night before we got married, Marvin got drunk. He'd been stabbed a few months previously and ever since he'd gotten stabbed, whenever he'd drink he'd start running a temperature. Well, the night before we got married, Marvin was hanging-out drinking. He came back home in the middle of the night and all night I could feel him getting hot and shit because he'd been out there drinking. So in the morning I had an attitude with him and I cursed him and I mean serious. All that day—our wedding day—man, I had to do everything. I had to get his shit together. *I had to dress him.* So we got married at my mother's house and like I was trying to keep his ass sober all day. But by the time we got married, he was already feeling a buzz from drinking. So I was disgusted with him. I felt like just fucking the whole thing right there. I think I knew that it was a real mistake. Even his mother said to me—and she was real serious, man—"Hey, you not gonna marry that shit."

He apologized but it didn't mean anything. Then, when we came home, the first thing we did was get into an argument about something that happened a long time ago. I remember he said he should pack his shit and leave, and I remember really thinking I wouldn't give a fuck if he did.

Anyway, a week after we were married, he got busted. It was really dumb. He was drunk and whenever he was drunk he'd go out there and do stuff that maybe if he was sober he wouldn't have done. So he robbed this woman and he put a knife on her. Now I've been robbed, raped, the whole bit, so I didn't dig him doing that to somebody. I guess because of my own past experiences I almost wanted to see him in jail for doing that shit. So he was sent upstate for two and a half to five years.

I'll tell you a little bit about jail. When he first went in, I missed him, you know, because I was used to having him around and shit. But jail has a different effect on men than on women. When a man goes to jail and he leaves his woman on the street, well, he starts having his feelings. He's wondering what his woman is doing out there and he imagines the worst. Marvin told me one time, "Jail'll even make you think bad of your mother." So if a guy's in jail and he's thinking this shit, he's gonna start putting a little pressure on his woman. He don't want her to miss a visit. And he starts telling her he needs things—like cigarettes and sneakers. And I was cool with all that for about a month. I'd do what I could do. But then, after a month, money started getting tight—welfare was shaving my check—so I started doing other things . . . hustling. Before Marvin went to jail, he'd always brought in a little money. He'd do little stickups and shit. But without his money, things got real tight.

I could always get money hustling. Like I knew people and I started hanging out a little more. I started getting hot. And it became very progressive. I started getting high first, and once I started getting high then I had more of a mind to go on the street and hustle. The people I was getting high with started introducing me to other people—so after a while I had a homosexual guy who I was hustling with. He was a drag queen. We hustled together, shot dope together, and lived together. And this homo taught me how to pickpocket, so after a while I didn't even have to give up my body to get money. We'd take people off, we'd rob 'em. We'd bring people to our room. But I didn't like violence. I'd always be the one who'd say, "Don't hit no more. Don't hurt him." But violence is kind of progressive and we were violent people.

In the meantime, what's happening is Marvin's in jail and he don't know what's happening. He doesn't know anything. And one day he calls me up and he asks me was I getting high. And he was like really fucked up because his sister had just told him that I was getting high and that I was hustling. By the time he called me—this was already a few months since he'd been in jail—I had gotten caught up in my things and I was just angry; angry at him and at the world. Just angry. And I was bombed out, spaced out. So zonked out that I used to bring my tricks, man, into my house, shoot my dope in my house. And my kids were there, my neighbors, my mother-in-law. So when Marvin finally found out, he was hurt and I was hurt because he was hurt. I didn't want to hurt him with this shit. So we both ended up crying. We had this crying session on the phone and I promised him that I was gonna stop. But as soon as I hung up the phone, I copped some dope and got high.

That's when Marvin started doing hard time. Before, when he was worrying about me, I was straight and he didn't even need to worry. But after that day, he really did have things to worry about. And by then, I was even starting to get high before I'd go visit him. And he knew it because he'd been a dope fiend himself once. But by then I'd reached the point where I just didn't care anymore.

This went on. I kept hustling. I kept shooting dope, hanging out. I mean, the whole bit, man. Marvin stayed in the city for like six months. They moved him to Riker's Island before going upstate. And by then, my visits started tapering off. And my phone got cut off too. I didn't want to rap anymore. I just wanted to shoot dope. And it tapered off until I just wouldn't go see him.

He used to write me, call me. He'd write me romantic notes and ask me what's happening. He'd tell me he was worried about me. But I was just paying no attention at all. When I was nodded out, that was it. I just wanted to be zonked out. I didn't want to have to deal with nothin'.

Then I lost touch with Marvin. I was just into dope. I had guys in the neighborhood who were my tricks and they would be ten-dollar tricks. This homo and me would shoot a quarter a day— and a quarter was costing us fifty and sixty dollars. First, we'd hustle our dope money, then we'd hustle cab fare, then we'd hustle food money. And this was like a day-to-day thing. This went on every day. That's where it was at.

After a year of all this, I was really disgusted with myself. You know, everything was like fucked up and I couldn't really see myself continuing out there—doing what I was doing. I just reached the point where I wanted to die. I'd walk down the block and I'd just be crying and shit.

Then I got hooked up with a pimp who was violent, really violent. And when I saw him beat his girls up, I said, "Shit, what the fuck am I doing here? This nigger's crazy!" I got involved with him because he showed a little concern. I was so spaced out. I felt like I had nobody, so I would latch onto these dudes. I don't know whether I was looking for love or what.

Well, one night I picked up this guy and I'd been feeling really suicidal, and I just said, 'I'm gonna off this dude.' I'd taken about thirty valium that day with a bottle of Yago plus my dope. So I'm with this dude in his car and while we're sitting in the car he reaches for me. And then I just went after him. We fought and shit. I was just stabbing him and cutting him. The dude was bleeding to death, and that's when the cops finally busted me. I was like covered in blood from my head to my toes.

When I went to jail that was the first time in over a year that Marvin knew where I was. And when I went to jail, he filed for divorce. By then, I felt kinda bad about the scene. I felt really guilty and really repentant about the shit I had done to him. I think after my first six weeks in jail I started undergoing some kinda change. I looked at the other women around me and they were in there for the same reasons I was there and they looked pathetic. They had nothin' to show for all the shit they did—for all the time they were out there.

I wrote to Marvin and as soon as I wrote him, he stopped the divorce papers. He didn't really want a divorce. He came to see me one time too. He came out on a furlough, and when we saw each other it was OK. But then when I came out of jail and when he came out, there was just too much animosity in him. I could understand his hate but I didn't want to deal with it. Like I met him at Grand Central Station. I'd been out a week before he got out; and the minute we saw each other he started drinking. And the hotter he got the more violent and hostile he got. He ended up slapping me that first day we got back together.

Marvin started this shit too, that he wanted me to hustle for him, but I was trying to get my shit together. He had this master plan about me and him making all this money. This is what he ran to me the first fucking day we were together. So I agreed to everything he said and as soon as he went to sleep, I left. When he woke up and saw that I was gone, he called me and apologized, the whole bit. But he was bitter toward me. He wanted revenge. He felt that I had really crossed him and shit, and he wasn't as

forgiving as he was seeming. Deep down in his gut he was mad.
You know, his whole thing was to get back at me.

All this on top of just coming out of jail is like really frustrating. And I had to deal with my mother, with welfare, with going to school, plus all of Marvin's shit. And he's going through
the same thing—he's looking for a job, he had to get adjusted to
being back in the city. So I started really feeling pulled apart. I
started feeling persecuted and paranoid and then I started fighting
back. Like I told Marvin. "Fuck it. I gotta do my own thing.
Ain't nothin' happening with us. I can't deal with your shit.
You gotta go deal with your own." So I got my own apartment
and I just told him we can't make it together. I couldn't deal with
him—his drinking and shit. I couldn't be sympathetic.

Whatever feeling there was between us, it had gone. He killed
it. Whatever it was, it went away. It was like self-preservation,
man. And plus, he was weak and I couldn't deal with that weakness. I just saw him as being incredibly weak and I lost all respect
for him. I was scared because I was saying all this shit to him and
I thought one day he was just gonna break on me, man. But
that's how I felt. I had no respect for him. And because he
couldn't see that about himself that made me hate him even
more.

After a while my life kinda fell into some semblance of order
and then Marvin just became an intruder. I resented him. He
came to my place and the first day it was cool. He came over to
talk and I had already told him I didn't want to be with him no
more. So he came over and we talked and everything was cool
because we can talk sometimes—but he stayed the night. And
after that, he kept on staying and that was bad. He wasn't doing
nothin'. I couldn't stand him. I hated him after a while. I wanted
him to go away and leave me alone. I had sex with Marvin the
first night but after that I wouldn't let him touch me. I knew the
shit had come to a head, man, because men have called me frigid
and cold in the past but if I was cold it was only because I didn't
know to be anything else. I didn't have no experience when I was

younger when it came to tender sex. On the street nobody had ever told me anything about sex. Nobody was ever tender. I was educated in the streets and I wasn't educated to any warmth. I was educated to a business. But I learned about sex and I learned about the difference between tender sex and the other—you know, the difference between hustling and making love. So I knew I wasn't cold. But with Marvin I experienced something that left me kind of shaky because even in the street with my tricks—even with them—I never felt numb and that's how I felt with Marvin—numb. It was weird; it really was. Then I just told him that it's best that he go.

Marvin calls me now sometimes and we talk. But I haven't seen him since I started messing with a new man. As long as I'm not juggling with him, I can keep compatible feelings for him. When I see him, I don't hate him. He still doesn't want to give me a divorce though. But the way he's living his life now, I won't need a divorce. He'll be dead soon enough.

Leslie

Leslie's thirty-six. She's attractive, witty, adventurous, and divorced.

My relationship with men has pretty much always been for them to think that I was uninvolved with anyone else and that each of them was the only man in my life. Which, of course, was never true. That's why I think marriage can be such a sham because you have to keep up that illusion—that you're not interested in anyone else and that you're not looking at anyone else.

The marriage I'd come from was not based on truth. I had so many frustrations. My husband came from the Midwest and he married what was in a way his ideal LA-type chick. And it turned out to be a thing he really didn't want at all. He would have been very happy with a nurse from Chicago who'd quit her job when she had her first kid and stayed home with the baby. I only realized all that after we were married for a couple of years.

At the beginning of the relationship we hardly got out of bed. It was really very passionate for the first six months. I was very proud of him; I was very proud to be with him. There were so many jerks, you know, in and out of my life and so many people who wanted to take from me because I had a lot of things to offer. I felt like I got badly used. With Sven, I felt he was my equal and I loved that. I can't really be passionate with a man unless I feel that I look up to him in a way. I know that's in the Doris Day school of sexuality, but for me that's a real thing. It's not a thing of me feeling smaller; it's just a thing of feeling feminine. If you're with a really strong man, it makes you feel good and Sven was like that. He was wonderful to look at and had a beautiful way about him. He was like part jock, part poet.

The problem was that the sex went out of the relationship after our baby was born. We lived together for a year, then we were married and I became pregnant a month later. At that point I figured I'd have an abortion, it was still too early for us to have a baby. We were still having a lot of fun and running around a lot. But Sven didn't want to have an abortion. I thought at that time that it was because he wanted to have the baby, but what I found out was that he didn't want to have the abortion because he just didn't want to have the abortion. He came from a Catholic family and those beliefs never leave you.

I know what was going through his mind. When we were living together, it was sexually like we were in his hotel room. It was just very taboo and wild for a guy from his background, which was very midwestern, very conservative. But suddenly all that intrigue went out of it and it was legitimate and we had papers to show we were married. It took a lot of the spark out of it. I suggested a few times that he sneak into my bedroom through the window and stuff like that, just to liven it up a little. But he was very conservative. Also, we had a lot of very attractive friends and I really wanted to get into things, like sleep with other couples and stuff. But we never did.

When Sven stopped making love to me after the baby was born, I remained faithful to him for about two and a half years. He was just impotent or so it seemed. He just wasn't a sexual creature.

We didn't fight at all; there was a lot of tenderness and a lot of love between us. I wanted to help him with his problem. I kept stuffing down my bitterness and I tried to talk about it. It was very hard for him to look at himself; it's much easier for me to do that sort of thing. I thrive on it. He was afraid of psychology; he was afraid of finding out what was going on with him. We slept together every night but there could be no touching because touch would be interpreted to mean that I wanted to have sex. I'd never been in that position before. I'd always been pursued and wanted, and suddenly here I was with the man of my life who I was in love with and married to and he didn't want me. It was very tough to deal with and I must say that I was probably as repressed about the whole thing as he was in acknowledging that the problem was there. I kept thinking, 'If I close my eyes, the problem will go away.' He was drinking heavily then and he was in a very high-pressured job, and those things combined—along with suddenly being a husband and a father—probably helped get him to that point.

There were a lot of men in our lives as a couple. We were friends with a lot of other couples and socialized a lot. Sometimes I thought we could get it on with another couple. We were in Martinique one summer and we met a beautiful couple, and I thought, 'How perfect, wouldn't they make great bedmates for the time we're here.' So one afternoon I was walking along the beach with the girl of this other couple and I suggested my idea to her and she started laughing and said, "Wait until I tell you about my husband." And she told me my own story, that her husband was impotent. So we were trying to devise ways to get our husbands into bed, but in the meantime we got sidetracked. There were a lot of gorgeous men there and Lynn and I wound up with the same guy one night, who was nuts about both of us, and he happened to be a psychiatrist. He knew our problems, had heard our stories, and so the three of us had sex together. Neither one of us wanted to cheat on the guys, but we couldn't get them moving.

It was such a difficult time for Sven and me because we both felt so shattered: this beautiful dream we'd had had just gone up in smoke. That was more of the pain than anything, the inevitability of the divorce. I loved him too much to make him face painful things and that, I realize, was wrong. I mean, if you love someone and he's a junkie, what you do is not give him any more heroin. In those days my thought was you give them all the bad things they want. So Sven became a spoiled kid and I fed him all the stuff he didn't need.

I was working for a fashion magazine at the time and I was looking pretty good. I'd put myself together and I'd gone from bohemian artist to nice clothes and all that shit. So I was looking great and I'd see all these guys checking me out and undressing me with their eyes and stuff, and here I hadn't had any sex in so long. I felt so bitter that I'd look at all those men looking at me and I hated them. I was just so angry I couldn't keep that bitterness down.

A friend of mine, a former college lover, was practically living with us during the last three months of our marriage. He became a good buddy of ours. I said to him that I wanted him to go out with Sven and that I didn't even care if they fucked other women. I just wanted him to get Sven going again. We leveled with Eddie about the problem. The three of us were like two brothers and a sister. We'd all go out together. We'd get all dressed up, looking to kill. And there I was with these two gorgeous hunks—this six-foot-three swarthy Italian and this six-foot-four blue-eyed Swede—and we looked like the sex trio of the century. But, in fact, the truth was that here I was, a totally frustrated woman not getting any, a plant needing water, traveling with these two supposed studs.

Sven went to a psychiatrist finally and he went six times and he came home one night and said, ''I think I'm OK. I don't wanna go anymore.'' So again, like the self-indulgent parent, I said fine. I protected him because I loved him too much.

Anyway, what happened toward the end was that I was at a pretty high-powered job where I was seeing a lot of men, photographers and models. So I met one model who seemed like the ideal sexual outlet for me. He was physically gorgeous and dumb like a bunny. I figured there'd be no involvement and I could just have a fling with him. With Sven, who was very intelligent, I always had to be on my toes. With this guy I could just lay back and relax and say dumb things and not have to think twice about it. It was just enjoyable. He was bisexual, with more leaning toward homosexual, which was good for me, too, because here I was trying to validate my femininity and here was this gay guy getting it on with a woman.

Looking back on it now, I think my goal was to make as much of a mess of everything as possible so that the divorce would be inevitable. I did, in fact, get caught with Ken—this model—in the house, and that was a crazy night. Sven was returning from a business trip in Iowa City. Unbeknownst to me he was bugging this little secretary out there. It was about 7:30 at night and he was supposed to arrive at 8:00. Ken was here helping me move some furniture. We weren't even touching each other; we weren't doing anything. I told Ken to leave here by 7:00 because Sven was coming home. So he's helping me move these things and then he wants to play around so he's grabbing me, at which point the bell rings and I thought, 'Oh, my God, that must be Sven.' So I whipped myself out of Ken's arms, at which point my entire T-shirt got torn open. Then the telephone rings and it's my maiden aunt on the phone. Sven is on the way up in the elevator, I'm standing there with a totally exposed breast, and Ken is standing there. I hear the key turning in the door; I tell Aunt Helen I'll call her back. It was just so unbelievable, everything coming together. I said to Sven, "This is Ken," To Ken, "This is Sven. Why don't you make some drinks." I didn't know who I was telling to make the drinks. And I ran into the bedroom to change my shirt. So I came back in and the three of us are sitting there and I figure this will be all right, it'll get Sven a little jealous, he'll know that there's a very attractive man in my life.

I was so fascinated with the scene. It was like watching an accident happen. Just as I secretly hoped, though I would deny to this day that I'd set it up like this, Ken opened his mouth and started saying very crass, dumb things like, "I know a lot about you, Sven," which led right into "I don't think you treat Leslie very well. Why don't you either let her go or do something about your sex life." And Ken, in his own flatfooted manner, really got Sven going. I could see Sven's knuckles turning white. Sven is a fighter and he's also mannered. And Ken had very bad manners and also cut him to the quick because what he was saying was true. So Sven sat there with his knuckles turning white and said, "If you don't get out of my house, I'm going to break your head and throw you through that window." He said it calmly but with so much fury behind it that I thought we were really going to have a scene. Well, Ken was smart enough to pick himself up and leave. This was the first confrontation that Sven and I had had. Sven slapped me that night and it was the first time that he'd ever hurt me physically. At that point I stopped resisting the fact that the marriage was over. But even then we didn't delve beyond the surface. The confrontation ended up being about the situation that had just occurred. So the relationship was really a lot of not leveling about what was going on and a lot of not telling the truth.

David

David is twenty-eight. His relationship with Bonnie, a relationship that lasted four years, was "a real roller coaster. Either real high or real low."

Throughout their relationship David and Bonnie always kept their own apartments. They did, however, spend most of their time—days and nights—together.

Right from the beginning, at least intellectually, she had always said, "I'm free. I'm not monogamous. I have to do what I want to do." She had this intense desire to be an independent woman. She wasn't going to get caught in any traps. She hated the whole idea of families. Yet our relationship was so intense that I couldn't reconcile the idea of how we could not be thinking of getting married. How can things be so blistering and we're not going to marry? It defied all my definitions.

Our first year was fantastic. Fantastic communication. It was one of the only relationships I'd ever really wanted. It wasn't something casual in my mind. I wanted the relationship to last. I wanted us to stay together, to live together, to have a kid. The whole works. Those were my kinds of feelings. I began to feel for the first time that the whole thing—living with someone—could be something other than deadly.

So she was opening me up emotionally with all of our talking and communication. And I was opening her up sexually. That was just such an ego rush for me. She had been with other men but none of the sex had ever been good. She gave me insane confidence. At the time when I felt good with her, I was really bouncy and happy. I was just really letting myself go. But then, she started seeing this other man and I was just thrown into the pits. My ego was just slammed into the wall. I hid. I went away. I disappeared. I just stopped visiting people. I was tightening up. It was an incredible loss. I felt ashamed. When she started seeing someone else I felt inadequate—inadequate in many ways. And I also felt that this guy she was seeing had a star personality and I didn't.

It all happened very fast. One night she met a guy and I saw them go into her house together. And right away I was very upset. I wasn't used to seeing her with other people and I just reacted. I immediately said to her that she could do whatever she wanted to do. I was reacting more on what my value systems were. You know, I intellectually felt that it was OK for us to see other people. I felt, who was I to stop her from seeing others? Yet, in practicality, we were both monogamous. This was the first time it was actually questioned. So I reacted fairly OK that first night. But I reacted from my mind not from what I was really feeling, which was just outrage, anger, frustration.

I remember I had to go away for a few days and when I returned she came up to see me and told me that she saw Bob again and that they'd gone out to dinner and that they'd slept together. And I was just destroyed. She was telling me this because we'd always been honest with each other. She was just trying to be as casual and honest and as open as she could. I don't think there was any ill intent on her part. It was just like this-is-what-happened-and-I-have-to-tell-you. I immediately interpreted it that she was being so fucking callous. You know, I'm crushed, I'm trembling, and there I was inside a projection room of a movie theater, having to stand there for the next six hours showing movies. I was all alone. And being in that booth is like being in solitary. You know, in the best of conditions, being in a projection booth isn't the best place to spend six hours. But to be having this thing eating at me in that booth was too much.

I want to tell you, I was hurt. I was hurt because I felt I was inadequate, that I wasn't satisfying her. And I was very willing to criticize myself about that. I probably have a great innate tendency in that direction anyway. I was really hurt—my image, my self. And my work, owning a small movie theater, was becoming difficult at the time. The theater had money problems and all. So I wasn't having any other satisfactions in my life other than this relationship. The relationship was my joy.

And this guy that Bonnie was with really hit me hard. It was the sort of thing where I felt that I underachieved but I felt that this person was really an achiever. He's like a graduate of Cal Tech in physics and he's got a master's in physics, and he was going for his second master's in astronomy. He was an achiever and I felt so outclassed. And another thing that really hit hard was that she said she was going down to the Caribbean with him, and I felt like, 'Wow, I can't do any of this stuff.' First of all, I didn't have the money. And I just felt so washed under.

Her feelings were still that I was the primary relationship. We'd even go so far as to say, and these things now seem so absurd, that we were going to live together, that we were still going to get married.

I was very confrontational. I didn't know what to do. I didn't know if I should like attack this guy, burn his car, or get a samurai sword and come through his window at night. And I did some of these weird things, too. I came up to them in the middle of the night when they were in bed together and I'd pound on the door. I actually came sneaking up one night—but they weren't there. I had this incredible vision of somebody dying and I had a knife and it was just lucky that no one was there. And I'd be walking around the streets at four o'clock in the morning, walking alone and feeling crushed. Just insane.

Then she told me that she was going to go down to the Caribbean with him, and as a reprisal I told her if she went I'd never see her again. She went anyway and while she was away I read her journal. And I was really hurt. In the journal she had written that I was pressuring her and she was wondering how I'd react when she finally started seeing someone else. Not that she had anyone in mind when she wrote those words, but she knew it was inevitable.

When she got back from the Caribbean I told her I couldn't see her for a while. It was too painful for me to see her. I was real confused and I was wasted by then. I was ruined. I had lost weight. I was pale, shaky. I was constantly upset. And I didn't know how to get out of this state. So I told her I just wasn't going to see her anymore. She didn't like that at all. She was really afraid that our relationship would end. She even said that if I was definitely going to leave her, then she would leave this other man. But I said that that would just fuck things up forever. It wouldn't be honest emotionally. So I didn't see her for a month. And then I saw her and the battle started again. Finally, we decided that we couldn't work this out, so we went to see a therapist, and after seeing him three times, he said, ''You know, each of you have your needs and it's not going to work. So forget it. You gotta end it.'' So we left there and she was very upset and I went on about how she had brought this on herself. I said, ''There's nothing to cry about. Don't cry to me.'' So she was really upset and I was really firm and annoyed. We were driving and I was just saying how it was all over, but then we ended up in a park and *I* got upset. So crazily upset. I was really insane. And I was just screaming and crying and shaking. Like never in my life. It was like a total breakdown. And I was just going, ''I wanted you to stay with me forever. I really thought we were going to stay together and now we're not going to see each other.'' And the sun was pulsing and the ground was shaking. It was such a real life event. So we ended up staying the night together. We just couldn't leave each other that abruptly. We were just feeling very fatal, like there was nothing we could do.

I was really sick at heart when we left each other, deeply sick about the whole thing. And I just wasn't getting satisfied. My friends, other women—nobody seemed able to satisfy me. There was so much unhappiness. And then I'd feel that, you know, life is too short. So I'd go back and see her. But then I'd run away again. So I'd see her a little bit and we'd go out a few times, but then invariably we'd get into some conflict. Like one night I happened to run into her in a bar. And here I am in the bar thinking about other women, trying to get out of the pit and get onto the road and go somewhere else, and I meet her and she's with a friend—a female friend—and so we're just standing there. And she's feeling insecure at that moment so she just attaches herself to me. And then she's feeling warm and loving again. So I feel like here's my hustle evening at the bar. You know, I'm supposed to be getting somewhere with some new woman and she's here. And at the end of the night she just says she's going home to Bob. And I just felt, you know, 'Get away from me. Get away from me, you bitch.'

Finally, last February, I said to her that I've been doing this back-and-forth relationship long enough. Now I really have to walk away from it. There was still a lot of pain, and I said to her some really horrible things one night—that we never had a really good relationship, that we never talked to each other, that she was actually dishonest. And we both reacted very painfully and we ran away from each other. And I didn't see her for six months after that.

I met her one day walking with Bob. And my reaction for a long time to this guy was like I just didn't want him in my sight. Anytime I'd ever be physically close to him I'd just be in a tense posture. I mean, I felt quite willing to kill him. And that's a whole other thing—dealing with violent emotions like that. But finally I got to the place where I could look at him when he was with her and be able to say hi. You know, that was pretty hard. It took me a long time to get to that.

When Bonnie and I were going through a lot of difficulty she sent Bob away a couple of times. And for me, if she had ever sent me away, then I'd go through traumas. But he'd just get up and walk out the door. He'd feel absolutely nothing. And I think that attracted her to him in a way. After a while, though, he wanted her exclusively also. But she'd say no and now she's dating someone else. She says, "I'm a free woman. I won't be with just one person."

I feel that now I'm in a process of sitting back and watching things. I'm working on myself. For awhile I was just going after relationships and I didn't know what the hell I wanted. So now

I'm trying to develop some interior confidence. You know, I was knocking around in absurd ways and getting no satisfaction. Now I'm trying to come out of that and I'm starting to feel that the world is not this hustle, this difficult thing. That it's just there and it can be OK. I still feel pretty hurt and alone sometimes, but I think I'm ready to experience things again.

Eleanor

Eleanor is sixty-four. She's an attractive, well-preserved woman. Her life, lived with a millionaire husband who died several years ago, was a tumultuous existence.

Victor was always very shy about sex. I don't think he'd had any sexual experiences until he was about twenty-seven years old, but somehow he was able to open up with me. I met him when he was just turning thirty—I met him on a blind date—and I found it very exciting being with him. There was a lot of necking and petting in the beginning, but it just wasn't in the cards then to do anything else. After two years we did finally have a premarital relationship that today would probably be laughed at by everybody. But in those days, physical attractions weren't what they are today. In those days you just didn't do anything about them.

He was a traveling salesman who hadn't finished high school and I think he was buoyed up by the fact that someone who had graduated from college was interested in him. I think he was really sensitive about the fact that he hadn't completed his education.

We were married on January 14, 1936, and after we were married, after Victor had the satisfaction of knowing that he had taken on someone who had a different background than him, he became very steeped in his business. Later on, the business became successful but in the beginning he was under intense pressure all the time.

We quarreled a great deal then. I say we quarreled an awful lot but with Victor you couldn't really quarrel. That was one of the very frustrating things about him: He was so closemouthed that the minute you tried to argue with him he'd withdraw or walk out. He was a very, very shy man, an introvert, and he never showed any signs of anger. You know, you had to tear the walls apart before you got any response to your anger.

When we were first married I knew nothing about sex and I think he knew even less. So our relationship was very, very difficult sexually right from the beginning. It was not a satisfactory physical relationship at all. It was bad in terms of frequency and in terms of satisfaction. Both of us were extremely shy people. Victor, if you can believe it, never once undressed in front of me nor I in front of him. I never walked around in the nude in all our years of marriage. Sex was always at night time and under the covers.

I did manage to become pregnant and I had Robert in 1939 and was very excited about it. He was the first grandson in both our families. But there were problems around this time because this was when I found out that Victor was having a relationship with another woman. It was "The Girl in the Office." She was a few years younger than me but not all that much. She must have been about twenty and I was twenty-five, or just twenty-six. Victor had an affair with her and the person who gave me an inkling that there might be something between them was my doctor. I had discussed with him the infrequency of my sexual relations with Victor and he said, "Well, if I were you, I'd start looking around to see what you can find because it seems to me that there must be somebody else in the picture. It isn't normal for a man that age to want sex that infrequently." We'd go a couple of months without having any sexual contact. So I started to snoop. Victor always tossed papers up on his dresser and I looked through the papers and one day I found a sales slip for a dress from Saks Fifth Avenue that was a size eight and I was a size ten. So from that point on I started to really snoop.

I remember thinking Victor was a little strange during the pregnancy. You'd think that a man who was going to have his first child would be absolutely thrilled about it; but by the time I began to show the fact that I was pregnant, Victor was almost embarrassed by it. He used to walk behind me or he didn't walk with me. I should have guessed then that something was happening but I just didn't think about it.

A friend of mine's uncle had a private detective agency, so I hired him to snoop on Victor. This detective was a horror. Anybody will tell you how depraved private detectives can be, and whatever anyone tells you about them, believe it. This detective was really an ugly, ugly person. I think he got a kick out of hearing all the sordid details of everybody's life. Anyway, he kept feeding me information about Victor and his secretary, how they were meeting at the New Yorker Hotel and all that sort of stuff. Victor would go up there during the day, in the afternoon, but he'd never stay out all night. Never. Which was probably why I never suspected anything.

So I found out about everything through this detective and one night we were all set to make the big catch—me, the detective, and my brother. In those days, the divorce laws required that you had to have someone other than a detective to be a witness to the adultery. This was all when adultery was the only grounds for divorce in New York State. I don't know if I wanted a divorce then or not but I thought that by threatening one I would really be punishing Victor. The plan didn't really work out because I didn't realize that Victor already knew he was being watched. Someone had tipped him off. So the night we were supposed to catch him, he'd already been warned. But, of course, by that time I knew that he knew, and I knew that he knew that I knew. So I just put it to him. I said, "This is ridiculous. I know how it is and you have to get rid of her or else." We ended up separating then for about three months.

After a few months, he'd come up to see our son. He'd hang around, and then it gradually got to the point where, you know, he'd say, "Do you want to go out?" He was lonely, I think. On the night of our fourth anniversary, he took me out and that's when we decided to get back together again. We went out very elegantly, and he was staying at a hotel, and I went back with him to his hotel that night, and it was really very romantic.

So we went back together again and things were pleasanter than they'd been. But it was never great between us. We tried a little harder to understand one another but, of course, there were things about the relationship that just were never going to get right. We always had problems about money, all throughout our lifetime. Victor never liked the idea of a woman having money of her own, so he doled it out to me. As a result, I was never able to save any of my own money. And everything he bought was always bought in his name. Also, and this was the biggest bone of contention in our marriage, Victor had bought a farm in upstate New York. I hated the farm from the minute we got it. I hated being up there. It was very isolated, but he loved it. He went up every single week. And buying the farm was typical of what was always happening in our relationship. We were sitting around reading the papers one morning and all of a sudden Victor said to me, "I bought a hundred-acre farm yesterday." He never discussed anything with me.

I don't know, maybe I was thinking that things weren't going too smoothly, but I decided after we already had two children that I was going to have another baby. Victor really didn't want it but, you know, the diaphragm wasn't being used when he thought it was and I became pregnant. But after our son was born, I had postpartum melancholia. It really hit me very hard. I was absolutely awful. I couldn't function at all. I went to a couple of psychiatrists and they didn't help me with pills and so in those days shock treatment was very much the thing. They gave what was called ambulatory shock so I had a series of shock treatments and it was terrible. It blanks out your memory and to this day there are a lot of spots in that era that I can't recall. Anyway, the shock treatments helped me because I was blanked out completely for a day or two so that when I came to I didn't feel quite as bad. I just felt physically and mentally so ill. I couldn't function. I didn't know if I should put this shoe on or that shoe on, and I used to stand in front of the closet and cry because I didn't know what dress to put on. So again, after that, our relationship got very, very bad. We hardly saw one another.

When I came out of my depression, I got very involved with organizational work. I was president of the PTA, and I was chairwoman of a number of charity organizations. I just got myself very, very busy. As far as our sharing anything, we'd go out on Saturday nights with other people and for years that was the extent of our relationship.

I guess I maybe started really seriously taking stock of the situation too late. Here I was in my forties and getting older and I started to sense that there would be something better out there for me if I were free. By now, we had this beautiful apartment on Park Avenue. It was a really magnificent place and Victor was very proud of it and I was very proud of it. Victor just loved it. He always loved possessions.

Anyway, I was in the apartment one day, getting ready to go to a wedding. I had my hat on and my gloves on and everything. I remember I was waiting for the maid to come in to tell her something or other and she was late that morning. Then the phone rang and I picked it up and a man's voice said, "Is this Mrs. Paulson?" I said, "Yes. Who is this?" He said, "I can't tell you who it is but I just want you to know that Victor is having an affair with Renée and I thought you might be interested in knowing that." So I said, *"Who is this?"* He said, "I can't tell you but I'm a friend of Jerry's." Jerry was Renée's husband, and they were both friends of Victor's from business. I found out later on that Victor and Renee's relationship had been going on for *eight* years before I knew anything about it. I sometimes thought there might be something going on. There were a couple of women I thought Victor might be interested in, people he'd known for years. But I never thought it was Renée because I knew Renée personally as a friend of Victor's. I had met her and her husband a number of times. I had them as dinner guests. She even bought tickets to my PTA theater parties and they would invite us to their club.

Well, of course, I nearly dropped through the floor after I hung up the phone that morning. And by then I had really had it. So I got busy again. The same rules still held—that the only grounds for divorce in New York State was adultery. I asked my brother to find me a good out-of-town detective. This time I got connected with detectives who had no contacts with any of the people who worked for my husband and they got me all the information I needed. I got a call one morning at four o'clock telling me that they had caught Victor in bed with Renée in some Connecticut motel. Victor was away, supposedly alone, on one of his monthly business trips. My brother had accompanied the detectives because you still had to have some relative there as a witness. That was still the law. Today you don't have to have anything. You just have to walk out on somebody and stay walked out for two years and that's it. Anyway, they took a couple of pictures, and that was it. The next morning Victor came back to the apartment, packed a suitcase while I wasn't there, and moved into a hotel.

Later I found out that Victor had been with a number of women over the years, and it was always women who would put him on a pedestal. I suppose this is what he needed because I didn't supply it. I'm taking my share of the blame for that because I sort of put him down because he wasn't giving me what I needed—sexually or otherwise. I don't believe Victor ever actually searched for any of these women because these were all fairly unattractive people. They weren't the kind of people he usually mingled with. He was such a good-looking man and he was always exposed to all these gorgeous models. I'm sure any one of them would have been very happy to have gone out with him, to appear with him. But a lot of the women Victor ran around with were just women who were after financial gain.

It's strange. In a sense I think I still didn't *really* want a divorce even after the second time. I felt that maybe there was something we could finally do about it. But it never happened, and when the divorce came through it was very painful for me. So much of my life had been spent with this man.

On the eve of our twenty-fifth wedding anniversary—January 14, 1961—I tried to commit suicide. I was very depressed. I was thinking about our wedding; our wedding had been such a beautiful thing twenty-five years ago. And I was thinking about all of the things that had happened over the years. I was all alone that night. I was very, very depressed.

Our daughter was the one who later found me after I had taken a bunch of sleeping pills. I took an awful lot and I was unconscious, and they took me out in an ambulance. I was in absolute agony. They pumped it all out of me.

After that, I didn't see Victor till much later. Eventually, he started coming to dinner to see the family, to see his grandchildren. But he didn't like the noise of the children. He didn't like disruptions. And I saw him a lot when we had problems with our daughter. She became a dope addict, a heroin addict. Victor's relating to her was always one of the difficulties in our relationship. I think I tried to favor her because Victor didn't like her. He really didn't like her. And it was very, very painful for her. It was a very bad time for her when she was growing up and I always tried to show Victor that his love meant a great deal to her.

He never denied the children anything but he was never really a father in that he never did things with the kids. He didn't want to take them out. He never made time to be with them or take them anywhere. And because he was so quiet and so difficult to get to, the kids preferred to regard him as sort of—almost as if he was a bumbling kind of person. They talk about him now with amused detachment. Really, that's all. And Carol, I think, of all of them, was fondest of him because she really yearned for a father relationship. But he was a loner, a real loner. He never should have been married.

About three years ago he died. Going to the funeral was like going to the funeral of someone you knew for a long time. Someone you loved, not because they were such a special person, but because you'd spent so much of your life with them, someone whose life had been so entwined with your own.

Mark

He's fifty-one and lives alone in Los Angeles. He's been divorced for nine years.

I needed attention from my wife and I never got it. I think I was as articulate as I could be about my needs to her. But if you just got hit by a truck and you're bleeding and your spouse is standing there reading the paper, well, it's kind of humiliating to have to say, 'Honey, I know you're reading the *Times* but I have a need that I think I should tell you about.' You know, there are just certain things you shouldn't have to say.

Our whole relationship was complex, as all relationships are. Eva could be very articulate, but whenever she was articulate she'd inevitably be saying things that were terribly offensive. She was really a cunt. I mean she was a bitch when she had the control, an absolute bitch. What amazes me now is how I took her shit for so many years. I was withdrawn and hurt all that time but I never left.

I'd say that my mistake, my tragic flaw in the relationship, was that I was so flattered that she loved me when we first met. She was so dependent, so needy, so helpless without me. She loved me, or at least I think she loved me when we first started seeing each other. And my pattern's always been to just start loving whoever's loving me. I need the reinforcement, the feedback, to be brought out by somebody.

I didn't marry young. I waited until I was in my mid-thirties. I wasn't one of those people who at twenty-one falls in love and then the next day they're married. I was always shy about long-term commitments. I had had a number of relationships—four or five before I got married. I always knew I needed a relationship but I was always scared about jumping into one. I think, though, I began to be afraid of just always living by myself.

I trusted Eva enough to marry her but I also felt that I was taking a chance. I was hoping it would work. She was very insecure when we first met and she needed my support and I was very willing to give it to her. But I suspected right from the beginning that I was playing a role—being her Rock of Gibraltar. She needed me to be that. She really did. I'm no doubt editorializing a little bit here but that's a lot of how it was. She was needy and I felt important because of how much she needed me.

In the beginning nothing made her happier than making dinner or, as she later called it, "the slave syndrome." She loved preparing meals, keeping the house immaculate. But then she began to talk more about her needs, her real needs. You know, she'd speak about her need to G-R-O-W. And this was okay. I knew she had locked herself very unnecessarily into the role of being a *hausfrau*. And sure, part of me liked that but there was another part of me that felt she was closing out the world, that she was a little bit *too* insecure. In the beginning, I really did want to do whatever I could to encourage her growth.

She was a good wife . . . until about two weeks after the marriage. I'm not kidding. Right after the honeymoon, in fact, is when it all started going bad. In the beginning, before we were married, whenever I touched her or whenever we were in bed it was like she was climbing the walls with joy and pleasure. She was very, very demonstrative and she came like the Fountain of Trevi. Sometimes, in the middle of sex, I'd feel that she was getting so off on the sex that she'd begin to lose me. She'd just go out on some fantastic trip and leave me behind. We'd be fucking and I'd somehow feel that things weren't quite right; like we weren't really close even though the sex was great. So I'd say to myself, 'Mark, what's the matter with you? You're so uptight and you're so distrustful that you can't even recognize a beautiful woman who's creaming all over the place. Shape up, Mark.' But I still always had that feeling of distance. No matter how things appeared, I sensed that sexually something wasn't quite right. The payoff came right after our honeymoon when Eva, for the first time, started talking about sex. First, she told me that I didn't know how to make love to her, and then she started telling me that she wanted it this way and that way, she wanted me to go down on her. Now there's nothing more destructive than to be told, without love or care, what to do sexually. I said to her, "Eva, I thought you were enjoying yourself?" but she only said, "I never climaxed." So I asked her why the hell had she made like she was coming a thousand times, and she said, "I can assure you, Mark, that if you think a woman has come with you, then it's only because she's faked it to be polite." This isn't verbatim but it's close enough. Her objections, her instructions were all said so coldly, so cruelly.

It was a power trip for her to do that. She's not a vicious person—only, I suspect, in a close relationship. And the only way it could be friendly between us after one of her cold, honesty sessions was if I crawled back to her and said, "I'm sorry. What do you want me to do for you?"

I didn't like her ultimatums because it was a power thing. It was a controlling ploy. But I was passive. I laughed it off. We lived together for seven years and we made love throughout the marriage. But right at the beginning of the marriage I started feeling that maybe I should end the whole thing. We'd just moved into a new apartment and I remember staring at a whole wall of closets that I'd built for her—nice louvred things—and I remember staring at those closets and thinking what a bitch I'd married. I thought of ending the marriage right then and there but I didn't. I think I was tired of running away from relationships and I needed to be with somebody.

The marriage was a time of great frustration. There was really no satisfaction. The only thing we got from each other was an occasional feeling of domestic tranquility. That's it.

I was conscientious about the relationship. The main thing on my mind during the relationship was 'What can I do for you" But that led to her dominating me—whether it would be sexually or in the kitchen. She really started expressing her power in such petty ways. Like I would always detect a lot of pride in her voice when she'd tell me, ''There's no more food in the kitchen closets.'' She enjoyed telling me that, she was proud that she could be so irresponsible. Or sometimes she'd announce, ''I'm not making dinner.'' And, you know, all I could say was ''Fuck you.'' Her power displays were on such a low, stupid, unproductive level. I mean what kind of real satisfaction can there be in saying ''There's no more food in the house.'' It was such a stupid rebellion. It was like women's lib was her gasoline but she was twisted.

I know I'm painting myself very favorably here but if I am objective I'd call it just not a good match. It screwed me up for a long time. I felt a lot of anger, a lot of frustration, a lot of misuse. There were times when I really needed to be held by her or petted but I never got that from her. I wasn't vicious in the marriage. I didn't have any other women until the very last year of the marriage. But she always played the role of never having been with anyone. Later, after we split up, I found out that she'd had lovers.

I'd say I have to take at least 50 percent of the blame for how the marriage went. If I'd been more together, I wouldn't have stood for a lot of the crap she doled out. I never told her what I was feeling. I was always assuming the short end of the stick. I was just too passive. I let myself be a schmuck for a pretty face.

We finally split up after seven years of marriage. She wanted the divorce and she didn't want to have any dialogue about it. I wanted to talk about it, to have some sort of communication. But she wasn't interested in talking. She wanted to, quote, *find herself* and just have the checks coming. She'd say, ''I'm only thirty-five and I still have my youth to develop.'' It was definitely a woman's consciousness thing—and raising women's consciousnesses I think is great. But when you have that mixed in with greed and with a parasitic attitude toward the world and men—well then you just create hostility. There's nothing I find more threatening than a woman who uses her femininity to the hilt and who's really just looking for a free ride.

Laurie

"My husband was a psychotic, obsessive perfectionist." Laurie told us of one incident where her husband whimsically insisted she grow two inches. Each night he pulled at her body, trying to stretch her. Their marriage lasted four years—was filled with these sort of bizarre and abusive incidents.

Laurie's twenty-six; her ex-husband, twenty-eight.

My husband was really fucked up and now that I'm no longer in that relationship—I've been away from him for about two years—I can see just how crazy he really was. I was scared of him most of the time because he physically abused me. He'd beat me up for no reason. I wouldn't do anything and he'd just take his shit out on me. He was always striving for perfection and if I wasn't perfect that really bothered him. Once he asked me when dinner was going to be ready and I said, ''I don't know, a couple of minutes.'' Well, that wasn't a good enough answer for him and that started him beating on me. In all of our four years of marriage not once did I ever stand up to him or show him my anger. Never. Because I was so scared.

His parents were real fucked up too. The fact that he beat me up was OK with them because his father used to beat up his mother. His mother told me that if he hit me too hard I should call the cops on him. That's what she used to do. But I knew I could never do that to him. I'd never have called the cops on him. And he used to say I shouldn't complain because I never had any broken bones or anything—only black eyes, sore feet, a sore head. He'd go totally crazy on me.

I knew it was very hard for him to live in the real world. He had a hard time for a long time, lots of times not being able to function. I understood his anger—not toward me but toward his friends and toward society. But the way that his anger manifested itself was all warped, twisted. It would come out physically or else it would come out in these fantasy trips of his. Some of them were very fun and exciting but I only remember the really sick ones now. One, I remember, was to own an island with slaves on it and we'd be the king and queen.

He was German and he was a Nazi in a lot of ways and he hated Jews—except for me, of course. Sometimes he'd say things like black people should be dead or old people shouldn't live past fifty. He was a sexist, a racist, every *ist*. He would say all of this seriously and I would be very quiet.

I was a child bride when I married him, only nineteen. He was the first man who I ever loved. When I was growing up my parents wouldn't let me go out with anybody who wasn't Jewish and there weren't many Jewish people where I lived. So I never really got close to a boy until I met him. And prior to our getting married he never treated me abusively.

I knew he was a little crazy but I could always forgive him because I understood him. I was into this whole thing that I was the only person in the world who could really understand him. I was in love with the old romantic notion of dedication and I think I thought that if I left him he'd fall apart. I kinda felt totally responsible for him and I think I realized that there was something in it for me too. I was needed very badly and I was very, very special. I was the only person in the world who he trusted. That's what made me feel so special.

There are a lot of reasons I stayed with him. When I look back on it and think that if I had the whole thing to do over again—if you put me back in that place and that time—I would redo it. It was something I had to do at that time, and I learned a whole lot.

I remember this incredible scene we had before I finally left him. It was all part of this very crazy weekend on an island off Massachusetts's coast. On our way back to the mainland, we were on this little boat and we'd been warned to be very careful because there were a lot of sandbars. Billy had been warned and he said, "Well, fuck it." He'd always wanted to defy nature anyway because he was better than God. So he said, "I can do it." Meanwhile, there was going to be a storm and that's why he wanted to take this shorter route that he wasn't sure about. But all these things were against us. He'd been really acting very irrational before that, all that weekend. He started telling me that I'd better tell him how far our boat was from the bottom. I told him I couldn't see. Well, he hit me for that because I couldn't see to the bottom of the ocean. I said, "Well, I can't see." He said, "I don't want to hear any negative things from you. You can do anything I tell you to do." So I still said, "I can't." Then I realized I'd better say I can because he was starting to beat me up and we were on this boat that was moving. This was, I think, the closest I've ever come to insanity, I mean, really breaking. I could have jumped overboard. So I started to scream numbers, "two feet deep," "six feet deep," anything to keep him satisfied. That was the only way. When we finally got somewhere, I was hysterical and I was waving to people to help me, and he was just laughing at me like I was foolish. We docked our boat and there was this Coast Guard guy, something like that, and I asked him to help me. It was the first time that I'd asked anyone to help me, that I'd ever admitted that my husband was abusing me. So I told him that my husband had just beaten me up and that I wanted to get out of there. And my husband just laughed at me and said to the Coast Guard guy that I was just a hysterical female who's scared of the storm, so naturally I'd been crying. So they both started laughing at me; the other guy hadn't believed me. So I just got up, took some stuff with me, and just walked away. Eventually I made it back to his parents' house and he didn't come home that night or the next night. I had a feeling he wouldn't. . . . A couple of days later we met at the house of a mutual friend of ours and I told him it was over.

A month later he tracked me down. I answered the door and he was standing there. I almost had a heart attack. I just said, "What are you doing here?" and I started crying. It was really the first time I'd cried or let myself feel anything since I'd left

him. Up until then I was busy just being really strong and dealing
with taking care of myself in material ways. So I asked him why
he was back and told him that he was making me cry. He said he
was back because he was buying me a store. I told him I didn't
want a store. He explained that if I had a store I would never have
to work for anybody again. I could be my own boss. I could make
all this money and buy an estate. I explained that I didn't want
that stuff. He said, "Come on. I'll show it to you." I was kinda
scared to go with him alone, so I said, "Well, I'll go in my own
car and follow you." So he showed me the store—it was in a
really fancy shopping center, a little clothing store. We went to a
restaurant afterward and we talked and he begged me to come
back to him and he cried and held my hand and I think it was the
hardest thing in my life to say no. He broke down and said he was
sorry for everything he ever did to me and he'd never be like that
again—that he'd never put me through that again, that I'd paid
my dues. I said, "I don't believe you, it's going to happen
again." And he said, "No. It won't." And he said other things,
too, like it had been him and me against the world. And it sort of
was. I mean, it was him against the world and I was sort of his
comrade and now I was leaving him alone again. And I still said
no. So we left the restaurant . . . sad and freaked out and scared.

Janet and Mitchell

They live together in a renovated factory building in lower Manhattan. Both of them work in advertising: Janet as a television commercial writer and Mitchell as a photographer. Janet is twenty-eight; Mitchell's thirty-three.

Mitchell: I would think our biggest conflict is a sexual conflict. The problem really is that we have no sexual relationship at the moment—and also that Janet doesn't like me blaming her for that.

Janet: I don't know why but for some reason, right now I don't feel like having sex. It's been going on for a while.

Mitchell: A year.

Janet: I really don't know why it's such a problem area. It's like a trigger whenever we start to talk about it. Mitchell will get angry quickly. I feel like I'd like to talk it over but it always becomes an argument and my reaction to the argument is to retreat and not to talk about it. Obviously, when we start talking about why I don't feel like having sex, I'm going to come up with some answers that Mitchell doesn't want to hear. Sometimes I feel cuddly. I kiss Mitchell. I hug Mitchell. I guess that's what I like now.

I guess I feel like it's not safe to talk about my sexuality with Mitchell. Maybe I feel I could get through it or past it or to it—to the reasons why I'm not into sex now—if I felt more free to explore it here.

Mitchell: I no longer express myself sexually here. It's just understood that it's not going to happen. When we cuddle, as an automatic part of my life, something else happens, and it gets crazy. I want to keep going in that sexual direction, both my heart and my genitals want to keep going, and I don't know what to do. I used to make advances but not now. It's like there isn't a human response from her.

I really feel two ways about it: I feel that she's rejecting me because she thinks I'm a creep and I also feel that something's wrong with her because I'm the same creep I was four years ago when we started living together. And for three of those years we had a healthy relationship. It was good. Now it's nothing. If she found me repulsive but she still had a sexual drive anyway, well that would be something we could work out—some psychological stuff. But she doesn't care. As far as she's concerned, it could go on like this forever. It's like some switch was turned off.

Janet: Yeah. It doesn't bother me. I enjoy our relationship without sex, but because it bothers Mitchell and because I think it's abnormal from what I know about people, I want to resolve it. I don't miss the sex. I don't know if it's normal or abnormal but I'm brought up to think there's something wrong with me. My only fear is that eventually time will run out and Mitchell will start looking around and find someone else. That's the fear. If in society there were lots of people who were nonsexual or who went through a year of nonsexuality—you know, where you didn't have sex—then I would think my thing was normal.

But I think the tension I have is about my relationship with Mitchell, not about my sexual thing. That's what it's all about. In my mind, I guess I feel that when Mitchell is my friend and stops attacking me, then it will come back—the sex. It's hard to discuss. This whole blame thing comes up. Whenever Mitchell says something that I feel is blaming of me, then I see this horrible side of him. Yet somehow the few times when he's given me the space to hate him, then I've stopped hating him. Like once he just didn't stop me. I wanted to express hate and he let me; he didn't attack me. And I said it and then I felt that I didn't hate him anymore. It became funny. It just went away.

Mitchell: The way I look at it is we're friends, not lovers. We spend a lot of time together but I'm really involved with that physical thing, the sexual thing. I mean my body needs it. Sometimes

I wish I could just go out and be with people I didn't even care about, just to have touching and get those tubes cleaned out. But I don't do that. I mean I'd like to do that. I like the idea of that. I even fantasize about it. But I haven't done it.

It's funny. Sometimes I value her out of my head. I mean I feel privileged to be with her. She's so wonderful, she does all these interesting things. Just her "isness" is so wonderful. But then the other times—and they're just about equal—I say I have to get out of this, this is ridiculous, it's all over, we're bored with each other, we have different interests, Janet's unhappy with me, I'm unhappy with her. It's really a mess. We can't seem to be happy enough together, but living without her is something I don't want to do.

Sometimes I think she really finds me revolting. I mean, she's even expressed that in several cases. There'd be times when she'd express disgust at my body.

Janet: No. Get out of here. That's not true.

Mitchell: Listen Janet, I'm not making this up. I remember this clearly. This is important to me and I feel very frustrated by it.

Janet: Not true. I believe that's how you see it but that's not how it is.

Mitchell: It only happened a few times but that was enough to get in there. It was like a whole facial expression . . . You know, it's almost illogical for me now to express my frustrations to Janet. It's crazy. It's like suicide. Right now, she gets plugged into my stuff, my feeling sexually frustrated. So we just can't listen to one another.

Leo

Leo owns a delicatessen in Brooklyn, a small, hole-in-the-wall deli. He's also a "type"—a talkative, down-to-earth guy who'll tell you his life philosophy right after he's told you his name. He's been married for thirty-five years.

My wife and I, we're two complete opposites. She's not as outgoing as I am. She's more introvert. She's the type . . . well, she's not an easy customer, let me put it that way. She's not as trusting of people as I am. And I'm too trusting. But then again I'm more temperamental than she. You know, I'm very outspoken. I don't hold back. I can tell people what I think and she doesn't like that. Say a customer gives me a hard time or I don't like the way they're talking to me, I'll just politely tell them, "You don't like it. Out." She thinks I'm wrong. This happened in 1949 when I was in my first store. I was partners with her brother-in-law then. And she thought it was a terrible thing for me to talk back to a customer. So we had a terrible fight. Terrible.

See, I come home and I like to relax. I enjoy watching television but she objects to that. I can just sit by the television and fall asleep. She can't see that. She doesn't realize that to me that's my way of relaxing. You know, I work twelve, fourteen hours a day. She's just not a relaxed person. She's a very tense person. You understand? Her ideal way of spending an evening is to eat, sit for awhile, then go right to sleep. No television. "You're tired," she says. "Why" stay up all night? Let's say I like to watch the news at eleven o'clock and then, all of a sudden, I'm falling asleep. She can't see that. She wants me to go to sleep.

Rest. But my way of resting is actually by watching something. Like I'm off on Monday—the only day I'm off—so I have a lot of things to do. But as far as she's concerned, why don't I just relax that day? But I enjoy going out.

You know, basically the whole thing between two people is to have one mind. You understand what I'm trying to say? Maybe we argue but in the end, everything should be one. I always say that to my daughter and my son. In the end, when you have to make a decision, it should be one decision. But our problem is we think different. See, I came from a family that was very free, free with money. Now I gamble a lot and that's against her principles. You know, cards, horses. I'm not denying that she's right. I'm not taking that away from her because it's true. If I hadn't gambled all these years we could have been semiretired today. But that was my outlet. What else is there to do? I mean, just work and sleep? So I felt that this was a way of enjoying but she can't see it. She hates gambling.

She wouldn't get angry but she hates it. She'll say why do I have to do it. Look at the things we could have had. We could have had a condominium. But, thank God, I haven't taken anything away from her. I mean, if I didn't support her, if I took away from the children, you know, their food, or if she didn't have a television or a piano in the house—I was what you called a compulsive gambler who deprived his family of the necessities—then I could understand.

She likes nice things and I've always given her nice things. I never forget a birthday or an anniversary. You understand? But she doesn't like when I get excited. She doesn't like screaming. So I get excited and start screaming and she hates that.

I feel that a woman shouldn't be a boss over a man. I'm against that. I don't feel that anyone should be a boss but I feel that a man must have self-respect and he should say something because he's still the provider for the family.

The whole thing of married life may be the fact that sex plays an important part. Not that you have to be sick about it and have it constantly but there must be some pleasure that you derive. That's part of life. Well, it was never really enjoyable between us. I don't know whose fault it was but she wasn't exactly what you'd call an oversexed woman. I don't blame her because every woman is built differently. Other women, if you just touch them, puff. My friend with his wife, she's like that. She mothers him and loves him in front of people.

You see, I came from a family that was given love and attention but in marriage I lack that sort of thing. I feel a woman should show a man some attention. You know, 'Honey, how do you feel?' when he comes home. 'Are you tired?' And I don't want to hear that *she's* tired. I know she's tired. I know she's put in a hard day's work. But if I come home from a hard day's work and I say I'm tired, she'll say, "Yeah. I had a hard day too." I'm not interested in that. I want her to say, "Yes. I understand you had a hard day. How was it?"

My wife's more frugal with the dollar. She thinks money's the most important thing in the world. But there's no such thing because what's life? Today you're here, tomorrow you're gone. It's true. I'm very easy with a dollar. They float through my hands. I never saved a dollar in the bank. I don't know what it is.

But this is basically the whole thing: I feel two people in a happy relationship . . . well, that one must give in. And my wife, she's never given in. She's very stubborn. When we were younger and when the children were small, she'd get mad at me and she wouldn't talk for five days and that meant nothing to her. You know, they say Tauruses are very stubborn people. They're bulls and I'm a lion. I'm Leo the Lion. You know, I'm king of the forest.

I'll tell you. I'm a very strong man in terms of ideas and speaking out but I've always felt that a man who marries must have a sense of responsibility. He has his children and children are basically the whole thing. Now I love my grandchildren. That's my life now. You understand? So to break up just because of what I'm telling you, I mean there's no reason. A man could have a relationship with a woman on the side. It's just a flare, it's over in one night and so forth. But just to leave for little things, then he has no sense of responsibility.

I'll defend my wife, though, even if we don't agree. If someone, God forbid, says something wrong about her, I'll fight them to the end.

With the kids my wife always had that fear that if they went to the grocery to buy soda, then the bottles would break when they were crossing the street. You understand? So she'd yell at me for sending our kid to buy soda. It was a terrible thing to her. So I'd be the one. She'd tell me to go buy what she needed, not the children. See, these are the things. That's what I'm saying. She's a good mother but she forgot to be a good wife sometimes. That's what I'm trying to say.

A woman can say what she wants but I don't like it when they're smarter than the man. This is the way I look at it. She should voice her opinion, she should say what she thinks, but I don't feel she should be the boss unless the man is a weakling. Then I can see it. I have a brother-in-law like that. He's a weakling. He doesn't talk. But I talk so I should be the boss.

Ava

She's sixty-four years old and has been a neurosurgeon nearly all her life. She showed us pictures of herself—a thirty-five-year-old snapshot of her and a lover, both of them tan and healthy looking at a beach resort in Italy. Another shot taken circa 1941 of her in a uniform: She was part of the Italian underground during World War II. She's young and vital in these photos and very attractive.

I met my present husband, my fourth husband, while I was still married. I was attracted to him but I was attracted probably because of circumstance—because I wanted a change. He was a good-looking man, and if you don't know somebody you can be easily impressed by them. He's a good talker, a good socializer, even a good bridge player.

I married him but I don't love him. It's just companionship. He's very nice and everything, yet I really have nothing to talk to him about. He talks very eloquently about everything, but I personally talk very little with him. Our interests are just so different.

Now I'm a senior citizen. What should I do now—leave him? That would be ridiculous. You just have to finish your life. He had a heart attack a few years ago. He had two major operations, very bad ones. So I care for him. I mean, you come to a point where you figure you cannot escape anymore. I mean, sometimes I feel like I'm in a prison and I can't get out. You see, the time is gone when I could do so many things.

I took my old age with not much dignity. Maybe because I don't have children. You know, I can't take a ride to see my children and grandchildren. I have sisters and some cousins who I see sometimes but somehow when you don't have your own family, your own children, and if you've had an interesting life—you know, with a career and men—then when you're old you feel like you're finished. I've been feeling like that for the last ten or fifteen years. So now it's just work, going to the hospital. No more money—I don't work for money anymore. And without work I wouldn't know what to do.

I had very interesting men in my life but I'm an old lady now. It's finished for me.

WORKING IT OUT

How's one going to get through it all?
How can you live if you can't love. And
How can you live if you do?

from *Another Country*
by JAMES BALDWIN

Jack and Liz

They work as therapists for families with alcoholic problems. They're each fifty-seven. They're been married for thirty-two years and have no children.

Jack: We're both depression kids, born in the 1920s. We worked together one summer on Cape Cod—I was doing the arranging and playing piano for an orchestra and Liz was our singer. This was back in 1939. We dated and during that time we were very much with each other.

Liz: I was nineteen then. It was a very shy kind of relationship. I wasn't really aware that it was going to be a meaningful relationship, although we did like each other.

Jack: That was the summer I started to drink. Musicians in bands are always heavy drinkers and I started drinking. So Liz was in on my boozing right from the beginning.

Liz: I can remember the night of his first drink. It's so clear in my mind. Somebody gave Jack a bottle of gin. It was a little pint. We parked the car and sat there and Jack took a drink—and there was a definite lift to his personality. For me, I had the usual reaction to alcohol. You know, ''It tastes terrible, let's get an ice cream soda instead.''

Jack: That was the first time I ever got a buzzing glow from a glass of gin. When I discovered the stuff it was sort of like where-has-this-stuff-been-all-my-life. From that day on I was a drinker. I drank every day if I could get it.

Anyhow, the war came along. Liz went into the army first. She was trying to save the world for democracy, and I was drafted sometime later. We didn't see or hear from each other that whole time.

Liz: Then the day I got out of the army, I called Jack and we arranged to see one another.

Jack: And a year later we were married. We went to New York, both of us to pursue the music business. I was writing and Liz singing.

By this time, and this is already about 1946, I was pretty deeply into the alcohol. I was in a sense obsessed with this state of getting high. I was drinking every day but very seldom drunk. I didn't get drunk in the way you might think of getting drunk. I had a high tolerance. But every now and then I'd lost control. No one ever said much to me, though, about my drinking. We were out on the road, swinging around quite a bit with either show biz or left-wing people, Village people. So my drinking wasn't noticeable. And Liz didn't bug me about it at all.

Liz: I didn't oppose it in any way. I didn't think of it as a problem. In our milieu everybody drank, except for me. I watched. So people drinking was just normal. It was simply the way we lived. I can remember within a week of our marriage, Jack trooping down to the bar every night. At one point I spoke to him a little about it—Why did he have to go *every* night, why not every other night? But I'd go with him most of the time and I'd force myself to drink something, anything that seemed like an ice cream soda.

Jack's behavior didn't get out of line. On a couple of occasions he would go into what I now recognize as a blackout state where he didn't remember having done things. He'd act in a kind of nonaware way. He'd appear wide-awake but he'd be repeating things or not remembering things. I was irritated by it but I didn't think of it as a symptom of alcoholism or even that he had an alcohol problem. I just tried to deal with it right then and there. I'd say, "Why are you repeating these things?" or "Why don't you remember this incident?"

Jack: Our troubles began when things finally started upsetting Liz. I began to get very depressed and that's hard to live with all the time. But even then we still weren't attributing the depressed moods to booze. We were attributing them to the war. You know, I was playing the returning, maladjusted veteran for all it was worth.

Liz: We assumed, and it was like a national viewpoint then, that returning servicemen were going to be a bit dingy. They'd be depressed or agitated, whatever. And Jack also had a personality style which included a degree of artistic depression. To be truthful, I loved his creative personality. I almost felt that he had a right to be unhappy at times because he was a composer. It was a lot of crap but that's what I felt. So just about whatever patterns of behavior that people might have considered strange were rationalized away by us. We just accepted them.

Jack: But then my mood swings led me into cross-addictions. I began to find other drugs to offset the effect of alcohol; that meant benzedrine, which was then offset by some other sedative—plus alcohol. It was like a little chemical game I was playing: a little of this, a little of that, and a little gin in the middle.

I'd drink all day long but basically I had a high tolerance—so things didn't get too complicated until I started using uppers and downers. This was now about 1950. Plus, I had a bad cough once and I discovered cough syrup, which has codeine in it, and I got myself hooked on the codeine, heavily hooked. I knew I was hooked, Liz knew I was hooked, and we talked about it.

Liz: We didn't fight about it, though. We just went about our business. And things didn't get too bad between us until Jack's behavior really started deteriorating. In social settings, he began to say and do things that weren't exactly suitable to the occasion, inappropriate kinds of behavior. Also, the way he was handling money was irresponsible, and he was getting more and more severely depressed. So when I finally lost my endurance, I persuaded him to go to some psychiatrists and he went. But all they ever said to him was to get off the addicting cough syrup. None of them ever picked up on his being alcoholic. And none of them ever realized that the cough syrup he was drinking was actually loaded with alcohol, 80 proof.

Jack: I went to a lot of psychiatrists but their training, even today, isn't always right-on when it comes to diagnosing alcohol-

ism. It looks like so many other things. I was called schizo-
phrenic, psychoactive, everything but alcoholic.

Liz: I knew by then that Jack had a problem. But like the
shrinks, I thought it was an emotional problem complicated by
the narcotics, not the alcohol.

Anyway, from then on in, it was a long, sad, downward course
for Jack, for me, and for our marriage. It was really a nightmare.

We were completely isolated from all our friends. My only reality was Jack's alcoholism. I was working and I was successful and
I was functioning, but the real world for me was back in the crazy
situation at home. And that's the way it was for years. I didn't
have any help. I had no one to contact. As a matter of fact, nobody knew what was going on. Not a soul. Our friends began to
drift away, which is classic with alcoholism. It's simply not pleasant to be around alcoholics. But somehow we adapted to all the
craziness. We made do.

Denial, depression, and isolation was what happened to us, and
it's what happens to every alcoholic marriage. First, we both
denied the problem, then we both got depressed about it, and
finally both of us were alone, just Jack and me—no friends, no
family. There was a time when our phone didn't ring once for six
months.

After a while we kind of achieved a homeostasis, some sort of
balance. Our relationship was crazy, we were depressed all the
time, but it was cool because it was familiar to us. It was comfortable because we'd created it.

We survived. You know, people survived in concentration
camps. You can adjust to any crazy thing. But one day, I remember I just broke down at work. The tension built up and I was
taken to a doctor and I sat in his office and cried from two o'clock
in the afternoon until six that evening. And that was kind of
groovy because after that I felt better. I was able to keep my san-
ity, but I'm not too sure how.

Jack: She even went to a shrink once. I convinced her that *she*
was crazy.

Liz: I was depressed. There was a lot of guilt on both sides. The shrink told me I had two choices: I could either adapt or get out of the relationship. And I kept kicking that around—that I'd leave Jack. But I sort of knew I never would.

Jack: We had a lot of really difficult times, really bad periods. But there was never any complete cutoff of communication during all those years. There was never any real question of us separating.

Liz: We had a very good friendship. We talked all the way through the alcoholism. There was only one point where Jack said to me, "I'm going to leave you and get us both out of this hell." I never forgot that statement. I was very apprehensive that he really intended to leave. But he was in a blackout when he said it and he couldn't even remember saying it later on. That was really the only time our staying together was ever in any real doubt.

It finally got to the point where Jack was so stoned all the time that he couldn't walk, couldn't eat, and his health was really deteriorating. By now he had a liver condition. So I could no longer deny that alcohol was the problem. But still—even *then*—I didn't say it quite that way. I'd say to him, "You're losing control," or I'd emphasize his career or his physical well-being. But I never put the focus on the alcohol per se. Only when he physically couldn't write music anymore, which miraculously was the last thing he was able to do, did we finally see the problem in all its ugliness.

Jack: The pencil I was writing with just fell out of my hand one day and that was it. I'd simply gotten to the point where I could no longer drink myself into shape to work. By this time I knew I'd been physically addicted to alcohol. I'd usually get to work about one or two o'clock in the afternoon. But one day, in the middle of working, my pencil just fell out of my fingers. That was rock bottom as far as I was concerned. It was the last thing I had left—my ability to work.

So I finally got to the point . . . well, I attempted suicide. One night I just got too depressed and there didn't seem to be any answer to any of it and I had a collection of Seconals and I took the whole damn mess and said the hell with it. That was in 1962 and we'd been married back in 1946.

Liz: I found him passed out on the floor that night.

Jack: She saved my life and somehow I ended up the next day tied to a bed in Bellevue Hospital . . .

When I got out of Bellevue, I jumped right back into the jug, and after that, the next few months of my life I can barely remember. I've pieced it together to the point where I know that Liz took me to another psychiatrist who, thank God, spotted me as being an alcoholic within fifteen minutes. This was twenty years after I started drinking. Then I went into another hospital and within days I was climbing the walls—withdrawal symptoms. And while I was there someone from AA came to talk to me.

To make a long and painful story short, at this point in my life the right people at the right time and at the right place came together and I managed to get well. I went into a rehabilitation center where I came into a whole different way of thinking, a positive way of thinking as opposed to my previous negative way of thinking. And Liz at that time got involved in the Alanon Family Program—which was for the families of alcoholics; and so things began to get better for both of us.

There was a period of about four years, right after my recovery, where there were a lot of changes, very dramatic changes both in myself and Liz and in our relationship. For the first two years it was all very confusing to me. It was sort of like, Where did my whole life go? And I saw Liz much differently now than I had ever seen her before. Both of us were involved in a sort of therapy in AA and Alanon. We were both involved in a kind of intense self-examination. And through that process I began to talk about some of my guilt feelings and angers and resentments. These feelings were all absolutely new to Liz. I'd never spoken about them before to her. I'd always had a sense of guilt for the whole damn thing. I thought I ruined her life, my life, everything. But now I was able to talk about my guilt and anger and I could begin to understand it.

Liz: It opened up a whole new dimension of our talking together. And now I had to accept myself as a separate entity from Jack. One of the curious things about being involved with alcoholism is that as long as you're not the drinking spouse, you think you're OK. You think that the person who's doing the drinking is the one who's doing all the negative things in your relationship. So I always saw myself as the good guy in our marriage. I was the white hat and Jack was the black hat. But once the drinking stopped, I had to start seeing things about myself. I could no longer blame all my faults and problems on Jack's drinking. I had to take responsibility for myself, for all my dissatisfactions and negativities. I could no longer be dependent on Jack-the-alcoholic as being the excuse for my failures. So it was a real process of reevaluation for me. I had to now assess myself just as I was, and it was appalling. I wasn't the integrated human being I thought I was. It was a wild experience.

Jack: There are some people, in fact, who even prefer being married to active alcoholics. There's a feeling of strength the nonalcoholic feels when they're in a marriage with an alcoholic. And once their mate sobers up, they can't be with them anymore.

After my recovery, the biggest problem I had in our marriage was to not let my feelings follow Liz's. It was the way I emotionally operated for so many years. I was so used to getting up in the morning and figuring out who she was, because whoever she was, that was who I was going to be. I'd just go along with her moods. If she was going down, I'd go down. If she was going up, I'd go up. It was a passive way of being and it's taken me a lot of work to get rid of it. Even after my recovery, that pattern was still operating in our relationship. I had to really be careful when Liz was going into a depression. And I still fight that tendency to this day. This was the kind of insight into our marriage that we came up with as a result of our therapy.

Liz: We really had to reconstruct everything about our being together. First, because of Jack's depressed behavior, which had been going on for years, my image of him was one of a depressed person. His feelings were always buried and he was very withdrawn. He had two moods—depressed and more depressed. But with sobriety, it was like seeing a new person emerge.

Jack: By this time, remember, I had been sedated with alcohol for more than twenty years.

Liz: I hadn't seen him smile in years. Then suddenly, after sobriety, he was smiling. It was like the two of us were starting over. No, it wasn't *like* we were starting over: It *was* starting over.

Jack: It was drastic. It was a miracle. The only negative thing, interestingly enough, was that our sex life got bad. There was a sexual letdown which, as we later found out, is classic for alcoholics once they're sobering up. During the alcoholism we were having a pretty normal sex life but then, after the recovery, it got bad for a while. It was because my whole body had to adjust, my entire nervous system had been affected. There wasn't one time in all those years together that I wasn't on some drug—booze, uppers, downers—when we were having sex. So without the drugs and the alcohol, all my guilt and anger and fear came up and it was hard to function sexually. Plus, I was twenty years older . . .

Liz: I feel like I've had two lives with Jack—like I've had two husbands, two different lifetimes.

Jack: We just dig being together. We enjoy pretty much the same things. She'd like to go to the theater more, I'd like to go to the hardware store more, she'd like to hang around dress shops more. You know, we have those sort of normal problems. But things are good now and we've been through so much hell in the past that whatever happens we know we can handle it. Interestingly, with a lot of alcoholic marriages once the booze is gone and the people start seeing each other more clearly many of these marriages end in divorce. You know, some of the marriages just weren't made in heaven; they were made in a bottle.

I haven't had a drink in fifteen years. It's not an issue for me. I never think about it. The first few months, it was a struggle, like breaking any habit. But now it's just something I never think about and now I can even feel some gratitude for having been alcoholic. If I hadn't had to come to grips with that problem, which forced me to learn how to live a normal, productive life, then Liz and I wouldn't be having the kind of life we're enjoying now. You know, by the time you're fifty-seven you're supposed to be thinking about retiring, about the rocking chair. But here we are—both of us in our fifties, both of us feeling fulfilled by our careers in alcoholic therapy, both of us still going to school and still learning about ourselves. This was because I was *forced* to learn how to live this kind of life. So sometimes I want to get through to alcoholics and tell them that what they're doing by drinking is blocking themselves from the experience of recovery, which is so far beyond any booze high. I found everything in sobriety that I was looking for in the jug. I found a sense of excitement, a reasonable amount of security, and a lot of satisfaction with my work. And I also found my wife again.

Geraldine

Geraldine's an associate professor of art history at a small college in Oregon. Her husband, Cliff, is a professor of law and her lover, Roger, an assistant professor of Asian studies.

Geraldine, Cliff, and Roger are each in their mid-thirties and each are devoted, hard-working academicians.

The summer I met Cliff, ten years ago, my emotional world was falling apart but I wasn't quite ready to deal with it. My relationship with my first husband was deteriorating. Cliff, at the time, was just coming out of a relationship and he was feeling really miserable. He was passing through Wisconsin on his way to Chicago and a friend of mine asked if I could put him up for the night. So Cliff came and spent the night and I was very drawn to him, sexually I suppose, erotically. Nothing happened that night except for the exchanging of long looks, etcetera.

A few weeks later I had a weekend conference in Chicago so I dropped him a note suggesting we have a drink. I ended up going and spending three days at Cliff's place and sleeping with him. While in fact, only years later it ended up in the relationship we now have, it was a marvelous three days, an extraordinary three days—it was different sexually than any three days I'd ever spent. It was much more intense. Sex itself was longer in duration. Cliff had more of a sense of giving me pleasure than any man I'd ever gone to bed with before. As I look back on it now, my previous experiences were when I was very young and I was—kind of fumbling around, having intercourse in two seconds, and calling it quits. It's hard to quantify but I doubt that I had had many orgasms before, and Cliff could make love all night. It blew my mind.

It was adventurous but it was also scary. The first night I was there he sort of asked me where I wanted to sleep, in the living room on the couch or in the bedroom with him. And as we were going to bed I still have this vivid memory of him saying, ''Well, I may have a hard time because I've already been to bed with two women today.'' It floored me and excited me; it was a strange kind of mixture. I think there was a need in him to kind of assert that our sleeping together didn't have to mean anything.

Even though I was rational enough to say 'this may not be the love of my life,' it made enough of a difference in my sense of a possibility of a relationship that I came back and told my husband immediately that I couldn't live with him anymore. The affair with Cliff was the catalyst that helped me leave my husband. The strange thing is that with the exception of a brief, two-hour meeting, Cliff and I didn't see each other again for another three years.

Every once in a while Cliff would write or call and so we kept in contact. One day, after one of his irregular phone calls to me, he just decided to come and spend the weekend with me. He was at loose ends and he was the sort of person who would get on a plane and go see someone he hadn't seen in three years. He was quite adventurous. He came for the weekend and it worked. It was marvelous. It was very clear that this man was really important to me. Yet at the same time in each of us there was a certain amount of calculatedness, of looking at each other and wondering if this was the sort of person that we could have a permanent relationship with. He was terrified of ending up with a woman who would be dependent on him and I was terrified of ending up in a relationship where a man would be dependent on me. We each sort of admired a sense of independence in each other. It made us feel safe and it also kept a kind of distance in each of us. There was a holding back or a sense that we were protected by the other's need for independence and for separateness. At first, and I mean for the first number of years, that distance troubled me more than it did him. I had to break through those walls in order to gather more intimacy. But Cliff resisted. Until we were living together—which was two and a half years after we started seeing each other—we both continued seeing other people.

At a number of points Cliff tried to withdraw. When we were living together we did it with the sense that it was negotiable. We were never quite clear how long we were going to stay living together. I had the feeling back then that Cliff would only feel safe and secure if I were fucking other people.

Anyway, after about two years of living together, we both were offered jobs in different places and we had to deal with that. We felt that we knew each other well enough to know that if we didn't make some kind of clear commitment, that if he went to one place and I went to another place, that the chances were that we'd get involved with other people and it would be difficult to hold the bond. We figured we'd get married and hold the bond, but live apart. There was a great sense of respect for each other's work. I think it was still a kind of self-protection, not wanting to give up the relationship but keeping a certain amount of distance and independence. So Cliff ended up teaching and consulting in San Francisco and I ended up here, in Oregon.

Cliff kept saying all spring before we were married that we shouldn't make a big deal out of this marriage thing, that we should just sort of do it, pretend it's not happening, that it doesn't really change our relationship. We had these sort of strange reasons for doing it and I kind of accepted that. But in fact the actual act of getting married for Cliff was very important and made an enormous difference. It meant a different kind of commitment for him. And for me I don't really think it did. I had become convinced that it wasn't such a big deal. In some way I felt as committed as I was going to be. And he felt much more committed. That summer a friend said to me, "For the first time I feel like Cliff's in love with you." I guess I felt it, too, but I was afraid to actually accept it, to believe it. So he went to San Francisco with a sense of commitment and security and feeling that there weren't things threatening the relationship.

After the first few weeks or so of his being in San Francisco and my being here, I really felt a need to protect myself. Some of what was difficult was that we weren't sharing a daily life. We saw each other maybe every other weekend, something like that. We'd have a ritual fight on Thursday night, it would wear off by Friday, and by the time he left on Sunday we'd have another fight. That pattern went on all year long.

Anyway, that's how I became involved with Roger. Part of the reason for my getting as involved as I did was wanting to have a shared daily relationship. He very much became a surrogate husband for me, even though he was married and was in fact one of Cliff's best friends. In a sense, for a year I had two marriages. We spent a lot of time together and we saw each other almost every day. His wife didn't know about this. A lot of where Roger was coming from was that he wasn't able to share his work with her, and he and I do a lot of the same kinds of work. I was helping him finish a book and I was reading everything he wrote. And I was falling in love with him.

Cliff knew about Roger in spurts. I initially told Cliff when Roger and I started sleeping together. It was a short affair that was supposed to end but then it started again. Initially, Cliff was just pissed off and sort of warned me of the dangers of getting involved with somebody who was a close friend of his. Eventually, I felt deeply involved and that got very complicated. For a long time I felt sort of able to handle it. There were various points at which I sort of retold Cliff and in the spring we had a big scene about it. Cliff was very clearly hurt that I was continuing it this long and he could feel how important it was to me.

The relationship with Roger eventually reached a point where I knew that I had to try to stop and I couldn't. There were times when Roger and I talked about, fantasized about, each of us leaving our spouses and having another kind of relationship. But it never quite got to that and we were both very confused. Roger was in love with me and I was with him and in a way we both still are. It raised all kinds of very basic questions about relationships because we all were friends and I was very troubled that Roger's wife didn't know and eventually that's what partially led to Roger's and my separation, that I sort of pushed him to tell her. I could no longer handle the tension between Cliff and me because I knew how much trouble Cliff was having handling it. And in a way Roger's wife couldn't handle it either. She knew things were really wrong between her and Roger, but she didn't know why. So it was unfair to her.

There were periods when Cliff and I didn't talk about it, but there were more periods when we did. The kind of ground rules we had set up when we started living together were that we were not going to make rules about fidelity. What was decided was that if we went to bed with somebody where it was not important, we need not say anything. We didn't immediately have to come and confess. If you wanted to talk about it, fine; if you didn't, fine. But if it was something important there was a commitment to talk to the other person. And so I felt I had to talk about the relationship with Roger with Cliff, but it was hard because Roger and Cliff were friends and because it was a threatening relationship. Cliff wasn't dumb and he could see that it was taking away from his and my relationship. That's what mattered to him; it wasn't that I was being unfaithful to him, it was that he didn't feel primary. And that was a fair thing for him to be upset about.

Cliff moved back here in June, after school was over, and that's when things got more difficult. I had very mixed feelings about Cliff coming back. In a way I dreaded it. Cliff had been offered tentatively a job here. I was very confused. Half of me did want him to take it, the other half of me didn't. Giving up his consulting work in San Francisco for a job here was a big gesture and sacrifice on his part for our relationship, and I didn't know if I wanted to accept that gesture, knowing how confused I was, being in love with another man. I was in love with Cliff at the same time and that's what was weird. I don't think I ever stopped loving Cliff. It was a different kind of love. It was in many ways a more reasoned love, that of shared experience and time. With

Roger, it was much more magical, romantic, adventurous, crazy, and intense. Roger and I had offices near each other and once Cliff had come back we'd work up there for a few hours and then go off someplace. I think all that magical stuff had a lot to do with the situation. If I didn't think that, then I'm not sure I'd be with Cliff now. But I don't really know.

My relationship with Roger is now over compared to what it was. We don't have the same kind of freedom to be together now as we did. His wife knows now too. It's been about six weeks since we've been together. We hardly even talk to each other—so it's been very strange.

I miss him an awful lot and of course that's something I have to tell Cliff. But at the same time what has happened is that I've turned my energy toward working things out with Cliff. While there's a lot of pain and confusion in me and longings to have both relationships, somehow a decision is being made.

Roger told his wife, "OK, I'll give this up. I want to make the marriage between you and me work." That gave me a kind of space to turn my energy to Cliff. What I recognized at that time was that if I had really wanted to give up Cliff for Roger, I could have just left Cliff at any point; and while at moments I may have felt intensely drawn to Roger, I had to face the fact that I'd never left Cliff and there had to be something that kept me there. Of course, there was still the big question of whether I was terrified of getting divorced for the second time, the sense of a weakness in myself of not really trying to work this out. And of course there was also my son Jesse's relationship to Cliff. He'd lost one father when he was very young and had now developed a relationship with another and he thinks of Cliff as his daddy.

For Roger, a main factor in his going back was his children. During our crisis time, when we knew that splitting up was inevitable, there were times when he would tell me he didn't think he loved his wife at all. Then there were other times when he felt he did but that the hard thing for him was that he still loved me. It was sort of that he loved me in a different way than he loved June but with June there was also the family. In certain ways, it was that way for me too.

My relationship with Cliff now is different than it's ever been. It's more intimate and we have tremendous fights and depressions. But I think some of the fighting was a working at the relationship and I think there's a part of me that really understands, more than I ever have before, what it means to say one has to work at a relationship and that relationships aren't only those miraculous moments. Out of that work has come some renewal of the magic that was there at the beginning with Cliff and me and some sense of pleasure in saying, "Yeah, we like being together," and "Yeah, we are married and maybe there's nothing quite so terrifying in that as we originally thought." We are in fact thinking about having a baby. It's sort of surprising to hear myself saying this but I think the relationship is going to go on. Part of me feels that if it was ever going to break it would have during this past year.

There's a kind of comraderie and sharing that in a sense I seem to have both with Roger and with Cliff. That part of me now would very much like to find some way of establishing a friendship with Roger. I don't know if that's possible. Cliff and I were willing to have the four of us sit down together and not necessarily make everything nice, you know, scream at each other, but still somehow deal with it. But Roger and June decided not to. As June later told Cliff, there was just too much pain that she didn't want to deal with.

I really don't know if Roger and I will ever be lovers again. If there was some marvelous way it could work out without Cliff and June being either terribly hurt or threatened and without the whole thing again becoming isolated and secretive, then I'd risk it. There's a part of me that's still troubling deeply over it. I keep being struck with how easily everyone can intellectually accept the idea of having extramarital relationships but how emotionally they just can't handle it. Cliff, before marriage, never appeared to be threatened. He always seemed to be the one person in the world who could handle it. But when this thing happened with Roger he reacted in all the typical ways. I guess I always believed that if people had enough respect for each other as persons and not as possessions then it might be possible to free ourselves of those tensions. But I'm not sure. There are moments when I wonder if Cliff and I are better off, for a while anyway, moving toward some kind of monogamy. We'd like to experiment with that one, especially now when we're planning on having a baby.

Ben Morgan

*Ben, who's fifty, and Phil, who's fifty-eight, have been
living together in the same apartment for the past
twenty-two years. They're both psychologists.*

I'm fifty years old and this is what I've learned about relationships: I think there's a whole cultural brainwash about relationships. When I was anything up to thirty-five years old, like all
Americans, I was convinced that the most important thing in life
was to have a successful one-to-one relationship. 'Oh, God! Have
a relationship. This is the big thing.' And if you don't, you're a
blob. But somewhere in the last few years it sort of dawned on
me. I read in Kate Millett somewhere where she says, if you can't
have a relationship then cut it out and do something else. And
that started me thinking. It's a lot like being a parent and having
children. That's a special talent. Some people like to grow and
raise children the way some people have green thumbs with
plants. Well, I think having a love relationship in the most stan-
dard tradition is a talent too. There's a horrible brainwash that I
suffered from for at least thirty-five years of my life, thinking that
this is a thing I must carry off, like balancing my checkbook.

So I don't think having a relationship is anything one *must* do,
anymore than anyone must be good at mathematics or have an
ear for music or an eye for color or be able to paint, write, or do
poetry or gymnastics or dance.

I'm not talking about just having a relationship. I'm talking
about having the gift to carry off a walloping, lovely, really
groovy, romantic, in-love relationship.

About a year ago, after my last affair, I realized that a love relationship wasn't for me. I've had about seven or eight very intense relationships in my life. I would say none of them were successful. Some were for a few months, and one was for a year. This one fellow, he was going to come and live with me. You know, he was getting ready to pack up and leave Philadelphia and move to New York with me and all that. And it was all very exciting. But I guess what happened was he was packing—he was from an Italian, South Philadelphia family—and his sister said something like, 'If you leave our dear home, our *mama mia* and everything, don't expect to be honored in this house again.' She'd been reading my letters, which she found in the bottom of his bureau drawer, and knew the whole story. So he appeared quite shaken and said he couldn't move in with me. And I said, ''Goodbye. Get out of my life forever.'' I was twenty-seven and very stupid. I've rarely had anyone so completely devoted to me and delightful to be with, and if I hadn't been so terribly young I could have handled it. But I said, ''How dare you do this to me. I've waited a year. Goodbye.'' And that was that. And I mourned for three or four years. You know, the vengeance of the young is enormous. The unforgivingness of the young is extraordinary. He did come back a year later and said that it was so wonderful to see me. He really felt as if no time had passed at all. And I said, ''Where have you been, baby.'' We didn't talk that way then but it was sort of, 'Where have you been, I'm in another place, fuck you and all that.' And I turned the guy off and spoiled the whole thing just to get even.

There were others, but the point is, in one's youth and all through life there's this whole thing that there's a one and only, there's a right person for me. I was still in that place—believing that shit—when I met Phil at the age of twenty-nine.

I'm a gay person who doesn't have a type. Age doesn't matter to me. But at that time there was enough of a type that I did like—it was something like Burt Lancaster and Rory Calhoun. Phil happened to be that kind of person. We met on a beach and had a great deal in common: a mutual interest in handwriting,

baroque music, art, sculpture, and neither one of us were particularly keen on ballet. So we got a dialogue going.

Phil was a body-builder, a magnificent body. Unbelievable.
Photographed all over New York. He was roughly eight years
older than me. He was about thirty-seven. He was an enormous
turn-on—burning blue eyes, wavy brown hair, the whole thing. I
was enthralled, absolutely enthralled.

But from the start, the sexuality didn't work out too well. Phil
was into the whole thing that, 'OK, we're lovers, but I can go to
the Y and cruise and pick up other people.' And I would simply
lie down on the couch in a catatonic state and go to my therapist
in a catatonic state. You know, I couldn't live with anyone who
didn't want me exclusively. That meant that I wasn't fulfilling
their needs. How can I stand it. How can I live. I mean, they're
my everything and I can't stand it, I can't stand it.

But somehow I began to be able to live through that. I understood that I was his loved one and that the others were just to
screw around with. Still, when we were together, I wanted something good to happen but that wouldn't work out. We had all
sorts of problems about sex and I've never figured out his sexuality to this day.

He comes from the S and M scene, and long before it was chic.
I mean this was when they dressed in leather and they did things
very seriously. Phil and his friends pooh-pooh at the current gay
chic at wearing keys on this side and keys on that side and going
to bars, the bandana here, the blue one and the red one, which
side it's on—that sort of current chic. But that's not what the S
and M people consider serious stuff.

Within the serious S and M set there are really two sets. One
group who goes for games. Oh, you know, run at me from that
corner and I must tackle you and you must get down on your
knees and say master and so forth. It's a whole game. You know,
a few whip lashes and a few things like that but nothing *too*
mean. Then there's another set of the old S and M people—like
Phil—who, I mean, rings through the tits, cigarette burns, and
cuts, and blood. Things approaching death. And they were

always known as the freaked-out S and M crowd. I don't know now how much he's into that anymore. As they get older, they kinda say, 'Oh, what's it all about anyway.'

I wasn't into any of that. Pain. I still haven't figured it out. I mean I've never understood how it could be a turn-on for anybody to get themselves decked out like a sausage in leather and beat somebody to death. It's just not sex as far as I'm concerned. I mean, it's something else. I don't know what it is. Coat hangers. Apricots at midnight with long silver spoons. Whatever it is, it ain't sex to me.

Finally, after four years, I decided to give up sex with Phil. It was really a sort of gradual atrophying of our attempts to make sex work. And that's a whole other thing: the thing of people trying to "make it work"—sex, their relationship, whatever. Tinker, tinker, tinker, tinker, tinker. They tinker all day with their relationship. Well—fuck it. If it isn't good, get rid of it. You know, if it feels good, hang on. Sure, you can have troubles, but if the general feeling is good, it'll wave you over the obstacles. But if it doesn't, don't tinker and fuss. Don't get out a monkey wrench or a screwdriver or some oil. Tinker, tinker, tinker, tinker. You know, we're taught to do this because the whole Judeo-Christian-western-modern-Freudian-religious and every other ideal says that one should be able to make a monogamous, one-to-one relationship work. Well, there are better things to do with one's life, so I stopped tinkering.

Phil and I, it's really just an arrangement now. You know, two can live more cheaply than one. We have an apartment, a place in the country. When we started this, that's over twenty years ago, we were both working, both of us busy all day, every day. So we hung in there. At that point, we were just so used to living together. We'd been living together for three or four years and Phil was OK to live with once we abandoned the idea of having sex together. Our arrangement, after we stopped being lovers, was that either one of us was free to have any kind of relationship we wanted.

My conviction now is that no matter who I'm in love with, I

don't want to live with them. I want them to have their own space and me to have my own and for us to meet because we want to be together, not because we're locked together. I just sort of said when I got to be forty-seven or forty-eight, after too many unsuccessful romances, that at my age it's undignified to fall in love and get into a passion. Just as I think it's undignified for people my age to go to discotheques and shake their little asses.

Neal and Carrie

They described their relationship to us as being "an open marriage." Neal's forty-one; Carrie's thirty-nine.

Carrie: Our marriage started off in a very traditional way. We met in college. I was twenty, Michael was twenty-two. We got married and had children—it was like instant family. I think there came a point in our marriage, though, when I started feeling that I was in the house with the children all the time and I found myself only relating to Neal. And I was jealous that he was outside of the house during the day—meeting people—while I was always inside. I just wasn't too sure of myself anymore. I didn't know what I looked like, whether or not I was a desirable woman. I really lost that sense of myself. I was sure that I was a mother and I was sure that I was a wife but I wasn't sure if I was an attractive, interesting woman.

I had met a man while I was walking my son to school one day and he asked me to have breakfast with him. I wanted to be with this man but I knew that I didn't want to be with him without Neal knowing about it, without sharing it with Neal. And I guess that's the point where our marriage started to really change. I remember that morning very well. Neal was about to leave for work and I said, "By the way, I'm going to have breakfast with a man named Gary." Well, from that morning on—and we'd been married for ten years—we started really sharing things. Neal came home from work early that day and we spent many, many hours just catching up on all the previous years. Neal told me about the times he'd wanted to be with other women and about the times he'd actually been with other women. And that talk kind of gave us both permission to have other relationships outside of our marriage.

It was very scary at first and also very exhilarating. The main fear for me was never that I was going to leave the relationship, it was always that I would be left. That's what jealousy is really about for me—being left. So it was hard for me when I first heard that Neal had been with some other women.

Neal: And naturally I was jealous when Carrie told me about having breakfast with this other man. But I was pretty skillful then at denying my emotions, at blocking them. When I heard it, I used my greatest defense—withdrawing. So I didn't feel all the jealousy that was actually in me.

At about this time in our lives we had gotten involved in a couples group which consisted of about eight couples. The group was really a support system for people who were trying to reexamine their marriage contracts. It was a group of people who were willing to look at their marriage contracts and then either choose them again or radically change them. So when Carrie and I started going through all of our changes, we had people to talk to. And it was really fortunate to have these people who could listen to our problems and who wouldn't be judgmental about what we were trying to do with our marriage.

Carrie: We saw that on a head level, on an intellectual level, we could say, 'Hey, we don't possess one another, we don't own one another'—and that we each wanted the other to be who they were. But that was all intellectual. Emotionally, dealing with all the jealousies and all the feelings of possessiveness, was another story.

Neal: The agreement that we worked out with one another was that whatever we wanted to do, we'd have to be open about it and willing to share it. Nothing would be done secretively. And that was tough. We were committed to letting each other know exactly what we wanted to do and then we had to act on our desires —with or without the other's consent. So in the beginning, there really were no reassurances that we'd be safe and stay together no matter what happened.

There were tremendous conflicts in the beginning. On the surface, it probably would have appeared to an outsider that Carrie had a harder time adjusting to the new freedom we'd opened up in our marriage. At least, she expressed her hurt and anger more frequently. But I kept a lot of that stuff inside.

One night I remember Carrie saying to me after I told her I wasn't coming home, "Neal, at least let me know if you're going to be at the breakfast table in the morning." And I responded with, "Breakfast? What's so important about breakfast?" And we spent a long time hashing that out.

Carrie: The reason I wanted to know if he wasn't going to be at our breakfast table was because of the effect it might have on our kids. If they woke up, what would they feel about him not being there? Of course, my concern wasn't just about the kids. *I* cared about waking up without Neal too.

Neal: By now, we're pretty sure our kids know that we live a different kind of life-style than most people. But we don't really get specific with them. If I were asked by them, I'd certainly explain everything. But as long as they don't ask, then we don't feel we have to be totally explicit.

Carrie: In the beginning, when I felt this need to exercise this openness with other people, I think I went through a lot of falling in love with different people. So sometimes my relationships with these other men were higher, more enjoyable than things were at home. There were love notes, packages—you know, lots of romance. But it was also very exciting to be allowed to share with Neal that I was a very interesting woman.

I never really thought of being with someone else as a thing that was replacing something that was lacking at home. I always thought of being with someone else as just being with someone else, just enjoying that new relationship. I'm not exactly sure how many men I've slept with since this all started—but about ten. It's really not numbers for me, though. It's not a party kind of thing. All the people I've been with, in fact, I've been with more than once. And they're almost all people that Neal and I are now friendly with.

Neal: When I meet someone and feel good about them, I immediately want to share what I'm feeling for them with the people who are important to me. So I want them to meet Carrie. I want them to meet my kids. I want to include those people in my life, and Carrie and my kids are part of my life. So the people I'm with and the people Carrie's with understand the built-in limitation to any relationship they might develop with us. They know they're not going to be the primary thing in our lives. But they also know that they're very important, not just casual affairs.

Carrie: You know, it's funny because we've been friendly with a lot of the people we've been involved with for a long time and now it seems as if the sexuality part of it is kind of diminishing. I think by now all of my fantasies have been played out and it's just not a strong need anymore. I still get excited with people but I'm much less romantic about it. It's not what I want to be doing right now. I guess what I feel now is that being with Neal is really where I like to be and that this is the fun place.

I've played out a lot of the exciting possibilities and though I know there are exciting times ahead, I'm more relaxed about it now. I'm not uptight about myself anymore. I *know* I'm a desirable woman.

Neal: There's really relatively little pain involved for Carrie and me now with these sort of experiences. This summer, for instance, I was out in Colorado with some old friends—lovers—and I knew that Carrie was genuinely joyful that I was with them. And I can support Carrie's experiences too.

Carrie: I've felt very close to Neal ever since we opened up our relationship. It's a very intimate thing to be able to share these things with the person you live with—all the fantasies, the fears, the jealousies. Being open about all the ugly and hard stuff really brings you closer.

Helen Bernat

She was anxious about us recording her. She wasn't used to sharing her feelings about her marriage with others. "I feel like there's another person in the room," was how she expressed her wariness of the tape recorder.

She's forty-seven years old, lives in a $65,000 home in a suburb of Boston, and recently celebrated her twenty-fifth wedding anniversary. In the past couple of years she's returned to college and recently completed her undergraduate degree.

I met my husband while in my first year of college. I think I was about eighteen and a half. He was five years older than I was and very dashing and he was already in business, which was unlike any other date I had ever had. We got married a year later.

I continued in college for a little better than a year. What had happened was that he had lost his father three months before we were married and his mother was an invalid, handicapped. And being very naive and very young, I decided we couldn't leave her alone. My husband pleaded with me not to move in with her but I was very proper and very idealistic and I said, "How can you leave your mother? We can't just leave her after your father died." So we moved in with her, which was the first big mistake in our relationship. It set very bad precedents which had their consequences and still do.

I feel resentment about that whole period in my life. I felt like we never really had an open time together in the beginning. She would get up in the middle of the night with one of her pseudo-asthma attacks and pound on our door. She is handicapped. She has osteoarthritis, but I think the asthma is psychosomatic. She was going through a hard time and didn't have any other children. She has an overwhelming personality and I came from a very loving, low-key background, very gentle people. She was just too much for me. I just couldn't handle it. It was nothing that she ever directly did or said to me, it was just her presence, her countenance, just her being there was too much for me. I felt very intimidated by her.

I feel that those early beginnings set up precedents for my husband and me. He had the trump card so to speak because it was his home and his mother. We lived in her apartment and we did our room all over with completely new furniture; and although everything on the surface was just beautiful, there was a lot going on underneath and I just couldn't concentrate on school. I felt so—it's hard to label the feelings I had at the time—just terribly frightened, not being able to function as a whole human being, intimidated. Because I was the kind of person I was, I wasn't able to express myself, and even if I had been able to I really don't think it would have mattered. I felt like I was on the verge of some kind of total emotional collapse.

I quit school and went to work for a dentist. I became pregnant while I was working for this dentist because I knew that would be my only way out. I did want to start a family eventually, but I knew that if I had a child right away I'd be able to get out of his mother's house.

Finally, we did have our first born and we moved out. Then things were much better and I was much happier. I was very anxious to make a new life, to move away from things that had troubled me, and I think Carl was too, because he had gone through quite a hard period, having a handicapped mother and being an only child. She lived by herself and she functioned amazingly well. She had amazing stamina. She's still alive today. And kicking.

I loved being a mother, those were some of the most joyous years of my life. There was nothing I left undone as a mother, but I was functioning better as a mother than I was as Helen Bernat, person.

When I was pregnant with my second son—I was about twenty-five—I started suffering from ileitis which I didn't discover for about five years. I was in and out of hospitals with this excruciating pain and all the doctors would tell me was that it was something mental rather than physiological. Finally we bought our house in Quincy and a year after we moved I needed major surgery. I could no longer eat any food at all, not even water. After I came out of surgery I guess all the anxieties and all the underdevelopment of my nature came to a head and I started getting that feeling again that I couldn't cope. I *was* coping, but under great stress. My husband came home one night and I just told him that I needed to get help, that I wanted to start therapy. In those days there was a stigma attached to it. My husband went crazy when I told him. He has terrible fears about money problems, although they're not rational in basis. He just went absolutely bananas. So he said, ''OK, we're going to sell the house.'' I was wise enough to know that I didn't care what he had to sell. I said, ''I don't care what you do. I'm going to get help.''

I was always frightened to take a good look at myself. If you ask me why, I don't really know. I guess maybe I couldn't deal with it. The early years of my marriage had been very bad for me and it frightened me. Therapy just helped me realize that there were the makings of a worthwhile human being there with a great deal of potential. My therapist gave me the ability to work on the potential I had rather than hate myself for being less than perfect. To this day I feel it was an invaluable experience.

Through the years, and I feel I have to add this because I've been evading it, my husband has had a very volatile personality. He has a lot of repressed anger, probably from being raised by his mother. For twenty-five years I've lived with a person with whom I never wanted to rock the boat because of this explosive personality which I guess frightens me, and I've learned to live with it in a way that hasn't been productive for either one of us. There are any number of topics that I feel I can't discuss with Carl because his rage starts to build up until it becomes overwhelming and he can no longer contain it. He can physically lash out and grab me by the arm and shake me. He's done it in front of the children and he's done it to the children too. When he gets into this rage, he knows it and it's only something he's admitted recently. When it starts coming over him, it builds up into a kind of whirlpool sort of thing and there's no getting out of it. It takes him hours to get out of it and after he's over it he goes into, not a catatonic state, but something like it where he's just completely drained of his energy. It stifles both of our feelings about one another. It creates unbearable hostilities that last for a very long time, and it really cuts him off from the person that he is because this is a part of him that he has not learned to control.

For example, we were discussing our twenty-fifth anniversary party that the children were making for us and there was one neighbor in particular who I didn't want to have come to the party for very valid reasons, personal reasons. And Carl wants to come off as a nice guy. And over this nonsense which had no direct relation to either one of us, I don't know if he was overtired that morning or if something else was bothering him, he started to work himself up over this one issue that could have been handled in a very, very simple way. We could have talked about it a little further or we could have come to a decision or let the decision rest until some future time. He became enraged over it, which he's done before on other occasions where other people are concerned. He can't handle any kind of adversity, whether it's with a neighbor or a child or his mother. He just can't handle it. When he becomes unhappy about even the slightest thing, he cannot work it through. This rage takes over. We had a terrible, terrible battle that day. He started using his hands, and his face was distorted with anger. It was all completely unrelated to the incident and out of proportion to what the discussion was about. That day my children were home. He took me by the arm and shook me. I was black and blue for several days after that. I decided that that was the last time I was going to tolerate that kind of behavior. I had to get out of the house. I just didn't know what he was going to do next. It was humiliating for me to know that other people in the community were hearing him. The children had seen him that day and I had strength in their having witnessed it. They had seen how it had started from nothing and they had tried to control it.

The next morning I called my internist and I think up to that point I was embarrassed to talk about it. It wasn't wife beating per se because he never beat me but it was just that I could no longer handle this terrible rage that came over him. I told the doctor exactly what had happened and he wasn't really shocked because Carl had always been on tranquilizers. He had nightmares when he couldn't sleep at night and so the doctor was pretty familiar with his personality. His only question was why did I wait so long? Once I took that step I felt much better about myself and our relationship. The following week I got Carl to come with me to the doctor and he had a consultation with us and it was his opinion that Carl definitely did need therapy. Carl knew at that point in our lives that I was no longer going to live with him that way. It was a tremendous turning point, very positive in that he, from that time on, has really tried. He didn't go into therapy, but he really learned to control his emotions. I almost feel now that he was like a bratty kid who whenever he felt angry he just let himself go crazy. He had to be given that ultimatum. I think that knowing that I was doing something constructive about it helped him try to help himself as well. He hasn't had any of these outbursts since. Of course he'll have little waves here and there, but he'll try to sit down with me and take it step by step until we'll both come to some kind of agreement.

I was speaking to a friend of mine who's a psychologist and she was married to someone like this, who lost control of himself. And she said, "It will come to a head again and he will test you again." That very well may be. I don't know how long it will take. But I think he knows my purpose was not to humiliate and embarrass him, but rather to help him see an aspect of his personality that needed alteration and which was very, very destructive, not only to himself, but to me and to the children as well.

I'm still trying to get him to go into therapy because I think he needs it desperately, but he's not quite ready for that. He feels he will not pay for therapy. His money hang-ups affect and color his every thought. Somehow I know, too, that this is related to his rage. There's really nothing he hasn't done for the children or for me, but it's always been a battle, a constant battle. He's never been able to do anything financially without a catharsis of crying about it or complaining about it or feeling sorry for himself about it. I think he has this feeling that tomorrow he'll wake up and he'll be penniless. He wakes up in a cold sweat. The most he sleeps is about four or five hours a night. There are terrible fears that he's not able to deal with.

What he does is he avoids any one of a number of topics. In one given day he'll say to me four or five times, "Let's not discuss that because it upsets me. Let's talk about something else, this is unpleasant." It saddens me because I think it just cuts him off from being in touch with himself.

Carl likes to think that everything that happens here at home is always on the up side, idyllic. If things are going well and I'm healthy and the kids are healthy, he can kind of put his energy into things he wants to do, such as business. When I'm feeling down or low, initially he will be supportive; but if it continues for what he feels is too long a period of time—which might be a half a day or a day or two days—then he can become sarcastic or argumentative with me, like "Again you're not feeling well?" or "What is it? You have everything you could want." He'll be supportive initially but if he gets beyond the point where he can handle it and it's starting to creep into his own day, he can become nasty about it.

After my mother died I went through a very low period and he was very disenchanted with me. Whatever great love he seemed to have for me seemed to have flown out the window at that time. He was disgusted. At the time I needed him most, he was not supportive at all. We really were not getting along then. I guess maybe I did push him out of my life at that time. I've come close to leaving him many, many times. I've said it's just not worth it. Life simply has to have more to offer.

I haven't really thought about leaving him in the past couple of months because he's really worked so hard at containing himself. Sometimes I feel I'm still not able to openly express myself. It's complicated because now I have a college degree and he doesn't, so I have to watch myself and not make him feel like he's less intellectual than I am. Truthfully, I think we are on different intellectual levels and it's not that he's not bright—he's very bright, very worldly and knowledgeable—he's just not tuned-in to the same things I am. I think all three of my children are very serious factors in my staying in the relationship. On occasion I've shared my thoughts about leaving Carl with them but it's so terribly frightening to them. What they say is that I'm just talking to them about it so that I can get rid of some of the feelings I have. I think there will always be a certain lack of communication between me and Carl. Perhaps he feels the same way. Perhaps there's certain things that he would like to talk about with me that I'm not terribly interested in. He can go into business in such great detail sometimes that I really am terribly bored by it. I've heard all the stories many times. I think I like to talk more about intangible things; he likes to talk more about things that are visible, something he can put his finger on.

I really do love my husband very much. I could never really picture myself living with another person. We do have a very strong, loving relationship. There's still a very strong physical attraction between us. We share many common interests. In order to keep this relationship going, which I have made up my mind that I am going to do, I cannot give vent to all the things that I might want to. I can continue school because that will work within the framework in which I'm living. But I cannot go completely outside of it and grow to the potential that I know I could. I've given that up. I give up that freedom because if I do all these things, I know that I will leave him behind and I don't want to do that. Also, there are many things about the relationship that I need, like my own sense of security. I'm not willing to give that up.

I think my husband is a chauvinist. I think it's very hard for him to accept anything that I suggest without the suggestion originally coming from him. It can be something very simple. For example, my son had to have a coat altered and I suggested he take it to the local cleaners. He was leaving for college and time was short and Carl kept insisting he take it back to the store where he had bought it four years ago. I thought it was ridiculous for him to drive all the way into Boston when he was pressed for time and they would probably charge him something anyway. We had a terrible argument about that. Just because I said it, it wasn't good enough. He really believes he must have the final say. If I tell my daughter to call at 9:30 from a friend's house before she leaves, he says she must call at 9:15. If I say 9:15, he'll say 10:00. I think that's an insecurity on his part. When a person is pretty sure of himself, he doesn't have the need to question and be authoritative about everything that goes on in the house. Or with the children—if they come down to breakfast and say hello to me first, he'll really start something. "You said good morning to mommy, but you didn't say good morning to me." When we're in mixed company he likes to give the impression that he's patting me on the head, like, you know, nice little harmless person. When we're alone together, it's never that way. His outside image has to be flawless, he's got to be the macho man. Tarzan.

I think the future is going to depend on what I'm going to do from here on in. If I'm able to get into the teaching field, it will fulfill a need that I have for myself. Carl's found his niche. He's very happy in business. He deals very well with his world. I can't see that he'll be changing very much. I think as far as some of my needs go, like intellectual needs, I'll have to fulfill them on my own. I'm willing to accept that.

If Carl has another one of his explosions, I'll really sit on him and he'll have to go for therapy or I'll leave. As much as it would hurt me to do so, and I don't know if it would be a permanent leave of absence, I would really physically pack up and leave. I know that if he started therapy it would open up new vistas to both of us. I think we could really explore our maturity to a much greater extent than we've been able to do. He has a part of him that has gone unexplored, that has a great potential for understanding.

Sharon

Sharon is twenty-six and has been married for five years. She works as an editor at a popular women's magazine.

I met Jerry when I was fifteen. I was crazy in love with him for like six years. He was my dream—the guy that never calls, the one that you wait for who never shows up at the right time. And our relationship was like that for about five years. Then I started growing up when I was around twenty and that's when Jerry really started getting interested. I think I married Jerry because it was the thing to do. It was the thing I always pictured myself doing. It's easy to do something once you've dreamed about it often enough. Plus, I figured I wanted him so much that I must really want to marry him.

I didn't love him when I got married, or maybe I loved him but I didn't want to live with him. We didn't know each other. We got engaged and we were engaged for about six months and I didn't find myself very excited about getting married, but I figured as soon as we got married it would all change.

Frankly, I did have thoughts about canceling the whole thing but it was more frightening to call up my mother and say, "I'm not getting married and you can take back your dress to where you got it." Also, what would I do if I didn't get married? A lot of friends said, "Don't get married, there's no reason to, you don't have to." But I was scared not to get married.

About a year after we were married I got really strung out. I was freaking and crying and went into all sorts of depressions. Nothing made sense to me. I was a nervous wreck. I didn't like myself; I had a lousy self-image. So I started with this therapist. She said, "Why are you here?" and I said, "I want a divorce. I want to kill myself. My life has no meaning and get me out of this.'' I also figured it had been a year, it was a respectable amount of time. You know, 'I tried, Ma. I really tried, but it's not working. We're splitting up.' So this therapist said, ''Maybe your husband is contributing to your problems,'' and I said. ''No. He's fine. He's a doctor, what could he be doing wrong?'' And Jerry came into therapy with me about a week later and within a half hour this woman had dethroned him before my eyes and I couldn't believe it. She showed me that he was really *asking* me to become the nag. Jerry was looking for a second mother and he wanted me to be as obnoxious and nasty to him as I was being. If I asked Jerry to help me with meals or something, he knew that if he didn't respond to anything I said I would keep at it; so I became this nagging wife. He never dealt with his feelings about whether he wanted to help me or not. He just let me yell. I became his alarm clock. He didn't have to do anything until I'd yelled at him for the third time, and it was an awful position to be in because I didn't feel like a woman who was married to a man who loved and cared for her and made her feel terrific. I felt like somebody's mother. I felt very old, ugly, horrible. And it showed. It seemed like everyone I saw on the street had something more than I did. But in therapy, Jerry's reasons for wanting me to be in that position came out. I've always enjoyed pushing people around so I got something out of the relationship too. It wasn't just as if I was forced into it. That was such a simple problem to solve I couldn't believe it. Within a couple of months, Jerry and I were functioning beautifully and really enjoying our time together.

We went deeper into therapy. We learned how to commit ourselves to our own feelings: Rather than saying, ''You ought to help me in the kitchen,'' I started saying, ''Why don't you help me? I'd like it. It would make me feel good.'' It all came down to the fact that we hadn't dealt with each other's feelings about anything. We didn't know what each other's feelings were. Through therapy I found out that I was really in love with him and the part of me that fell in love with him when I was fifteen is now living with us and it's incredible. And he's also become a friend because therapy was a growing process and the fact that Jerry went through it with me makes him closer to me. I know that he knows where I'm really at. There's very little that I can't talk to Jerry about and the things that I can't talk to him about are things he doesn't want to hear. He doesn't like to talk about my sex life before I married him, my days of promiscuity and fucking around in college. It would mean a lot if I could share that with him because that would be the very last secret and it would feel good for me to know that I have deposited my life with somebody else.

Jerry has told me that I can even go get laid because he really believes that I love him. But there is the understanding that I would not get involved with anybody who I would have an emotional affair with. I will not cheat on Jerry emotionally. I would just never go to bed with somebody who could jeopardize our marriage and relationship. The frivolous me is capable of going to bed with somebody because they're just into having fun that night, because somebody crazy asks me. It's like having a drink with somebody—almost. But the truth is that I haven't slept with anyone other than Jerry—except for my brother-in-law. And that's a whole other story.

About once every six months, Peter, my brother-in-law, would make a pass at me. Many years ago, before I was married to Jerry, I had modeled for Peter—he's a photographer—and we'd gotten into a sexual space together. I say we fucked but Peter has tried to convince me many times that we didn't. Anyway, he was on top of me without any clothes, I'm sure of that. We kept it from my sister, Karen, for a long time. When Peter finally told her about it he didn't mention the sex, just the fact that I'd modeled nude for him. She was very sweet and understanding about it and that was pretty much the end of it. Except that every once in a while Peter would make a pass at me, kind of for old time's sake. I didn't think he was really interested in me and I really didn't think anything was going to happen. My husband and Peter didn't like each other too much anyway, so I figured if Jerry was going to let me fuck somebody, it sure as hell wasn't going to be Peter.

The four of us went to a hotel for a weekend, a ski lodge, got very ripped, had a good time. I'd always thought of my sister as very sweet, someone who led a very sheltered life, never did much of anything. So we were all just rapping and someone said to Karen, "What do you feel like doing?." And she said, "Sucking off Jerry," And I was supposed to be the cool one. So I said, "OK. That's fine with me." And Jerry, who never committed himself to *any* feeling—like even, 'Yeah, let's play monopoly'—just sat there and decided that the rest of the group was gonna decide whether Karen was going to suck him off or not. And my sister sort of slithered over there and the next thing—there she was and I could not believe it. My sister, who I really think of as my younger sister although she's older, had the balls to do that. Peter and I were sort of sitting there looking at each other half smiling, and I don't know whether I felt like going to bed with him at the time or not, but we did. After that we just exchanged rooms. Peter went back to his room, Karen went back to hers, and we never talked about it. We all had breakfast together the next morning and we never said another thing about it. We saw them a week or two later, went to their house, and the same thing happened. What would happen from then on was that we'd start out playing some game like strip poker or monopoly and we'd say the loser has to fuck so and so. I couldn't believe this was happening. I really was appalled, disgusted, sickened by it all because it was so stupid. And I felt I was the only one in the room who was into being honest about what was happening. No one else even wanted to talk about it.

I went along with it all. I wanted to be cool. I didn't want to be accused of being uptight. But when the games started going on, I started talking to the three of them and I said, "Why can't we just be honest about what we're doing? I don't like the games. I don't want to play them anymore, and if we feel like fucking,

can't we just say that?'' And I really appealed to them all on that
level and they all agreed. But then we'd all start to play monopoly again.

It was crazy but I really don't think any of them had really
thought about what they were doing or wanted to think about it.
Maybe Peter did, but I think his attitude was 'I'll keep my mouth
shut and get laid as often as I can.' He didn't want to rock the
boat. That went on for a few months—at first every week, and
then every other week. Then, as time went on, I knew I didn't
want to be doing this. I'd invent excuses not to see them. I'd
make sure we were busy, booked up for parties months in ad-
vance so I wouldn't have to face them. And then when they'd
want to come over I'd tell them, ''Sure, bring the kids.'' I knew
if Karen's kids were around, nothing would happen. The whole
thing got more complicated when we started suspecting that
Peter and Karen were getting it on with other couples. That
didn't bother me at all except that they'd say to us, ''We do this
with you because we feel so close to you. You're our brother and
sister and it's more than fucking that's going on here. We're exchanging feelings. A relationship is happening.''

At the time it started, I think Jerry really felt affection for my
sister. She's a very affectionate, beautiful person. She's cute,
she's adorable, she's fun to be with, she's intelligent. I had
always been in competition with Karen, so the thing with her and
Jerry annoyed me a bit. But I was sharing a part of Jerry's life
with him that she could never come close to so I didn't really feel
like my marriage or my relationship was in jeopardy. I was
peripherally jealous. After the whole thing ended, I told Peter I
wasn't really into him sexually, and he told me I was full of shit,
that I was just copping out because I couldn't cut it. Then my
sister told me that she'd been thinking a lot about what was happening and she wanted to get into something with me. I thought,
'Oh, my God, what is happening.' Karen and I had always been
very physical together. We'd hold each other for an hour at a
time and it's beautiful because she's my sister and it goes back to

us being kids together and loving rolling on the floor together and doing what little girls do. Given time, I think I might have gone into it because I was curious about it and I'd never been in a physical relationship with a woman. But the only real reservation I had was that I didn't know what to do; I'd be embarrassed to take the initiative. Anyway, I turned her down and said I was really uptight about this and I had to think about it and I didn't want to do it now. Well, within a week she was in bed with her best friend, Peggy. She told me about it and she kind of broke the news to me gently. I kind of felt like a date had just dumped me, like I'd been rejected. I felt that she hadn't given me a fair shake. She didn't give me a chance to say yes. Now, if I went ahead and did it I'd have to compete with Peggy—so I wouldn't do it. Jerry was kind of turned off to the fact that Karen had done it.

Anyway at about the time Karen started talking about whips, Jerry got really turned off. Jerry doesn't like to talk about having been with my sister, and I don't really like to ask questions either because one of my fears is that if I ask him, 'Was she better than me,' he'll say yes. How could I deal with that? But I think now that however good a lay she might have been, I'm the one that he shares things with. I'm the one that he loves and only I could fuck Jerry the way I do because I love him that much.

The occasions we see them now are few and far between. We've avoided them because they make so many demands and pressures. The sexual stuff is over. One of the things they constantly say is don't be uptight. Whenever they don't like what you're doing, they accuse you of doing it because you're not loose enough to do something else. There's no way that I could ever convince them that there's anything wrong with them because they're snobs, they're the elite. They're very manipulative. But she's my sister and before Jerry and Peter came onto the scene a lot of love passed between us. I really do wish I was closer with her, that I could share things with her. I love her; I just don't like her right now. I hope the situation will change.

Allen and Beverly

Allen is thirty-two, Beverly's twenty-nine. They're both clinical psychologists in Chicago.

Allen: I had a sense that I was going to marry her pretty early on. It felt pretty solid. We had both had a number of relationships before we met and we both pretty much knew that the next time was going to be *the* time. You know, we weren't playing around and we had both reached the point where we had some sense of our own vulnerabilities, fuck-ups, dynamics. It was all very *adult* in the beginning, very mature. But then some of the junk started coming out.

About five months after we met we were going to Canada, and as we're packing, Beverly all of a sudden started getting crazy about something. I had never lived with someone who started screaming. Screaming, screaming, screaming. It was about whether or not to buy a chicken and she's running her mouth off like a maniac. So I pulled her out of the car and I never found myself wanting so much to absolutely slam the living shit out of a woman. So I'm yelling, not realizing all the time I'm becoming a bigger nut. I had gotten angry before and I had screamed and I had gotten hysterical but I never had anyone become a nut and turn me into one. And that's what began to creep into our relationship. We had already worked through a lot of stuff in order to be honest together but there was a lot more stuff to get into.

Beverly: My getting crazy with the chicken wasn't just my getting crazy with the chicken. It was me reacting to something in Allen and him reacting back. Allen goes through periods that are kind of immersions in work but in a way they don't feel just like an immersion in work. They feel like a real pushing away of me. And it always happens right before we're about to take a big vacation. There'll be two weeks when we're supposed to be getting maps, packing, but somehow it just so happens Allen has a mammoth project to finish. And he's literally up twenty-four hours a day for two weeks.

One of the things we've discovered about some of the anger that used to go back and forth between us—and sometimes it was really crazy and rageful like the chicken incident—was that it was our way of getting away from ourselves. The rage that was generated was from things that I wasn't wanting to deal with about myself or that Allen wasn't dealing with about himself. Getting angry was just a way of getting away from our own skins. In our early days, too, the highs were so completely involved with the lows that they never felt really good.

Allen: Yeah. Like the high you get after two weeks of fighting and then, you know, you finally fuck and you're crying and then twenty minutes later you're fighting again. And then finally, if you have any presence of mind, you just plead not to talk. "Can we just do something where we don't have to talk?"

Beverly: We try to remind each other when we're fighting now that we're both fragile and that we shouldn't say anything for a while.

Allen: We've already had three divorces. One lasted three and a half days. It was horrible. You know, when you can't get off the phone but when you're yelling at each other. You're seething but you can't get off the damn phone. When it's 'I can't hang up on her, she'll call me back anyway so if I try to hang up on her and the fight's not settled, well, I'm not going to be able to do my work anyway,' it's terrible—terrible because there's just something in those moments when you realize you're not autonomous in this world. There's somebody linked into your guts at a very primitive level and if you don't get it OK with them, then nothing else is going to work. You realize you're totally helpless. The last time that happened was about two years ago. We separated for three or four days and we went through things where she was threatening suicide and all that.

Now we're finally at a place where if we can't talk to each

other, if we're starting to fight, we'll just not talk until things are calmer. It's less crazy. We're just not going to do that other stuff anymore. There's just no point to it. You don't get anything out of it.

Beverly: We used to be able to extend a fight over a week. Now it's like an hour. So I guess we've made some progress.

Jonathan and Claire

Jonathan is a psychologist and former college clergy-man. Claire works as an administrator in a nursing home.

Jonathan: We've been married thirty-three years. That's three months and six days short of a third of a century. We have three grown children.

Claire: I'm fifty-five and Jonathan's fifty-three. When we were first married we had a great deal of things in common and we spent an awful lot of time together. There were no really big challenges to our marriage until after our first daughter was born. Up to that point, I'd been a part of everything Jonathan had done. I'd been a very important part of his work. So after six years of being so close, all of a sudden I was tied down with a baby and couldn't do a lot of the things I'd done with him before. I went through a kind of questioning of my role and I realized I really wasn't happy just being a mother. I loved being a mother but I did resent to a certain extent the restrictions it put on me, on my mobility.

Jonathan: I felt a little detached from Claire at the time because we did have less time together and the time we had wasn't quite as free. I think we lost the art of playing for a long time and we had to rediscover it.

Claire: The distance between Jonathan and me really increased when our kids were very young. Jonathan developed a summer program for his students that took him away to South America every summer. So that meant that for three years I was alone all summer with the kids and he was off in Peru. I found that extremely hard and we're only now starting to talk about how difficult it was for me. He left me with the full responsibility of the house and the family—all the major decisions that had to be made, including selling the house. It was a tough time and there were some very difficult things to go through. Plus, it was hard for the children.

During one of those summers, I discovered I had a lump on my breast and I didn't know whether or not it was going to be really serious and be a mastectomy. That's an emotional kind of thing that's hard to go through alone. It turned out to be just a lump and everything was OK. But after I wrote to Jonathan and told him about it there was never anything more said about it. When I told him everything was OK, he didn't even write back and comment on the fact that he was glad that it wasn't anything serious. That was very painful. I didn't really tell him about my feelings, that I was so hurt. I always sort of brushed it aside.

The times when our relationship has been as its lowest ebb have usually been when we're both hurting inside and we don't want to show it so we cover it up. And once we begin to close up, it becomes easier to cover up and then our communication breaks down.

Jonathan: Recently, we went through a period of strain where we questioned whether we wanted to stay together. When I had my fiftieth birthday, I realized I wasn't getting any younger and it was quite a painful time. I knew I wanted more out of life than I was getting. It became clear, too, that I wanted a lot more from our relationship than I was experiencing. I wanted more sharing, more openness, more freedom, and more laughter. I knew that I wanted these things from our relationship and I felt that if I couldn't find them here, then theoretically I wanted to anticipate another relationship. I didn't want to stay in the relationship just because of a moral or legal bind or out of force of habit or social expectation.

Claire: That was painful for me to hear. I was feeling like some kind of a drudge. I had a full-time job. I was putting Jonathan through a doctoral program and my kids through college. And on top of all that, I was starting menopause and having a very rough time. I felt that Jonathan wasn't being understanding.

What I needed to be told then was that life wasn't over for me and that I was still a desirable woman. But he just wasn't able to tell me those things. I really needed to be cuddled and loved but Jonathan was needing a great deal at that time too. In spite of all his bravado about being fifty and never feeling better, he was also having some real thoughts about being over the hill. I guess you could say that in a sense both of us were going through menopause.

Jonathan: It was unfortunate that we both had to go through it at the same time.

Claire: In addition, Jonathan was going through a very difficult time in his job. There were weeks on end when he didn't know if he would have a job come the next week. So the last thing he needed to come home to was a bitchy wife. He needed to come home to love and care and concern.

In times of strength, I had always come through for Jonathan, realizing that his needs were almost more critical than mine. I would usually be able to muster up the support that he needed. I'd just try to let him know that he was OK. So during this trying time, I managed to realize that this was no time for sniveling around. He needed my strength.

Over the years, it seemed that when one of us had been in a low period, then the other one would be the source of strength. But when we both hit a low period it was rough.

Jonathan: Part of the problem, too, was that my awareness of the importance of the relationship varied. I'd get really involved in some project and really excited about it, and if Claire wasn't involved, I'd kind of lose interest in her. At those times I'd feel that the relationship wasn't that important and I'd take it for granted. And then home would just be a place to come back to to change my clothes. But because of her strength, Claire's always brought me back to reappreciating what we had.

Claire: I started screaming that we should spend more time together. Every summer on vacation we'd make great plans and vow that next year we weren't going to get so busy, that we were going to spend more time going out to dinner, to plays, things like that. Then, on our vacation the following year, we'd end up saying the same thing. Well, during this crisis, we started taking more seriously the time we spent alone with one another.

I saw that you have to be very careful about making assumptions about your spouse. Jonathan had made assumptions about who I was as a result of my not being able to participate in what he was doing. My commitment to raising a family, for instance, had to take priority in my life. I wasn't able to do certain things I ordinarily would have loved to do with him. That didn't mean I didn't want to be doing them or I wasn't interested in what he was doing. It simply meant I didn't have the time. But Jonathan had this image of me as being very dull, a boring little *hausfrau,* and I didn't like how he was seeing me.

Jonathan: Our relationship had started out being very powerful with a definite life-long feeling to it. Very seldom in the thirty-three years did I doubt the strength of the relationship. But much of the time we didn't really think that much about it.

Claire: During this last crisis I realized that we were doing so much negative analyzing of where we were at that I had the image of a chain and we were hammering away at one of its links and it was getting weaker and weaker. And I suddenly realized we had to stop hammering at that link and strengthen it. That's when we started talking to each other and hearing each other. In the past we never really heard each other, especially when we argued. We would just talk past each other. So then we shifted gears and began thinking about and doing all the things we loved doing together.

Jonathan: We're aware of our dissatisfactions now and we work at them. But we don't dwell on them, and that's helped make things a lot better. I've been experiencing the buoyancy of the relationship, the space to feel comfortable, a lot more energy, a lot of affection, a renewed sexual relationship . . . and I've been remembering how very strong and resourceful my wife really is.

Claire: There have been some very rough times, but I wonder about the people who don't have the kind of solid base, the kind of foundation we have. If a marriage isn't on solid footing to start out with, how in the world can people face up to these things?

Rufus

He's a rock 'n' roll star: groupies chase him, managers swindle him, and journalists hype him. Before making it, he was married for ten years.

His house is an oceanfront duplex. Its interior resembles a nightclub more than a home—soft red lights, piped-in jazz, bar stools and bar.

Success brought him lots of money, lots of women, a movie contract, and, as far as he's concerned, "an overdose of kinky sex."

(At his request, his name has been changed to protect his privacy.)

I was twenty-one when I got married and I was married for ten years. We separated a couple of times during those ten years. We met in college, at Pennsylvania State University. We were both music majors and we'd go to the music department to practice music and, you know, to practice being married.

It wasn't magic with her. I don't know. I'm such a weird person. I never talk about this stuff with anyone. It was my freshman year and I was in the post office one day and I said to one of my friends, "Man, who is that girl over there." And he says, "That's Betty and you don't want to do nothin' with her. Stay away from her. She's the meanest girl on campus." And I had to prove a point to him, you know. So I got to know her and she was pretty mean. She was tough. She grew up in Harlem. She was an only child, raised by her grandfather. Her mother died when she was very young and she never knew who her father was. So she had a tough life. And she made it to college—that's makin' it to college out of *Harlem* and that's saying something right there. It was a lot tougher back in those days. And so she was a real tough

219

chick. But I understood her, I saw her softness. She had a warmth that was in there—way back in there, but it was there. She didn't let you see it often, but it was there.

We were together for two years and then we got married. We got married because I came from a very rigid background, a religious background from Virginia. I come from a long line of Baptist preachers. You just got married, you didn't mess around. So we got married, that was the thing to do in those days. But looking back on it I'd never do that again.

You know, I'll never forget it. I had a bachelor party and her uncle said to me, "I can't let you do it. You don't want to marry her. I'll put you right on a bus and just get outta here." And, man, I wished I had listened to him. But, you know, I felt an obligation to my mother who I told I was getting married. She'd bought a new dress and all that. It sounds stupid but that's what it was.

We never fought. Never anything physical. No abuse. No yelling. We'd just say a few words and that was that. And that's the worst thing, really. No intimacy there. Cold.

I was into music. I was playing rock 'n' roll in Pennsylvania in all these clubs. You know, you have a few drinks and when you play in a band there are like a thousand chicks. So my wife would never go to these clubs. She was a teacher by then and she didn't want her students to see her at these clubs. That sort of stuff wasn't cool back then. So my wife would send her friends along with me. You know, to help me drive home and all that. And I ended up getting it on with one of her friends. See, if my wife would have come to these clubs with me from the beginning, our relationship wouldn't have gotten the way it did.

You know, I'd come home and she wasn't the warmest person in the world. She didn't express her affection outwardly. She didn't come on and say, "Dear, here's your dinner. I love you." And I've always been a romanticist. I love the warmth. You know, big people are like that. You'll find that most big guys are teddy bears. So anyway, we stuck it out. We should have separated earlier but we stuck it out because of the insecurity of separating from each other.

There were no men in her life, to my knowledge, other than me. And I didn't tell her about me but she knew. But she never pursued it. We'd just talk about bills.

I never even had a hope that the marriage would work. It was just an insecurity thing. I was just afraid of what it would be like to be without her, you know, because she took care of everything. She had a business mind. I could make bucks but I couldn't keep money. So it was a dependency we had on each other.

We moved to Connecticut and I used to get really bummed out at home sometimes because of the lack of affection there. So I kinda started not coming home. Sometimes I'd stop at a bar and have a drink and at this one bar there was this girl working there. So eventually the girl and I became close friends. I would come to the place, have a few drinks, and then just kinda cry on her shoulder. And I even thought I was in love with her and eventually it did turn into love. So I was seeing her for about five years while I was still married.

I'd stay out all night and Betty would never ask me anything. I even wanted her to say, 'Where have you been?' I wanted her to get angry or something. But maybe because she grew up without a mother she didn't learn those tender ways, those womanly things. You know, the tenderness. So Kathy substituted everything I missed with my wife. I could sit down and talk with her.

Betty couldn't have kids. She had some sort of plumbing problem. But once when I was away for a few weeks she had it fixed and I didn't know about it. And then I came back one night, I'll never forget it. I don't even want to talk about this . . . but I conceived my first kid. I didn't know it. It was heavy, man. I suffered. I didn't want kids. There wasn't enough love there, you know. I didn't want my kids to grow up in a home without love. I was freaked out, man. And my parents were telling me that God isn't gonna love me if I didn't get back to my wife. All these things going on. And I almost flipped out over it. And then Kathy started running around with another guy, which was natural. You know, I was a married guy. She wanted a life for herself.

So I walked down to the jetty and I started to jump off. . . . But I was a coward and I chickened out. So anyway I got it together and I came back. We tried to make it work but it didn't work. People don't change. She still remained the same and she's still the same.

Then I met this girl Mary. She was married. She had three kids. But there was something we had that was real good that I can never ever match again. But it was too much. She became very jealous of my music. She wanted me, you know. She didn't want me to have nothin' else. Like I love the music thing and I had started my band by then. And all her friends started telling her what would happen once my band started going out on the road. She started freaking out. She wanted me to give it all up.

It got so weird. I met her husband after they were separated and he'd tell me, ''I feel sorry for you.'' And sometimes I'd want to tell him he was right. But it was good when it was good. I really, really loved her. But she wanted me to give up something that meant a lot to me, and I couldn't.

Now Mary was bisexual. So we had really weird relationships with different people. Mary would be with other women but, you know, I wasn't jealous; a man doesn't get jealous of another woman. But that started me off on a whole trip—being with gay chicks. Makin' it with two women. And I still dig that and I know why. It keeps me from getting too involved with any one woman. I don't want to give myself emotionally to anyone else in life 'cause I've been so fucked over. Everytime I get involved with anybody it always ends up as a hurt. I don't want to hurt and I don't want to get hurt. And it would hurt me if I hurt somebody. I run away now from the single woman who's looking for something heavy. I can spot it thirty miles away. I don't want that.

It's amazing how pairs of gay chicks pick up on me. Like I know two chicks who hitchhiked thousands of miles just to be with me and to hear my band. Whenever the band plays, it happens. I guess I project it. You know, one time I was with six chicks and we all went to bed together. I was the only guy. It sounds like I'm bragging but that's how it was. And it's cool because I'm not threatened. I know I'm not going to get involved. You know, I used to go to the beach with these three chicks all the time and guys would come up to them and try to pick them up. But they'd just say, "Get lost."

Man, I've had chicks who've just wanted me for the scene. And, you know, sometimes I wanted what they had and they wanted what I had and I gave 'em what I had and they gave me what they had. But then it was over. And, you know, different people have different sexual needs and I'm a very flexible person. You haven't seen my whip yet. It's like different strokes for different folks and I go with anything. Some chicks get into physical spankings—but I'm tired of a lot of that. I think I want something a little more normal now. Spankings, whips, chains—all that kinda stuff. I was never into a real pain or blood thing. I can't make that. You know, one time I got into a spanking thing with a little riding whip and I put a bad welt on this girl's leg that lasted for two months. And she was just so proud of that damn thing, man. But I'm not into getting pain. Only if somebody I know wants it, then I do it. I'm an adaptable person to whatever's going down. If you're into tenderness and you want to cry, I'll sit there and let you cry. Whatever.

I think by now I've seen everything there is to be seen. I have friends who are into ponies and dogs and that kinda thing. I've been through every kind of sexual thing, man, you can think of.

Meanwhile, I have one girl now and she's been keeping me at home. She keeps it all straight. And with my new girl, well, I think I just might want to get hooked again. I'm getting tired, tired of the whole scene. It's too much of the same scene and you don't get enough of the one to one. I think I'm falling in love and I didn't think it would happen again. But it's happening. It feels like I'm going back to the beginning, like a circle. I want to try the one to one again.

My piano player, he's married, and ever since we've been going out on tour I've never seen him with a chick. He's never once cheated on his ol' lady. And that to me is the greatest thing in the world. I want that and I can probably do that. Or maybe I can't. You know, I'm a horny old man.

The road kinda keeps you strung out there. You get the urge for new experiences. You're moving, moving, moving, and you want different experiences all the time. We've been cutting an album so we haven't been doing any gigs. Maybe I want all this normal thing now because I've been off the road too long.

LEAVING

Many years ago when we had decided to be divorced, we sat holding hands in the marriage counselor's office. He asked why we wished to separate if we were such good friends. "Just for that reason," we replied cheerily.

from *Changing*
by Liv Ullmann

"Did you ever know, dear, how much you took away with you when you left? You have stripped me even of my past, even of the things we never shared."

from *A Grief Observed*
by C. S. Lewis

Betty and McKay

Betty is twenty-five years old. She's a Phi Beta Kappa graduate from Stanford University. Approximately three months before this interview was conducted, she left the man she'd been living with for the past three years.

It was like a feeling in my body, this lack of love I had for McKay. And I had it all the time, from the minute we started the relationship to the very end of the relationship. It was like a constraint on my heart.

I experience a lot of emotional things in my chest, in the muscles or something. You know, when people talk about feeling things in their heart, well, I would really feel this constraint in my chest muscles, especially when I had to say ''I love you,'' or ''You're good,'' or ''You do good things for me.'' Most of the time I would say those things when he asked me to say them. And that was automatically wrong because I should have said them on my own but I never did.

It's interesting. I don't know how much McKay knew about my not loving him. See, I don't know how much McKay knew because some of the things McKay knows are sort of stopped almost at their inception and are like stored away somewhere. It's really hard for me to know if McKay knew how much I was suffering those last few months. According to him, he really didn't know. He didn't know at all. And that time was the height of that thing—that pain in my chest. It was total constraint.

Now he was doing his own suffering all this time. He was doing his graduate school adjusting trip—not being a renowned personality the way he was as an undergraduate. And that's a hard

thing for me to experience too. I'm used to being a renowned personality. And he was getting people to know him but it took
them a long time. I wasn't able to support him. But these were
things we never discussed. He never said, "Why the hell aren't
you giving me support when I'm having this hard time getting
people to know who I am and love me?"

One of the things that McKay has said to me in one of his more
resentful moments, when he's telling me what a fucker I've
been, was that I never gave him the support he needed. And I
didn't. And I knew it. And I couldn't.

I couldn't give him support because in order to give him
support—support from my heart—I had to first be feeling that I
was close to him. And I wasn't feeling that closeness. I was feeling very distant.

What kept me there? Well there are certain things that people
think they need at different times in their lives. I was thinking
about all this today because of a phone call I had with Angela,
one of McKay's old girl friends and a close friend of mine. And
the way Angela responded to me—at least, the way I interpreted
her response—was, 'Well, it's about time, Betty. It's been three
and a half years. You know, I have nothing more to say. We both
knew what was going on and I have nothing else to say.' So I was
thinking and I had this really bad feeling inside myself. So I went
off walking and I tried to figure out what that feeling was. I knew
it had something to do with that conversation I had with Angela
And I kept thinking, 'OK, if that's what she really thinks—that I
wasted three and a half years by living with McKay and that it's
about time I left him—did I really waste that time? If I knew I was
going to eventually leave, why didn't I just leave?' I had thought
about all this before but it was never very immediate.

And I just think, you know, that at different times people think
that they need different things. And for that period of time I
really felt that I needed McKay to supply me with certain things
—to be my lover and to hold me. I mean, that's a big priority in
my life. It still is. I need to hold someone. I love physical contact.
It's everything to me. It means so much to me.

OK, it means so much to me. I just said that. So if it's every-thing to me, then it was a good enough reason for me to stay with McKay even when I didn't want him. And there were lots of times I really didn't want him at all. I mean long times when I didn't want him. But it still mattered enough to me to have someone to hold, someone who found me attractive, someone who thought I was great and wonderful and who respected me.

Another thing is I really like having a home and I could do that with McKay. You know, I could make a home with him because he was into a home. At later times, though, making a home was pretty much of a bullshit thing. I knew I was going to leave. Like I bought curtains, curtain material, and I never made those cur-tains. I knew I was going to leave and it hurt—wanting to make those curtains but knowing it would be stupid to make them because I knew I was leaving. But I felt I really needed McKay. I'm so intimidated by my physical reality. McKay really cut the intimidation down, really protected me from that stuff, like daddy and mommy. He made everything OK and that was something that was another priority for me. And I think the most important thing was that I had to get to the point where I could believe that I could really have what I thought I wanted and needed in terms of a man. I had to believe that it existed. And I got to the point where I did. And I do. And then I could let go of the old relationship.

I had to believe that if I left McKay there was going to be a man somewhere who was going to be right, someone I wouldn't have any heavy reservations about. And now I believe it. And it took me a long time to believe it. Friends who I saw in good relation-ships made me believe it. And I had an affair that made me believe it. That was like my first hit of brain ecstasy. My brain went crazy, like I couldn't have enough of it. It was like heaven in my brain when I would talk to this man. That was my first hit of real relating and I wanted it. And I knew it wasn't happening with McKay but I didn't know how much it could happen until I met Sean. And then it was so intense. I mean, I couldn't talk enough to Sean. I just couldn't talk enough.

And sex hadn't been too hot between me and McKay for a long time. I could get off on it in a very simple sexual way but the thing about me and McKay was that for the first year and a half of our relationship, the sexual space was our space. It was great. I mean I didn't hold back at all. Then all of a sudden it just stopped. And the reason why it stopped was because I fucked Sean and something clicked inside of me. I never really understood that completely. I felt something I hadn't felt with McKay and that was scary.

On Christmas day I knew I was going to leave. Finis. That was really the first time I knew I was going to do it. And as soon as I knew I was going to do it, there was no turning back—ever— from that moment. I'm willing to give myself a lot of slack because I know that when I finally get around to doing something or feeling something or whatever it is, then I'll do it OK. I'll do it clean. And that's the way I've lived pretty much. And so I'm willing to let myself ride something out as long as I have to until I get to the point where I'm hooked. And so that's how I rode that relationship out. That's what happened. All that time I was just getting closer and closer to leaving and finally the blanks were just filled in and that was it.

It was always there—that feeling of not having a real heavy love for McKay. It was. Always. But now there are times when I hug McKay that that feeling is not there. There are clean hugs now. Like friends.

The best way I can describe the whole thing is how I described it before. It was an expression in my body. My stomach was constricted, my chest was constricted, and hugs—hugs should be reaching outward. But I could be hugging McKay and the energy would not be going out. It would just stay inside of me. And that was the thing, that's what made it so painful.

About three months after Betty was interviewed, we met with McKay. McKay is a twenty-six-year-old MFA candidate at Boston University.

This interview was conducted under slightly strange circumstances. The night before the interview, McKay, without our permission, had gone into our tape files and listened to Betty's tape. (Both Betty and McKay are close friends of ours—so McKay's breaking into our private files was not seen as a criminal act but rather as the easily forgivable and easily understandable behavior of a recently abandoned lover.)

Betty's tape, to put it mildly, devastated McKay. This interview was conducted during a momentary lull in what was an otherwise painful and tearful morning.

Betty's leaving me came as a total surprise. I had just come home from Italy where I'd traveled for a month and I'd been home for only a week. We woke up one morning and we made love and then we were lying together and holding each other. We held each other and then I started fantasizing about a house I'd like to build. I always talked about wanting to build a house and what it would be like—all the ideas I had for it. So I was going through this fantasy, relating it to Betty, and all of a sudden she started to cry. And, you know, I said, "Wow, what's going on?" And she said, "I'm leaving you." And the words just didn't compute in my head. Didn't register at all. There was no way—I couldn't—I didn't believe it.

And she just said, "I'm leaving you." So we were in the bed and it was such a . . . the reality of what she was laying on me was so overwhelming that I couldn't even begin to talk about it, you know, to even ask her why she was leaving me. I couldn't integrate it. It was beyond me. Like sometimes when you think you know what's going on in your reality and then all of a sudden—*smash*—you find something that's totally out of whack with what you thought was happening.

There had never been the slightest mention of Betty ever moving out. Sure there had always been talk about what our relationship wasn't giving her. We always talked about her reservations about the relationship, the lack of communication and all. But we never actually considered not living together.

So finally I asked her that morning why she was leaving and she just said, "Because I can't stay with you, because it isn't right, because I'm not getting what I want."

I don't remember how many hours we stayed together that morning. We talked for a couple of hours. And I knew that she said she was going to leave me but I didn't know exactly what that meant. I didn't know if that meant she was going to leave next week or next month or whether she was going to start looking for a new place. But then she just got up, got dressed, and there—under the bed—were her bags, already packed. And she just said goodbye and that was that. She had already set up a place to live.

Frankly, I've pretty much repressed those first few days. Like they're gone. I have memories, though, of being in a supermarket and having a hard time walking—losing my depth perception, my body being so discorporated and my balance being really terrible and my vision really screwy. Just the weight of it all.

So I dealt with it by not dealing with it. It was too much of a hit at one time. I just said it wasn't real, that Betty would move back with me in a couple of months. I even remember telling people that she'll be moving back with me in a few months. I just believed it was going to work out. I loved Betty and I believed that she was in love with me and that she was interested in us getting back together. And if I hadn't heard her tape, I'd probably still be thinking that way. Even having heard her tape, I still can't totally let go of my love.

See, Betty always complained about our relationship. Essentially what she always said to me was the same thing. "You don't talk to me enough, you don't respond to what I'm thinking and feeling, and you don't tell me what you're thinking and feeling." And I never knew what to do about it. What she really wanted to know was what was I feeling, what were all the different ways I was feeling, what made me feel one way then another. She wanted to know just what was happening with me. But I didn't know what was happening. I just went through my days so unconnected from my feelings. I was obsessed with what I was doing, with my sculpture and classes. Not even that I was so into what I was doing, just that I was so focused on all the things I had to do during the day. So my pattern was really to suppress what I was feeling, to not examine myself that closely. And those were the things—my feelings—that Betty wanted to hear from me. So she kept saying "Talk to me," and I couldn't. I just couldn't talk to her about the things she wanted me to talk about. And the whole situation was always complicated by the pressure I always felt, the pressure that was always there for me to respond.

I never really understood how serious it was. Other than talking, our relationship functioned smoothly. The details of the day-to-day stuff were fine. We had no conflicts with cooking, shopping, cleaning, and our schedules didn't really conflict with each other. And we both relied heavily on the physical presence of one another. Just having someone to love and to hold and to be with and to wake up to. And both of us were very much into the idea of a home.

I don't know how I might have responded to Betty if I'd known how seriously she thought I wasn't giving her what she wanted. I don't know if I could have given her what she wanted even if I understood how badly she wanted it. There were changes I had to go through before I could begin to see what she meant by "really talking to one another." I think it took this whole business of her leaving me to open me up to my feelings and perceptions.

I always accepted that what Betty wanted of me was right, that it was something I should give her. And I always felt inadequate that I couldn't talk to her the way she wanted me to talk to her. I accepted that it was fair for her to be asking for it but I just didn't know how to give her what she wanted. And I never really knew how serious it all was. Not until I listened to her tape.

With hindsight, and I guess this is how it is for a lot of relation-ships, it was the classic case of not enough communication, and this lack of communication started very early on. I say that now, having heard Betty's tape, having heard her say that from the first moment she ever held me she had reservations about me and that she always had the feeling that I wasn't going to be the man she would be with forever. That's hard stuff to hear but I think maybe I'm starting to hear it.

Harriet Kantor

She's a fifty-three-year-old painter who lives alone in Soho—a well known artists' community in Manhattan.

My marriage lasted a long time, twenty-four years. I married a very nice man. He was very good to me, good to the children. Very kind. I suppose one of the problems was that he was as nice as he was. Otherwise I probably would have left him earlier. It was very difficult for me to not want to make it work with him— and I did work very hard at wanting to want it to work.

I never really wanted to get married but my mother expected me to get married. So I got married. I wasn't quite nineteen and then my mother died six months after I got married. I've always felt that for me it would have been wiser not to have gotten married. But it took me about thirty years to act on that. I loved my mother very much and I was very anxious to please her. But she had the usual set of expectations. You know, because I was a girl she felt I just couldn't exist in this world if I wasn't married. I always felt that if she had lived and we could have talked about my frustrations about being married, then I could have left the marriage much sooner. But I had children and that was that.

I remember the day I got married. I told my mother I didn't want to get married and she said, "It's OK. You'll get over that. Everybody feels that way." Only I didn't stop feeling that way.

My husband never objected to anything. He was very passive. He was also very nice. But the nice, I learned, are never just nice. I learned very early that the tyranny of the weak is the most tyrannical, because if you feel in any way morally or ethically connected to the world, then it's very difficult to be rotten to a nice person. When I say Ben was a very nice guy I mean that he was also very weak. But I knew that and I knew that if I was going to get married I'd probably be better off getting married to somebody like him so that I'd be able to be in control of things. I ran the marriage. I decided to have children. He didn't care one way or the other. You know, whatever I did was fine.

I always knew there were gay women but I didn't know who they were, where they lived, or what they looked like. I had an idea I was gay but I wasn't threatened by it because I figured I wasn't going to do anything about it. Not in this lifetime anyway. But I ended up having an affair with a woman fifteen years after I had gotten married. I thought I was safe by then; that I could just have a homosexual affair and that would be that. But I wasn't safe.

I went off one summer to a summer camp. I taught arts and crafts. You know, I wanted my kids to have a summer in the country, so I did this teaching number. Meanwhile, Ben stayed in New York and he'd come up to visit us on weekends. In this summer camp there was a woman who was the drama counselor and she had two boys, like I did, and she was gay. Well, to make a long story short, by the end of the summer we were having an affair.

It became an obsession for me. And honey, it was dynamite. I was thirty-six years old and I was sure that it was not going to happen to me. I was just going to go through my life, children growing up, and living my usual fragmented existence. You know, my art here, my kids there. And I really didn't expect to leave my husband. I figured I'd make some kind of an arrangement with him. I felt I had a commitment to him. I mean, after all, he didn't do anything to me. I did it all. And if I had been really fair to him, I would have left long ago. I should have given him a chance when he still had some kind of self, when he could still make another life for himself. So I was not going to break it up with Ben just because I fell in love with this woman.

Well, it was a great summer. The kids were all in their own bunks and we had our own rooms. I was getting all the vibrations from her at the beginning of the summer but I wasn't giving them back. I thought it just wasn't my thing. I figured not me. I had gay male friends and they used to kid me that thirty-five was the cutoff point: that by the time I was thirty-five I was going to be gay.

Anyhow we started this affair and I was like . . . well, the world had opened up. I was ready to take off into the sunset with her. I was obsessed by the relationship. She was in love with me and I was in love with her. We had it made. Each of us had two children and each of us had husbands so we could socialize together in our heterosexual life. And we even started working together.

I was living in the Bronx and she was living only five minutes away. It was the ultimate, ideal situation. Nobody ever suspects women, particularly when they're mothers. I mean *lesbian mothers* is a contradiction in terms. So as soon as the kids were off to school, I'd go over to Shirley's house and we'd get into bed and we wouldn't get out of bed until three in the afternoon. This went on for practically five years, five years of straight fucking. We were inseparable. It was just five dynamite years. It was like the ultimate escape. Tahiti.

But Shirley was a very sick woman and it fed right into my own neuroses. Our neuroses dovetailed beautifully. First of all, she would only have affairs with mothers. You know, because mothers would understand that she wasn't going to leave her children. And secondly, her needs were overwhelming. When Shirley met me she was trying to stop being homosexual and her therapist was trying to help her do that. In those days that's what it was all about—you know, everything stems from your being gay and that's the cause of all your neuroses.

Now when she met me she thought I had been gay. She was floored when she found out that I had never had any homosexual experiences. She really thought I was going to be a role model for her, someone who could show her how to lead two lives—being gay and being married.

I knew for a long time that there were women who I was in love with but I thought that was perfectly legitimate. It's interesting—I never had any guilt feelings about my sexuality. No shame. No feelings that anything I was doing was wrong. No nothing. I mean I had been seduced when I was ten years old by my grandmother's boarder, a man. We had an affair for six months. Of course, it wasn't an affair. I was too little. But I loved it, I loved it. I kept going back for more. I was being molested and I only stopped it when he tried to penetrate me. He was forty. So I was highly sexual—always—and I never had any hang-ups.

With Shirley the sex was dynamite. And interestingly, it was always good with Ben. In fact, the only time that I ever stopped having sex with Ben was when the whole thing with Shirley was breaking up. But that's when I stopped having sex with anybody. I was a virgin when I got married and Ben was a wonderful sexual partner. He was patient. He was the most gentle, the most considerate, the most involved lover. But that didn't make me think I loved him—it just made me think that he was a marvelous lover. I can't blame Ben one bit. It wasn't his fault. As a matter of fact, I feel badly because I took twenty-five years out of his life.

What made it so difficult for me to leave the marriage were the expectations of women in our society. They're incredible. And in my early life I was a classic example of someone who suffered from those expectations. Nobody made me do anything and yet the societal thing made me do all the things I didn't want to do: marry, have kids. It was an incredible oppression in that it was so unnoticeable. It was so fucking invisible. I look back on it now and I see all the things I said to myself—I can't leave my husband, my kids. Well, I can only blame myself and I really can't blame myself. I grew up in a society that had so many expectations.

In my relationship with Shirley I was the aggressor. It was the first time she ever had a relationship with a woman where the other woman was the aggressor. Now I'm not a butch in the traditional, old role-playing but I've always been an aggressive woman. I was an aggressive woman with my husband.

Anyway, in the last year of our relationship Shirley started having an affair with another woman—a woman who had cancer.

Now when this whole thing with Shirley and the woman with cancer was going on, well, I said to Shirley, "You're falling in love with her. Be careful." I was pushing Shirley hard, too hard, to get out of that relationship. I think unconsciously I wanted to get out of the relationship myself. It was eating me up. It was too obsessive. It was so intense—and I really couldn't do anything except be in the relationship. It was like an addiction. But, you know, how could I reject this thing that I needed so badly. The only way to do it was for me to set it up for Shirley to reject me. Which, of course, is what happened.

The relationship was zapping me of my work and it was painful—a lot of it. I would feel that if I wasn't with her then she would disappear. That's painful. So I literally had to touch her, I felt, to hold on to her all the time.

Both our husbands were the most passive guys in the world. Neither of them ever said anything, but they suspected. They had to. But both of us were hooked. It was crazy. I couldn't believe it. I mean here I was in my late thirties. I mean, for Christ's sake, there was a part of me that was always saying, 'What are you doing?' You know, 'What are you doing with yourself?'

So the split with Shirley was absolutely horrendous for me. I was so obsessed that I wanted out. I didn't want to continue it on a part-time basis. But I couldn't let go of it. I was unutterably saddened by the breakup. I just couldn't work it out. I was hysterical. I was a mess, a mess for a year.

And I'll tell you something interesting in regard to Ben. Before I left for camp one summer—I went with Shirley every summer to camp—Ben said to me that he got a call and the caller said I was having an affair with Shirley. And Ben accused me of it. This was just about the time when Shirley and I were breaking up, and he knew it. He could hear us arguing on the phone. So I denied it. I totally denied everything. I figured—'Fuck you, Ben. If you don't have the guts to tell me straight on—I mean this bullshit about some mysterious person who's making telephone calls.' So I said, "No way, buddy." I just denied the whole thing. I said he was crazy. I was furious. I pushed all the guilt buttons. I

.said, "How dare you." I had no guilt about lying to him. I figured if he was going to be dishonest then I sure as hell wasn't going to level with him. Ben picked a time when I was weakest to tell me about it. If he had done it when I was feeling strong about the relationship with Shirley, then I could have told him, you know, 'If you don't like it, then leave.' So he really tried to get me when I was down, wiped out, when Shirley and I were splitting up, and he knew that. But eventually Ben just backed off and assumed his usual passive role.

I was forty years old and so vulnerable and very isolated. Abandoned. Shirley broke it off with me and we didn't see each other ever again. I did a real cold turkey withdrawal.

A year after the break with Shirley I had an affair with another woman. And at that point when Ben accused me of it I admitted it. And I also told Ben at that point that he better get himself together because the kids were growing up and while we might live together, I was going to do my own thing and he better get used to it. I told Ben I was going to continue this affair I was having with Paula and I told him that I didn't intend to hurt him. I was really at this point no longer angry with him. I was just going to do whatever it was I wanted to do.

But Ben continued to give me a hard time and I told him he'd better stop, otherwise I'd leave. But in a few months he was beside himself with fury about it because I was obviously doing what I wanted to do. He was so threatened. He knew that if he said stop, I'd just say forget it. So he told our older son all about me being gay and we had this great big drama in our foyer in the Bronx. It was Ben's last attempt to keep me cool. Ben wanted me to stop running around with women. He knew *he* couldn't make me stop but he thought maybe our son could.

There I was, up against the wall, and Rob standing in the doorway of the kitchen and Ben standing in the doorway beyond the archway to the living room. And I said to Ben at that point, "You blew it. You blew it." I said to him that the only reason I was staying with him was that there was no reason for me to leave. The children didn't ever have to know. We could just go

on doing what we'd always done. So I said, "But you blew it."
Meanwhile, Rob is saying to Ben, "What kind of a man are you
that you'd stay in a marriage when you knew that your wife was
homosexual?" Instead of getting support from Rob, Ben's plan
was backfiring. Of course, Rob was furious about me but not as
furious as he could have been because it wasn't a man I was sleeping around with. He wasn't as threatened as he would have been
if I'd been with a man.

Well, what's happened is that Ben's now living with his
mother and we have absolutely no communication. He's extremely bitter.

You know, what I really remember about that whole period of
my life was that I was shocked to see how many married women
were gay. It fucking blew my mind. I didn't think anyone ever
got married who was gay. I mean, as sophisticated as I was, I
knew that there might be some gay married women around but I
thought I had an idea of who they were: They were wealthy, very
upper middle class, very sophisticated, very cultured. But I'd go
to a gay bar and there'd be all these women from Great Neck
there with their teased hair and all the rest. I mean it blew my
fucking mind. The stereotype I had was of some chic types being
able to do both—be married and be gay. But I never thought it
was going to be all these middle-class ladies from Queens. I mean
it was just unreal. I remember walking into a gay bar on Four-
teenth Street in the old days and seeing the women with the
blond-tipped hair and the diamonds. It blew my mind.

Barbara Hankins

When we asked her how old she was, Barbara responded, "I'm going to say fortyish and leave it at that." In the twentieth year of her marriage she decided she "wanted out." This interview took place only three months after her divorce came through.

Barbara is a bank teller in a small town in southern New Hampshire.

I feel very bitter, very resentful about it. Right now I can't even remember the good years. But there were a lot of them. Lately, though, they've been very bad years. Say, in the last four years. The divorce was a very hard decision for me to make. We had separated one other time and then had gotten back together again.

My husband has a drinking habit that's gone from bad to worse. Economics also had a lot to do with it. We used to have a lot of money and I think it was mainly through his drinking that he lost his business. His drinking affected everything. He became very moody, abusive, both mentally and physically. He'd do things to get me upset. He'd yell and scream at the kids. His mood would change from one hour to the next, from really up to really down.

I went back to work after not working, after not having to work. I went back to work about two years ago. When we first got married, I worked for the six years before we had our son. Then we waited four more years and we had our daughter. All planned children. And back years ago you didn't really plan for it to happen. But these two were planned. So when the kids were older and in school, I went back to work. It was all okay when I was looking for work, but when I actually got the job I think my husband resented it because before I was more or less dependent on him. I think he sort of resented me being out among people, dressed up to go out.

We'd have fights. I'd have the cops coming down and I took him to court twice for assault and battery. I pressed charges. I was all black and blue. He'd do all this when he was drunk. When he wasn't drinking he was a completely different person. It just affected his whole personality, his outlook on everything. A Jekyll and Hyde personality.

Our son got sick four years ago. He had a very serious illness, Hodgkin's disease. He had several major operations and spent a whole summer undergoing radiation treatments in Boston. His father would take him down daily, drive from here to Boston daily. And that was a drain on us emotionally and financially. He's much better now—he's been in remission for several years now—but when he was ill, the way I coped with it, I guess was the way my ex-husband accused me of coping with it, was shutting myself off, going into a shell. And he coped with it by drinking more. To me, that was the beginning of everything going downhill. I felt that he took our son for his treatments out of duty, not out of love.

We separated almost a year ago. I went to court, had a restraining order against him and so forth, and he was told to move out of the house which he did.

I wasn't certain I wanted a divorce. I hadn't made up my mind. But I was certain we had to separate and sort things out for a while. I had lived in this town all my life. I know everyone in town—lawyers, policemen. I know just about everybody. At first, it was embarrassing. You know, dial 911 and have a cop arrive at the door that I'd known for years, that I'd gone to school with, that I'd gone out with. That was my initial feeling. You know, embarrassment. My husband, too, was from this area so he knew, more or less, everyone from town. But as I said, as time went on, it didn't matter if I was embarrassed at being separated or being embarrassed at having his name in the paper for going to court for assault and battery. It was just something I couldn't take any longer. And so we separated last summer.

We'd get together once in a while and he'd *visit,* in quotation marks, and we'd end up fighting and then he'd leave. And I'd say, "OK, *we're* having problems but at least keep in touch with the kids." Well, he didn't seem to want that. When he was mad at me he was just mad. Period. And I could tell that he was drinking all the time.

He had a truck that he had in his business and we had a real nice LTD station wagon that I used for work. I kept it up. It was my pride and joy. If there was some little thing wrong, I'd run and have it repaired. So to sort of keep me in control after he'd get mad at me, he'd come down and take the car. That was his way of saying, 'You're dependent on me, you don't have this car, you can't go to work, you can't do this, you can't go shopping and so forth.' All I would use it for was to go to work and to come home. Other than that the car would just stay here. Well, the last time—I think it was back in September—it was the straw that broke the camel's back. He came down here, got mad at something or other, and took the car. The next morning I called and said, "Can I have the car back? I gotta go to work and both our kids have dentist appointments that I made like six months ago." He says, "No. You're not getting the g.d. car back. It's your problem." So I said, "Fine. You sit there in your motel room and you look at that g.d. car and that truck and you decide which one you're going to drive." And I think it was that day that I called my lawyer and said, "OK, I've had it. File for divorce."

I'm not saying it was all his fault. I can be very stubborn. But I just got to the point where I couldn't take anymore. There was no more point in discussing because it wasn't a discussion—it was a fight. So finally I said to my lawyer, "You know, that's it. I want the divorce."

My ex-husband was totally shocked, totally unprepared for that move. I think he expected that in the end I'd probably take him back as I had done one other time. He called me and wanted to talk to me but I just said I'd had it, that my mind was made up. It was a very difficult decision but once I made the decision, I realized it was right. I just plain didn't want anything to do with him. And on top of everything, he smashed up that beautiful LTD. He'd been drinking and it was icy and he smashed it up. Totally demolished it.

One day the kids came home from school and they could tell that my ex-husband had been in the house. He still had a key. I should have changed the locks but I didn't. So the kids came home and found these things smashed, sentimental things—a picture of my dad, something my daughter had made me, and snapshot albums. He ripped out pages in our album, pictures of our several trips to Bermuda and the Virgin Islands, places we went in our better days. Things thrown around, glass on pictures smashed, and it was all done on my birthday and all done so consciously. He took his foot and smashed in our radiator units in the bedroom. Plus, he left his calling card, a beer can, on the table, so I'd know it was him.

The phone would ring late at night and I'd pick it up and nobody would be there or else somebody was breathing on the other end. One time I remember he called up and we had a fight and then he purposefully left his phone off the hook so that the connection could not be broken. Know what I mean? So here I was all night long with no telephone—another way of him stranding me. The telephone company ended up fixing it the next day. That's the sort of thing he would do.

Recently I found out that he's moved out of his motel room and that he's found himself a lady friend who he's moved in with. So here I am left with all these financial problems, with the two kids, and he's going merrily on his way, living with this dame. I'm screwed, to put it bluntly. He sends me forty dollars a week which you can't even walk up two aisles in the supermarket with. So I'm left with all the bills, all the problems, and having to support myself and our two kids.

I think the divorce itself has made me a stronger person. It's certainly made me more determined, liberated, if you want to use that word. More outgoing. I can kid with men now. I can make remarks and have remarks made at me. I've even been propositioned a few times.

I'm not a superstitious person but this house is a jinx. From the minute we moved into it we had problems. So I think once I move out of here and resettle in an apartment things gotta get better. They gotta get better. How could they get worse? Here I am—I've lost a marriage, I lost a house, I lost financial security which had always been important to me. I feel that once I move out and get the kids and myself settled that things will go forward. I've thought of joining Parents Without Partners and those sort of organizations. But just now I'm not ready to tackle anything. I have to get all this bitterness and hurt out of me and get out of this house and then maybe I'll be ready for something.

Right now the way I feel, I don't think I'll ever get married again. It just doesn't appeal to me now. I hope I find somebody I can care about or maybe love. Now, though, I'd live with a man before I'd marry him. When I told my seventy-year-old mother that, it totally shocked her. But I would, I really would.

Once I made the decision to get divorced, it was a big relief. Never once have I questioned if I did the right thing or not. I'm positive I did the right thing. I just couldn't go on in that situation any longer. And I'm sure if we had gotten together again it would have just kept on happening.

So I'm happier now. Not happy, but happier. But sometimes I feel like here I am—I'm single—I'm free to do all these things. But there's nobody to do them with.

Robert Boyd

He's thirty-seven and lives in Chicago. At the time of this interview he was emotionally disengaging himself from a man he'd been in love with for the past five years.

I was always a whore at heart. I didn't ever want a permanent relationship. I'd have little flings but I would always run if I thought someone was getting too attached to me. I just didn't want it—a long-term relationship. Too many complications. I'd seen too many friends who'd been through traumatic affairs. I had friends who'd buy houses and cars and furniture together and I said, "I'm never going to get to the point where I have to saw the sofa in two if we split up." You know, "The dog is mine, the cat's yours." But I think as you grow older you change and in my early thirties I met this man and I did all the things I said I'd never do—namely, fall in love, especially fall in love with a married man.

I think in your teens, in your twenties, your outlook is different. You're younger and you call the shots more or less. But when you're thirty, you think differently. So when the right person came along, I was ripe for it.

A house guest of mine picked Jim up in a bar and brought him home. We met the next morning, and over a period of months we started falling in love with one another. Jim was married and had three kids, and I accepted the fact that he was married. I knew all along what I was getting into and I knew he had no intention of ever leaving his family. And with his position—Jim was a big executive with one of the airlines—he needed a wife.

Jim hadn't come out until he was thirty-five years old, out of his closet or whatever. I was his first serious homosexual affair but not the first man he ever went to bed with. And his wife was always aware of his homosexual tendencies.

In the beginning, Doris, Jim's wife, was jealous but she controlled it very well. There were times when I'd be a little jealous, too, but over the years I've come to love her, love her the way you'd love a sister. She and Jim and I even had sex together once and all of us have traveled throughout Europe together.

Jim traveled all over the world in his work. I lived in San Francisco and so he'd come to visit me twice a month. That would be like our honeymoon. Occasionally, Doris would come along and I accepted her. I wasn't jealous of her coming along. Of course, I loved Jim more because I'm homosexual but I always felt she was a very wise woman. She sometimes would say, ''I think you two need a night out. I have things to do.'' She'd actually insist that we go out together alone.

Anyway, a few months back, Jim expressed to me that he was against my moving to Chicago—where I was planning on opening a restaurant. In San Francisco I had my own house and an OK business. For Jim, San Fransicso was really a little oasis. He could go to the finest restaurants, know all the waiters by name, and be given the best tables. Or we'd go to the swim club with a rooftop solarium and bask in the sun. We'd be invited to dinner at the beautiful houses with the beautiful people. Jim had this idea that some day he was going to retire and move to San Francisco and we'd be together.

Well, one day I realized that maybe I was fooling myself, that even though I loved this man I couldn't stay in San Francisco, planning on his eventually coming to live with me. I realized that it might not happen or if it did happen it wouldn't be for a long time. And I had this good opportunity in Chicago that I couldn't afford to let go of.

He came through Frisco a few months back and stayed with me for five days and four nights. And during that time, right before I left for Chicago, the last night he was there, we were out at a bar and against my wishes he went home with some other people. We'd met these people in the bar and they wanted to go

home and have a fivesome, but I wanted no part of it. I didn't like
them, physically or anything. And it was the last night Jim was
going to be in town, so I wanted to be alone with him. Jim and I
had had threesomes and foursomes before, but it was just the last
night we'd be together and after that night I wouldn't be seeing
him for a long time.

We did manage to have sex once before he left and a few days
later I came down with gonorrhea. I hadn't been to bed with anyone else so I knew it had to be him. Well, when I went to the
health clinic, two of the guys who Jim had gone home with that
night were there and they both had the clap. Jim had obviously
given it to them.

On top of the clap I also developed a bladder infection. So
there I was—sick in bed—and in the meantime this letter arrived
for Jim in care of me. I opened the letter and I guess when you
read other people's mail you get what you deserve. It was a love
letter. There I was with a fever, nausea, I couldn't work, and here
are these love letters from someone else. I had asked Jim the day
before he left if there was anyone else. I sort of felt there might be.
I knew that distance didn't make the heart grow fonder. But he
denied it. Then two days later these love letters started arriving.

I called him. I was so angry. I told him he'd given me the clap,
and I told him about the letters. He said he'd only met the man
once or twice and that this man must be in love with him. Then,
after that, I wrote Jim a very nasty, mean letter. I told him I
thought he was running scared and trying to live in two different
worlds and that he wasn't being honest. Finally, I called Jim and
said, "Look. I've vented my anger," and he said, "Well, I have
too." And since then I've received letters and cards from him
saying there's too much love, too many beautiful memories—
Madrid, Paris, Rome—and that we said these things in anger and
now they're said and done with. About all the accusatory things I
said to Jim, about his being dishonest and lying, well, he said
they were probably all true but he just didn't want to hear them
from me.

I still love the man but I'm more realistic now. Our relationship just isn't the same anymore. I can see flaws in Jim that I never would admit before. Jim's very selfish really. He was carrying on a relationship with a wife, a lover on the side, and boyfriends in every port. I realize now, too, that we probably won't ever live together but we'll be friends always. You just don't give up when there's so much. But I'll be more realistic in the future. I know I have my life now and he has his.

Bernice

She's sixty-eight years old and lives alone in Manhattan. Her expensive upper East Side apartment—parquet floors, billowy drapes, oriental carpets—has been her home for the past twenty-five years.

"How my marriage ended," she told us, "is such a strange story."

My husband was a quiet man, introverted. He lived on his own little island. He was one of those passive guys who just went along with things. We had no terrific struggles, no real money problems. It was a placid sort of life. But we didn't communicate. We never seemed to reach each other when we talked. He was almost like a stranger to me. And he wasn't quite impotent but he was not good sexually. The minute he got into bed with me, he was like a jack rabbit. The man would be on and off of me. There would be no playing. I never had an orgasm with him. My sex life was practically ruined by him.

He was a very secretive man, very repressed, very passive—in business, with his emotions, in sex. And I was the type of woman who wanted an aggressive, successful husband. I wanted my husband to be at the top of his field. But Paul just didn't have that certain push that men have, that bit of larceny, skullduggery, whatever you want to call it. He was so low-key, so terribly withdrawn.

There was a real sense of monotony living with him. I wanted someone who was stronger. I wanted someone who would make decisions for me. I was always the decision maker. I was always the social arbiter. I made all our plans. We never went on vacations together. He'd always say he was too busy. The result was that I never went on any vacations—never the islands, never Europe, never anything.

I married him because everyone was getting married and it was the thing to do. It wasn't like it is today. I can't really say that I was ever madly in love with him. But, you know, things happen and after a while you accept it. I even thought of leaving the marriage after a few years. I told my mother but she brainwashed me out of it. She said, "Who's gonna grab you if you leave him? You're an old lady." I was thirty-three at the time. So I stayed.

After we'd been married for many years, I started a romance. I needed something to spice things up. This was probably in the fifteenth year of my marriage. And it was exciting. It was like forbidden fruit. Call it what you want, it made me a happier person. I'd have to do a little lying and a little maneuvering but I had steady help so I was as free as a bird. I'd meet this man in the afternoons but I'd always be home for dinner. The affair went on for more than twenty years, and it helped me get through my marriage.

There's a story I have to tell you. My husband and I had been to a party, and coming home from the party, we were in a car. I think I must have said something about one of my husband's friends who was at the party. To this day I don't know what exactly I said. Well, my husband turned around and he started to pummel me. Maybe we had a few drinks, maybe we didn't. But there was nothing I could have possibly said to excite him that way.

The man had been so locked up all his life that he didn't know how to get his temper out. He didn't know how to explode—even a little bit. And this was the first time he ever really hit me, the first time in more than twenty-five years of marriage. And I said, "Let me out of this car." I remember hurrying out of the car and going to my sister's house which happened to be nearby. The next morning, this was Saturday morning, I went home. My son had gone out. It was a gray, foggy day—terrible. My husband was in the bedroom sleeping. The blinds were drawn. I went into the bedroom and got out of my clothes. Then I took a look at my husband and I immediately said to our maid, "I don't like the way Paul looks." She said, "Leave him alone, he's sleeping." I looked again . . . and . . . he was dead. A heart attack. Now the thing I was thinking at that moment—and I wasn't being dramatic—was that if I had gone home with him that previous night, with his temper or whatever he was going through, then I'm sure he would have taken me with him.

We were both so locked up emotionally. I know that's what killed him. My husband was corroding inside. Somehow, something that night possessed me to get out of the car. We'd never slept a night apart before that. But I just knew something wasn't right. It was like years of rage had swelled up inside him. Maybe he knew about my affair, maybe he didn't. But if he did, he never once spoke to me about it.

Neither of us ever talked to anybody. I led my own little life. I was slightly alcoholic, too, throughout my married life. And it's only been afterward, with friends, that I've been able to unburden myself of some of what I went through.

Virginia

After eighteen years of marriage, Virginia separated from her husband. She's thirty-eight.

We always had a hot and cold marriage. It would either be high or very low. Some of that has to do with the fact that my husband is a very independent person and I'm a very, very dependent person.

I was very strictly brought up. My father was born and raised in Italy and as a result I was brought up very sheltered. I went from one sheltered environment to another—from the sheltered environment of my parents to the sheltered environment of my husband. And my husband comes from a very bad background. His mother left when he was thirteen years old and he hasn't seen her since. He was not shown love as a child and in order to show love you have to be given love.

In the beginning there were letters from him when he was in the service that really showed love and desire and understanding. Maybe I leaned on him and he leaned on me because we came from these backgrounds that were less than perfect. Maybe that's how our relationship developed. Anyway, we got married. I was twenty, he was twenty-one. And a year later, I got pregnant . . . unexpectedly.

I was always trying to be perfect in his eyes. I just loved him so much. I would do anything to please him. And that's not so good because maybe, without my realizing it, he began to step on me. Being so naive or immature, you just don't see these things. I really lent everything I had to the relationship. I always tried to look my best, I'm a good cook, I kept a spotless house, I'm comparatively well-spoken, and I work as an executive secretary so I was in tune to what was going on outside the household world at that time—totally interested in his welfare, divorcing myself from my welfare to give him what he needed. When he'd spend evenings out entertaining clients there would be rare times when he'd come home and he'd talk about them with me, about pressures of his work, etcetera. I used to thrive on his coming home at one, two, three o'clock in the morning and talking about his evening. That used to be my whole life really, when he would come home and talk to me.

The main thing in my husband's life was always to be successful because he came from a family where money was spent on other women and clothes for his father, who prided himself on being well-dressed. The money was never there for the kids to go to the doctor or to go to college, but it was always there for that new suit of clothes. So eventually, after his first couple of years of working on Wall Street, my husband began making an awful lot of money for an average boy with no college degree who came from a poor background. By the time he was in his late twenties he was making $32,000 a year—and for him this was a stupendous amount of money. But making the money was a constant strain on him. He was constantly wining and dining clients. He'd come home late every night of the week. I remember him coming home from work and me luring him into bed because I didn't want him to go out that night.

All the pressure and tension led to us having heavy arguments. Twice he hit me out of total frustration. And I remember him crying once after he hit me. He'd sometimes drink a lot too, coming home with too much under his belt. So things were difficult, and added to that was my mistrusting him. I guess I always had a basic mistrust of men. When we'd been married for only two months I wondered if he was playing around with someone else. But in the beginning he was very wonderful about reassuring me. So I began to trust and then he began to go the other way. I think he started his indiscretions when our son was about four or five years old. At that point I only had suspicions. I never had anything to put my finger on. As a result, if he walked in at four in the morning, I'd curse him at the door and walk back into the bedroom. But that's all I could do because I didn't know anything else. . . . I can't believe it was all my fault. Sure, in the beginning I had a basic mistrust, but I think it goes much deeper than that. I think it was a total insecurity within himself, wanting to show himself and his family and his friends how much he could do. An ego thing.

There was one woman, Melissa, with whom I discovered he had a deep involvement. She was very, very attractive. I remember wondering then but never knowing. I remember one afternoon I was preparing for a dinner party and I looked like death warmed over—my hair was still in curlers, I was hanging starched curtains in the kitchen, setting the table, just doing a million things in preparation for the dinner party that evening— and in walks this impeccably dressed young woman with nobody to think about except herself. And I just thought . . . I kind of thought but I didn't know. I didn't present it to my husband because I would have been called everything in the book. 'How dare you accuse me! What's the matter with you.' He even said to me a couple of months ago, "I got away with it because you allowed me to." His indiscretions became *my* fault in his eyes.

We had a three-week separation once when our son was five or six years old. He had walked out and then he came back three weeks later saying, "I don't know why I do this," crying, "Please take me back, forgive me." He wined and dined and romanced me. "Please let's try it over again." I loved him so much that, you know, I just took him back. I loved this man.

When the stock market broke in 1969, he went from making $30,000 a year to making $6,000 or $7,000. He was with a firm that went into bankruptcy. Jimmy did absolutely no business that year. Finally, he left the brokerage business three years later and those couple of months while he was unemployed I can remember as being the happiest months of my life. He wasn't working, he wasn't so compulsive, and there was lots of closeness between the two of us at that time. We were very open with each other. I was backing him one hundred percent in whatever he wanted to do. I remember telling him, "Jimmy, I don't want the world. I just want another child. I just don't want Bobby to grow up alone.'' I was always involved in what he was doing. I wanted to know everything. I only wanted love from this man. Nothing else.

I'll tell you what I really wanted out of life. I wanted another child and I wanted to move out of our small apartment. I wanted to buy a little house. That's all I wanted. I wasn't looking for diamonds, furs, all the things he gave me. It didn't have to be a grand house that was paid for in cash, which was the only way he would ever buy a house. I just wanted something small, simple. But the type of goals he set for himself were unreachable, not a step at a time type of thing. It was always hot and heavy.

Anyway, he started working as a manager for a bar and grill. He began working twelve to sixteen hours a day, and because the restaurant was quite a ways from here, he'd stay overnight a lot. It was during this time that he met this gal who was a barfly. And it was also right about this time that I got pregnant. To be very blunt, I put a hole in my diaphragm. I really wanted another child. I don't know if Jimmy knows that now—about the diaphragm—but he knows I did something. They say a lot about women who try to have children to save their marriages. Whether or not I was trying to keep the marriage together, I don't know. I really don't think I was doing it for that reason. I knew that the marriage would always be hot and cold.

When Jimmy found out I was pregnant, he wanted me to have an abortion. I found out I was pregnant in July and I didn't tell him until September. I wanted the baby. I told him about it one morning in September and that night he came home drunk and told me he wanted a divorce. He kept on insisting on an abortion and I wouldn't have it and I almost thought he was going to blow his mind. He said he couldn't handle the responsibility. He felt he wouldn't live to be fifty. He said how could he have a child. You know, by the time the child would be fifteen years old, he'd be fifty. But there was nothing wrong with his health and up until then he'd always been very responsible.

Frankie was born on his father's birthday. I called Jimmy from the hospital when I was ready to have the baby. He wasn't there when I delivered but he did manage to get there when he finished work. During the pregnancy I cried a lot. Jimmy wanted nothing to do with the baby, nothing to do with even naming the baby. There were times that he never came home during that period, weekends when he'd be away. He'd just walk out to stop an argument and not return.

I brought the baby home from the hospital and Jimmy would have very little to do with him. Sometimes I'd go out at night and leave the baby with him, but he showed very little interest in the child. Jimmy finally moved out about six months after Frankie was born, and during those six months we didn't make love once.

When he first moved out I wanted so much to still be a part of his life. I think I still do. And that was more than two years ago.

Later on I found out that Jimmy had moved in with this barfly. She was just a woman who I guess didn't think anything of walking into a cocktail lounge and picking up a man. I found out about all this through a mutual friend. I called this friend on the phone and I told him that I knew he knew what was going on and that I had to know. I told him I knew I was putting him in a very bad position but I told him that he was the only person who could help me. So the next day he came over and he spent the whole afternoon with me and he told me the whole thing.

Well, two weeks after I found out I arranged to meet Jimmy and talk. He agreed and we went to a cocktail lounge. You have no idea how much I planned this. We sat down—this was about a year after Frankie was born—and Jimmy ordered me a drink. My first question to him was—and it was a dumb question—"Jimmy, are you involved with anyone?" He looked straight into my eyes and said, "No way." So I said, "OK, Jimmy. Let's try it a different way." I said, "Let's play chess." We used to play chess. "I'm going to make the first move." And I said to him, "Betty McArthur?" I gave him her address, her telephone number, her background. He put his eyes down and didn't say anything for a few moments and finally we began to talk and we sat there until about four o'clock in the morning. I wasn't nervous, I was very calm. Maybe because I had the upper hand.

I gave him an ultimatum. I said, "I'm giving you two months to decide what you want to do. If you can't give me satisfaction one way or the other, I'm going to file suit for divorce." But there was no way I wanted to file suit for divorce.

The few weeks after I found out about Betty McArthur I was hysterical. One evening I took my wedding portrait and broke it. As a result, my son suspected that something had happened and he was questioning me. When I told him, he cried. He was totally, totally disenchanted with his father. He couldn't cope with the fact that his father was anything less than perfect. It was like flying off a building for him.

Jimmy's still living with this Betty McArthur. I've asked him if he feels this thing with her is a lasting relationship. His answer to me was, "No, I never thought it was going to be a relationship." My husband's a totally independent person. He likes to do his own thing and I'm sure he's just going to do his own thing whether or not the woman he's involved with wants him to or not.

I've joined several organizations through which I've met some people. I began entertaining friends again, which is another move in the right direction. But after eighteen years of marriage it's very hard for me to go to a social gathering alone.

I feel now that I really want an in-depth relationship. I need it. But I'm very frightened, still very frightened. I still cry. I don't cry half as much as I used to, but I have not made a real break with my husband. If I had made a break, I would have filed the divorce papers a long time ago. I don't know. I don't know if I really want a divorce. If I met someone that I could have a good relationship with, possibly that could help me make the break. But for now I know I still want my husband.

To be truly honest, if I were to threaten him with divorce proceedings and that didn't frighten him, if he didn't protest and the divorce was actually to go through and he married this woman—that is my fear, the terror of the total break. I think I'd just die.

Florence

Florence is forty-four and has been a widow for four years. She has two teen-age daughters. She spends much of her time counseling women whose husbands have recently died.

I was married to Barry for seventeen years before he got sick. Both of us had already graduated from college and were teaching when we met. We were both high school English teachers. We went together for about six weeks and then we got engaged. We had both gone out with enough other people so it didn't take very long for us to decide that we loved each other. And that was that.

The funny thing was that all the fights and the squabbles and the things that are supposed to happen during the first year of marriage never happened to us. We had no trouble adjusting. It was mostly an intellectual attraction at first because we talked more than we did anything else. We talked for hours and hours and hours. He was someone I knew I could spend the rest of my life with because I'd never be bored. It wasn't the kind of thing that was this mad, fantastic, physical attraction. I really don't think I ever had that with Barry. Not that it wasn't a satisfying relationship sexually, it was. It just wasn't the grand passion where you're constantly on fire.

Barry was a very easygoing person. One problem we had was that I could never get him to fight. That was very frustrating. I have the kind of temperament where an explosion every once in a while is necessary. I blow up all over the place, get everything off my chest, and feel a whole lot better. But I could never get Barry to fight back. He'd say, "You finish whatever you have to say and when you get finished, I'll talk to you."

About the last year or so that he was teaching, he began to have problems with his classes. He was complaining that the kids were getting rotten. He said that he wanted to stop teaching and he started going to school at night to become a librarian. Right before he went into the hospital, he started the school year—teaching his English classes—and I don't know exactly what happened but his supervisor took him out of the classroom one day and said that he wasn't able to cope with the classes. I later learned that one of the symptoms of a brain tumor is that you stop being able to cope with things. You sort of start to ignore everything. He would come home from school and go to sleep and just be out for the night.

The school suggested he might be in a depression and they sent him to a psychiatrist. He'd never seen one before. The psychiatrist finally decided that it might be a good idea for him to be in the hospital because after a month things weren't really changing. So he went in as a psychiatric patient. He was in there for about two weeks and the neurologist and the psychiatrist examining him said that his problem wasn't mental, that his reactions were normal and that it wasn't a depression but there seemed to be a physical cause. So he started having some very unpleasant tests and the doctors discovered something they said was about the size of a walnut right on the outside of the brain, something they could peel right off and then that would be the end of it. So he very happily signed all the consent forms and we figured this was better than having mental problems, that he would be operated on and everything would be fine. I figured this was the easy way out and that he would soon be well. Foolishly, all my worries were allayed.

Before the surgery, I remember we felt that we were helping each other prepare for it. I sat by his side that whole night before the surgery and held his hand while he tried to sleep. We talked about what things we were going to do after the operation was over and how this was going to make everything better. He wouldn't be sleeping as much as he had been, so we'd have more time together. We had all kinds of plans about the things we were going to be able to do. We talked about being able to go to the theater and museums, which we both loved, and that we would go away on weekends and leave the kids with my parents. That was going to be a reunion. Well, that was one reunion we didn't have.

He never came home. He was in the hospital for ten months. The surgeon came down after surgery and said to me, "It's a massive brain tumor. We removed as much of it as we could but we couldn't take it all out. It would have meant removing almost all of his brain. It's terminal."

I was in a complete state of shock. The doctor met me in the lobby of the hospital. Everybody was coming and going all around me and he just told me that flat out and then left me there. Fortunately, I had somebody with me. Otherwise, I think I would have just passed out on the floor and that would have been the end of me.

Barry was in a coma and they never expected him to come out of it. So at that point, as far as I was concerned, he was dead. But what happened was he did wake up from the coma within twenty-four hours and although he wasn't able to speak, he was alert enough to pick out letters on a blackboard and tell the nurse that he wanted to see me. So I got a phone call and here I was expecting to sign for the release of his body and instead I'm told to come back because my husband wanted to see me, which was another complete shock. It was like a bad movie with one turn-around after another. I thought maybe the doctors were wrong. He seemed to be responding. He seemed to be aware of what was going on. I don't really know how to describe it but it was as if we were starting all over again. It was like it was a reprieve and everything was going to be wonderful because he was back. I hadn't really ever expected to see him again.

But it got progressively worse—and very quickly. He never regained the faculties the doctors said he might regain. They thought maybe he would have a good deal more time than they had expected. They said the speech centers were not affected and that he'd regain the use of his speech. But he didn't. He'd try to speak but he could never speak coherently. And when he tried to write, it was a question of decoding his letters. He could read, but when he'd try to write it came out jumbled.

We could never bring Barry home because he couldn't function outside of the hospital. He couldn't walk without assistance, he didn't have complete control of his bowels or bladder, and it was a question of not being able to take care of him. And after a short while, he couldn't even get out of bed anymore. My kids went to see him and it upset them both very much. So I told them that if they wanted to go and see their father, I would take them; but if they didn't, it would be all right. They decided not to see him anymore. That first time had upset them too much. Besides, Barry could hardly communicate with them anyway.

It seemed to me as if his mind wasn't there anymore but I didn't really know if it was or not, and I felt that if I didn't know then I had to behave as though it was. What still disturbs me more than anything else is that I still don't know how much he knew about his illness, about what was happening to him. We couldn't communicate in the end. He couldn't communicate with me and I was afraid to communicate with him because I didn't know how much he knew and whether he could think about all this. The idea that he was locked inside his own mind and that he couldn't talk about it made me not want to put any more thoughts in there than were already there.

At least a couple of months before the death I started wanting Barry to die. He was being fed through a tube in his nose and he wasn't even opening his eyes most of the time. I would say to him, "I wish I knew what you were thinking." I would do dumb things like bring him pictures of the kids and tell him what the kids were doing in school, things that I knew he couldn't have understood or even hear. But there were pictures of the kids posted up on the wall near his bed so he could see them if his eyes were open. And a picture of me. And there were cards that people had sent and I had them pasted all over the wall. I went every day. For ten months I never skipped a day.

I would do the things for Barry that the nurses did for him. I'd feed him, take care of his bedsores, and turn him. He wasn't my husband by then, he was somebody that had been my husband but he still had to be taken care of. And he was somebody that I needed to take care of. He *was* my husband in the sense that I still owed him my presence and I still loved who he had been and he needed me. Or at least I thought he needed me. There was no real way of knowing if he did or not.

I don't know that I have any mystical feelings about essences communicating with essences. I think I believe that when you're dead, you're dead and that's it. So I don't know why I had to be there with him but I just did. I couldn't be the one who was going to break whatever there was between us. The only thing that would break it was his dying.

They called me one night and told me that he was likely to die at any time. So I went to the hospital and slept in a chair near him. That was probably the worst night I ever spent in my life because I slept by his bed and every time his breathing changed I was up. I kept looking for a nurse to help him. There was a siphon gadget that would siphon fluid out of his sinuses so that he could breathe more comfortably. I remember running and asking the nurses if they could use that on him. I remember one of the nurses telling me that they really shouldn't do that because it would irritate his throat. And I remember yelling at her, ''Goddamnit. The man is dying. Can't he at least die comfortably? What the hell difference does it make if his throat is irritated? He won't live long enough for it to be any bother.'' But priorities are different for different people and the nurses had better things to do than worry about somebody who was on his last legs.

I missed his actual death. He died later that day while I was at home trying to get some sleep. I'm glad I missed it.

The most difficult thing after he died was the fact that I didn't have any purpose anymore. I didn't have any place to go. And before his death, even at the point where I didn't feel that he was really with me anymore or that he was comprehending, I still had someplace to go. I had to be there and I had to be there with him.

Once he died, even though I had my kids at home, I didn't really feel I had a purpose anymore. I would sit on the couch at home and do absolutely nothing.

I had had enough sense to start therapy while Barry was still in the hospital. Not that I thought that there was anything particularly wrong with me. I thought I was thinking very clearly and that I was coping very well but I couldn't stop my hands from shaking and I figured if I can't get myself together enough not to shake, then something might be wrong with me.

I wouldn't do anything on my own. After Barry died, there was a panic in me because he wasn't there anymore and I had never realized how much I had relied on him as a backup for so many of the opinions and ideas and decisions I thought were my own. He had been so unobtrusive about it and he had always let me feel that I was doing what I wanted to do, so I didn't realize until after he died that he'd done such an awful lot of guiding in our marriage. And besides all that, I just missed him an awful lot.

I was afraid of the whole world. I was afraid of what would happen if I had to take the car in to be repaired. Going food shopping was too much for me. Anything at that point was too much for me. I think I probably frightened the kids a lot more with that than their father's death did. I think they thought that they were going to have *me* as a casualty as well as Barry.

One thing Barry and I had always planned on was to go to Europe. My therapist suggested I go with the kids to get it out of my system. So I did go, though I was still very panicked about it. That trip to Europe was really what did it for me. After that I began to function pretty normally again. My friends say that I came off the plane a different person than I had gone on. It was enough that I found out that I could function and get things done and that I didn't fall apart if there was any kind of situation that had to be coped with. Once I'd done that, which was about a year after Barry died, I stopped needing therapy.

I think the most traumatic loss one can have is losing a mate. I think that's the worst thing that can happen to anybody—if it's a good marriage. You're a part of a whole and when you lose your mate, you're not only losing a part of yourself, you're losing the person with whom you learned to deal with everything else. If you lose a child or if you lose a parent, at least you still have your mate. There are so many things that human beings do to each other out of a sense of false pride that get in the way of their love relationships; things like being spiteful and holding grudges. I hope if I'm ever in a permanent relationship again that I won't make the same mistakes, that I won't let petty arguments get in the way of our closeness. You just waste too much time that way.